Listening to Listeners

Listening to Listeners
Homiletical CASE STUDIES

John S. McClure • Ronald J. Allen

Dale P. Andrews • L. Susan Bond

Dan P. Moseley • G. Lee Ramsey, Jr.

CHALICE
PRESS
ST. LOUIS, MISSOURI

Biblical quotations, unless otherwise noted, are from the *New Revised Standard Version Bible*, copyright 1989, Division of Christian Education of the National Council of the Churches of Christ in the United States of America. Used by permission. All rights reserved.

Cover art: © Getty Images
Cover and interior design: Elizabeth Wright

This book is printed on acid-free, recycled paper.

Visit Chalice Press on the World Wide Web at
www.chalicepress.com

10 9 8 7 6 5 4 3 2 1   04 05 06 07 08 09

Library of Congress Cataloging–in–Publication Data

Listening to listeners : homiletical case studies / John S. McClure ... [et al.].
   p. cm.
  ISBN 0-8272-0500-7 (pbk. : alk. paper)
  1. Preaching–United States–Psychology–Case studies. 2. Listening–Religious aspects–Christianity–Case studies. 3. Laity–United States–Interviews. I. McClure, John S., 1952-
  BV4235.L57L57 2004
  251–dc22

                                               2004005322

Printed in the United States of America

Contents

Preface

In 1999, the Lilly Endowment agreed to support, through Christian Theological Seminary in Indianapolis, a study of how people listen to sermons. The study, which is described more fully in Appendix C, seeks to identify elements in preaching that engage and disengage congregations. Essentially, the study team asked more than 260 laypeople in twenty-eight African American and Caucasian congregations to become our teachers. We also interviewed preachers in these congregations. We asked these folk, "Teach us how you listen to sermons so that we can help ministers become more effective preachers."

This volume is the first of several that report findings from these extensive interviews. Each volume is distinct in that it reports data from different points of view. Yet the different volumes work together as a kind of informal series called "Channels of Listening" and are identified as such by the presence of a common logo on each volume. This present book takes a case study approach by exploring in detail six interviews from the study and offering methods that pastors can use for interviewing their own congregations. Other volumes in the series will include the following:

Hearing the Sermon: Relationships, Content, Feeling, by Ronald Allen, discusses the three main settings through which listeners process sermons: ethos (perception of the preacher), logos (logic), and pathos (feeling).

Believing in Preaching: What Listeners Hear in Sermons, by Mary Alice Mulligan, Dawn Ottoni Wilhelm, Diane Turner-Sharazz, and Ronald Allen, focuses on the diversity of responses to specific questions and issues raised in the interviews. For example, this book reveals how listeners think God is active in the sermon.

Make the Word Come Alive; Lessons from Laity, by Mary Alice Mulligan and Ronald Allen, summarizes principles for preaching that significant numbers of listeners report encourage them to want to pay attention to the sermon.

All these books rely extensively on the words and interpretive perspectives of the laity and clergy themselves.

We deeply thank the pastors and laity who participated in the study. They devoted much time and effort and were the epitome of grace and helpfulness.

From the standpoint of authorship, the current volume is a hybrid. It is a jointly authored work in that all six writers contributed extensively to all chapters. John McClure and Ronald Allen served as coordinators and editors. Individual authors took a primary lead in particular chapters and are identified in that connection in the book. We also asked persons who are not on the writing team to read individual chapters as a check on the sensitivity of the commentators to the social locations of the interviewees. We greatly thank these outside readers for their careful and insightful work: Annie McClure, Barbara Brown Taylor, Jicelyn Thomas, Edgar A. Towne, and Dawn Ottoni Wilhelm.

For multiple forms of help while putting together this volume, we thank Mary Alice Mulligan, Associate Project Director, and the two Project Assistants who served during this time—Owen Cayton and Kara Brinkerhoff. We also express appreciation to Melissa Green, who patiently transcribed the interviews from tape recordings. We underline our gratitude to the leaders of Christian Theological Seminary who have supported this project: Edward L. Wheeler, President, as well as deans who served during the conception and carrying out of this project (D. Newell Williams, Clark M. Williamson, and Carolyn M. Higginbotham). We are grateful to the Lilly Endowment, which made this project possible, and especially the two members of the Religion Division who worked with us most closely, Christopher Coble and Craig Dykstra.

We are grateful to Lucy Lind Hogan and Robert Reid for the phrase "listening to our listeners" from their book *Connecting with the Congregation: Rhetoric and the Art of Preaching* (Nashville: Abingdon Press, 1999), 87.

We are most appreciative of the guidance given to us by Nancy Eiesland, Professor of Sociology of Religion at Candler School of Theology, Emory University.

Authors

John S. McClure is Charles G. Finney Professor of Homiletics at The Divinity School of Vanderbilt University. His most recent publications are *Otherwise Preaching: A Postmodern Ethic for Homiletics* (Chalice Press, 2001) and, with Burton Z Cooper, *Claiming Theology in the Pulpit* (Westminster John Knox Press, 2003).

Ronald J. Allen is Nettie Sweeney and Hugh Th. Miller Professor of Preaching and New Testament at Christian Theological Seminary. He is coauthor of *One Gospel, Many Ears: Preaching for Different Listeners in the Congregation* (Chalice Press, 2002) and edited *Patterns of Preaching: A Sermon Sampler* (Chalice Press, 1998).

Dale P. Andrews is Frank H. Caldwell Associate Professor of Homiletics and Associate Professor of Homiletics and Pastoral Theology at Louisville Presbyterian Theological Seminary. He has written *Practical Theology for Black Churches: Bridging Black Theology and African American Folk Religion* (Westminster John Knox Press, 2002).

L. Susan Bond is Assistant Professor of Homiletics at The Divinity School of Vanderbilt University. She is the author of *Contemporary African American Preaching: Diversity in Theory and Style* (Chalice Press, 2003) and *Trouble with Jesus: Women, Christology, and Preaching* (Chalice Press, 1999).

Dan P. Moseley is Herald B. Monroe Professor of Practical Parish Ministry at Christian Theological Seminary. He is the editor of *Joyful Giving: Sermons on Stewardship* (Chalice Press, 1997) and served as Senior Minister of Vine Street Christian Church in Nashville, Tennessee, for fifteen years before joining the Christian Theological Seminary faculty.

G. Lee Ramsey, Jr., is Associate Professor of Pastoral Care at Memphis Theological Seminary. He is the author of *Care-full Preaching: From Sermon to Caring Community* (Chalice Press, 2000), an exploration of how preaching can help develop the congregation as a community that expresses prophetic care for its members and for the world.

Introduction

Many preachers have a double-focus moment that happens occasionally in the midst of a sermon. They become simultaneously aware of preaching a sermon but also feel as if they have stepped outside of themselves and are observing the event. In the outside-the-self mode, a preacher sometimes asks, "From the perspective of the listeners, what happens when I preach?"

This book responds to that question based on interviews that allowed people to describe for themselves the experience of hearing sermons. Preachers who are aware of what actually takes place in the congregation during a sermon can develop sermons that make use of patterns of communication that encourage positive interaction with the sermon, and can avoid modes of speech that frustrate many listeners, as long as such adaptations are consistent with the preacher's deepest theological convictions.

Preachers typically get minimal feedback on sermons. Parishioners do sometimes make meaningful comments on sermons at the door of the sanctuary after worship. Occasionally a listener sends a note or stops by the office. From time to time congregants remark on a sermon during a pastoral call. Clergy sometimes hear language echoing a sermon in a committee meeting. Books that teach preachers how to develop sermons tend to be based on ways of preaching that have worked for the author or on philosophical approaches to language and understanding that arise more from theoretical abstraction than from the actual experience of listeners. Few pastors have a "thick" understanding of how people are actually affected by preaching or of the roles the sermon plays in the community.[1] A minister almost never has an opportunity to hear listeners describe for themselves how they are affected by sermons.

If you are curious about how listeners describe what actually happens in their feelings, thoughts, and actions during and after a sermon, this book may be of interest in two ways. (1) You can read several transcripts of in-depth interviews with ten laypeople who regularly listen to sermons. The interviewees open their hearts and tell us what they think is most important to them when they hear a sermon. Five of these people were interviewed one-on-one, and five in a small group. (2) The book suggests some methods you might adapt for making similar discoveries in your own congregation.

In these early years of the twenty-first century, we are ever more keenly aware of the particularity of each congregation. Consequently, the authors of this book would not presume to prescribe a method for ascertaining listener preferences that can work in every single congregation, but we offer some approaches that may help you think through ways to move towards a thicker understanding of your listening community and to name and think critically about how preaching functions in your context.

This book is based on one of the first empirical studies of people who listen to sermons in North America. While this study is described more fully in chapter 1 and in appendix C, you might like to know now that in 2001 and 2002, we interviewed more than 260 African American and Caucasian congregants of diverse ages and genders in various sized congregations and settings in twenty-eight Protestant congregations. These congregations cover a range of denominations, and are located for the most part in a circle geographically, with Indianapolis at the center and with a circumference bounded by Chicago, St. Louis, Louisville, and Columbus. The sample, while not randomly selected, represents many persons who listen to sermons in the middle part of the United States.

Of course, people cannot articulate everything that happens to them either as individuals or as community in preaching. Some of the deepest aspects of experience are intuitive and emotional and cannot be fully expressed. Nonetheless, we have discovered that, when asked, people can articulate many things that are instructive to preachers.

This book will not give you ten easy principles to improve communication between the pulpit and the pew. Each congregation is a particular communication context and calls for sermons that are appropriate to its people and dynamics. The book could help you as a pastor learn how to listen more carefully to the particularity of your own congregation and setting, to name and reflect on qualities of listening, and to adjust your preaching accordingly.

In this initial publication to come from the study, rather than generalize from the data or about congregations, we take a case study approach. We look intently at five interviews with individuals and one interview with a small group. Each case study presents key excerpts and interpretive comments from an interview with a person who regularly listens to sermons. The persons whose individual interviews appear in this book roughly represent the people interviewed for the study in terms of race (two African Americans, three Caucasians), gender (three women and two men), age (two younger persons, two middle-aged, and one older person), setting (two suburban, one urban, one small town, one rural), and denomination (three in long-established denominations, two from more recent Christian movements). We also consider an interview with a small group of five people (one African American and four Caucasians, three men and two women) in an urban congregation of a long-established denomination. Each case study concludes with a brief interpretive essay highlighting what ministers might learn about preaching from the interview.

Each case is discussed by a different member of the advisory board of the project.[2] We do call attention to an aspect of finitude that impacts our work. The writing team for this book is made up of one African American male, one Caucasian woman, and four Caucasian males. The writing group is thus weighted toward Caucasian males while the transcripts on which we comment include, as mentioned above, an African American male, an African American woman, two Caucasian women, a Caucasian male, and a small group comprising one African American male, two Caucasian women, and two Caucasian males. The members of the writing team are painfully aware of their limitations with respect to interpreting the remarks of persons who are in quite different social locations. All the transcripts and interpretive remarks have been read by all writers and thus benefit from the range of social locations in the interpreting community with respect to matters of gender, race, ethnicity, theological orientation, and other matters. Furthermore, scholars from outside the project board, and whose social locations correspond closely with those of the interviewees, have read the transcripts and our interpretations with an eye toward assessing the appropriateness and plausibility of our perspectives.

In chapter 1 we briefly recall the process of interviewing parishioners that led to this book (and the other books in this series) and we describe the perspectives through which we analyze the interviews. Chapters 2–6 are the heart of the book. Each of these chapters contains a case study as described above. Chapter 7 contains a case study from a small group interview. In chapter 8, we identify surprises and insights that emerged in the interviews. In chapter 9, we discuss methods whereby pastors can discover listener perspectives in their own congregations by conducting such interviews, by initiating other forms of discerning congregational responses to preaching, or by pastoral listening in various phases of the life of the congregations. Appendix A provides two interviews with no annotations so that readers can practice listening to these listeners. What does one learn about these listeners and their responses to preaching by attending to these materials? Appendix B lists the questions that the project interviewers used when interviewing laity. Appendix C sketches key elements of the larger project, including a demographic summary of persons interviewed, the characteristics of the congregations in which interviews took place, and other information.

In all these things we hope the reader will gain both a deeper understanding of what happens when people listen to sermons as well as some practical ideas for putting together sermons. Furthermore, as the Epilogue makes clear, we also hope this book strengthens the confidence of ministers and other readers in the witness to the gospel that takes place through preaching. As these case studies repeatedly emphasize, preaching is a lifeline for many people.

CHAPTER 1
_____

Listening to the Heart, Mind, and Will of the Congregation

Many preachers long to understand the dynamics of thought, feeling, and behavior at work in congregations. For example, some preachers organize "feed-forward" groups of laypeople in the congregation to help prepare sermons that intersect with the actual experience of the congregation. Other preachers imagine particular individuals from the congregation with them in the study as the sermon is being prepared and ask, "How would this sermon sound to Amy, Joan, Peter, and Charles?" Occasionally preachers may use survey instruments to develop a profile of congregational preferences in preaching.[1]

This book invites the preacher into still another mode of pastoral attentiveness to the congregation: interviewing people in the congregation with regard to what engages them in preaching. The book rests on a simple premise: When we ask, people who come to worship regularly can tell us quite a bit about the characteristics of the preaching event that help them take the sermon seriously, and characteristics that work against entering the world of the sermon. The authors of this volume believe it will be of further value in helping pastors learn how to listen pastorally to the congregation's perceptions of preaching while encountering people in routine ministerial life—in committee meetings, in the hospital, carrying out mission projects, and even in the parking lot.

To be sure, a listener cannot say everything about a sermon that is meaningful (or not meaningful). As Bernard Meland reminds us, "We live more deeply than we can think."[2] Some of the most profound insights cannot be expressed satisfactorily in conceptual thought, but are known primarily through intuition and feeling. Nevertheless, while hearers may not be able to describe everything that is important to them in the act of preaching, they can tell us much, even in what they do not say. Indeed, without drifting into amateur psychology, a sensitive preacher can often

5

hear qualities in listener self-descriptions that listeners themselves cannot name with precision.

This chapter begins by stressing the importance of taking account of how the congregation and its context influence how listeners perceive sermons. We then turn to the major categories used to interpret the six case studies that follow.[3] The chapter concludes by offering guidelines for listening to sermons from the points of view of what we learn about both preaching and theology. The guidelines pertain to listening both to the cases in this volume and to congregants in your own settings.

Listening in Context

People who regularly hear sermons in a congregation do not hear the messages in a vacuum.[4] The congregational context affects what people expect from sermons, the issues on their minds and in their hearts when the minister stands up to preach, and other aspects of receptivity. Indeed, in an important respect, preaching differs from most other forms of communication: Preaching takes place in a local community over long periods of time. While other modes of communication take place in particular contexts (every mode has its context, by definition), few other contexts are as long-lasting. The preacher, therefore, is called to have an unusual depth of awareness of the congregational culture and to think strategically about how sermons interact with that local setting.

In chapter 9, we offer extended practical suggestions for getting inside the heart, mind, and will of your particular congregation. For now, we call attention to the importance of hearing congregational remarks in resonance with the wider life of the congregation.

In the last twenty years, an approach called congregational studies has emerged to help pastors achieve a thick description of the congregation and its context. A thick description includes who is actually present (by race, gender, age, gender orientation, values, education, class, politics, theological convictions, world view) and their interaction. It also takes account of the dynamics of the congregation's contexts (e.g., neighborhood, community, nation, and world). Congregational studies dwells particularly on the character of the congregation as community and its understandings (formal, informal, and tacit) of its purpose, the significance of important places and events in the congregation's life, as well as the fabric of feeling that runs through the congregation.[5]

Some authors in congregational studies suggest that interviewing parishioners may be a significant component in moving toward a thick description of a congregation. However, to our knowledge, preachers seldom give members opportunities to identify qualities of preaching that motivate parishioners to engage sermons, and qualities of sermons that prompt disengagement. This book draws on one of the first large-scale attempts in North America to do just that.[6]

We do not regard our methodologies or interpretations to be the final words on how to understand what happens in listeners around the sermon. To the contrary, we publish these cases in the hope that you, as preachers, will find them suggestive for developing perspectives and methods for attending to your own congregations. Our hope is less that you will reproduce our work in your setting and more that you will use this book as a conversation partner in thinking about how you might move toward deeper awareness of the dynamics of your own listening community.

Categories to Interpret Listening

We used interview questions to explore listener perceptions of different aspects of preaching. The questions were inspired by categories from the field of rhetoric. Rhetoric, in this context, refers to the use of written or spoken language to persuade a person or group to adopt a particular point of view. It includes all the means and modes of persuasion.[7] Although Aristotle, one of the prime movers in the field of rhetoric, defined the basic categories used in this study more than two millennia ago, they continue to provide useful frames of reference for analyzing events in which people communicate with one another.[8]

The traditional rhetorical categories derived directly from Aristotle are the listener's perception of the character, personality, and trustworthiness of the preacher in the event of preaching (ethos), the appeals to reason in the content of the sermon (logos), and the role of feeling in the event of preaching (pathos). In addition, we created questions that probe the relationship between the congregational culture and the ways in which people process sermons, and the embodiment or delivery of the sermon.[9] Our understanding of these categories, along with the more comprehensive rhetorical category of identification, is discussed below.

While we discuss these notions separately, our study revealed that they are nearly all at work in each listener and community during a sermon. The study further showed that different categories are more forceful for some congregants than others. For instance, one listener perceives the content of the sermon as more important than relationship with the preacher or feeling, while another listener may think the sermon has been inconsequential unless that person is moved to tears. One of the preacher's tasks is to determine how the different categories function in the congregation. In the case studies in chapters 2 through 7, we highlight the roles played by different categories in the different listeners and how such awareness on the part of the preacher can help the preacher calibrate the sermon accordingly.

Through much of the twentieth century, preachers (and the literature of preaching) focused on communicating with the listeners as individuals. In the last thirty years, however, some thinking about preaching and the congregation has shifted toward the church as community. How can preaching effectively help a congregation become a genuinely Christian community? While this study is interested in how individuals listen as individuals, we are also interested in how the congregation as community is affected by the sermon *and* by how the congregation as community affects the sermon and the preacher. Consequently, some interview questions are geared more to individuals, while others specifically seek to help the persons in the study reflect on how the congregation as a group responds to the sermon. In the case studies, we lift up both aspects of listener response.

Ethos

In classical rhetoric, ethos refers to the role that the listener's perception of the speaker plays during an event of public speaking. From this perspective, the speaker "persuades by moral character" when "a speech is delivered in such a manner as to render" the speaker "worthy of confidence."[10] A congregation's perception of a speaker's character contributes to its willingness to take seriously the content of the speaker's address. The congregation's perception of a speaker's worthiness contributes to the authority it assigns to the speaker's words.

Lucy Lind Hogan and Robert Reid, contemporary scholars of preaching who are also rhetoricians, note that ethos includes qualities related to the credibility of the preacher that the congregation perceives within the event of the sermon itself. Positive ethos occurs when the presence of the preacher during the sermon creates a sense of trust on the part of the congregation.[11] Ethos particularly results when the congregation feels in the moment of preaching that the preacher represents its values and best interests, and when the preacher communicates that she or he respects the congregation.[12] Ethos can also come about because of qualities in the preacher that the congregation perceives outside the sermon. Such ethos includes the community's perception that the preacher is virtuous, reflects deeply on life, has professional credentials, and is pleasing in appearance. In the case of the guest preacher, being introduced convincingly to the congregation contributes significantly to ethos.[13] David Cunningham, a teacher of theology who works extensively with rhetorical categories, adds to qualities that reinforce ethos, such as the preacher's associations (e.g., the groups with whom a preacher is identified and their place in the congregation's worldview), and reinforces the importance of the preacher's actions in everyday life, particularly continuity between the preacher's stated values and the preacher's lifestyle.[14] Ethos is usually strong when the congregation perceives that the preacher is associated with groups that members respect, manifests respect for the congregation and the subject matter of the sermon, and lives outside the sanctuary in ways that demonstrate integrity between what the preacher says in the pulpit and the preacher's style of life. The congregation tends to be distrustful of a preacher whom they perceive to associate with groups they do not respect, who is distant from the congregation or constantly critical, or whose lifestyle contradicts what he or she says from the pulpit. Behaviors and attitudes such as the following, though taking place outside the moment of preaching, often contribute to a positive ethos between preacher and people: evidence of serious study of the topic of the sermon, genuine sensitivity to the congregation, personal honesty shared with the congregation, doing what the preacher says she or he will do, and regular pastoral care (such as calling at hospitals and homes).

In the optimum congregational setting, the congregation's perception of the preacher coincides with the way the preacher really is. The fact is that in settings outside the view of the congregation, the preacher may not actually be knowledgeable or trustworthy. Unless the congregation discovers this incongruity, the people may continue to perceive the preacher as a reliable companion on the journey toward religious wisdom. When a congregation becomes aware of the minister's lack of integrity in any area of life, members typically find the preacher's sermons less credible. Indeed, a preacher's shortcoming in an area of life or ministry some distance from preaching may cause the congregation to disregard the sermon even if the content of the sermon is theologically apropos. A breach of ethics in financial or sexual matters, for instance, can undermine the ethos of the rhetorical situation, i.e., the sermon. The questions in the survey focused on ethos were grouped with questions on congregational culture. These questions are listed together at the end of the next section.

Congregational Culture

Aristotle did not develop a major focus on how community culture affects the ways in which people receive and process communications. However, as noted earlier, preaching differs from many other modes of communication in that preaching takes place in a local community over long periods of time. While other forms of persuasion occur in particular contexts, few other contexts are as long-lasting. Indeed, the discipline of congregational studies demonstrates that the congregation's perception of the preacher and the sermon is affected by (and affects) the culture within the congregation. This culture includes factors outside the service of worship that affect the listeners' willingness to take the sermon seriously. Congregational studies helps us understand the preacher and the sermon in the context of the congregation as particular community. The congregational system orients the community to expect qualities that are specific to each local congregation.

Of course, such matters are dialectical. The preacher and the sermon contribute to congregational culture. The ways the preacher relates to people in the community during the sermon and in other parish (and trans-parish) settings, as well as the content of the sermon, help shape the qualities of congregational life. When the congregation trusts the preacher, the people may take the content of the preacher's sermons to heart, even when the message calls for a change in culture. The people may also follow the model of the preacher's own life in relationship and witness. From time to time, of course, the pastor helps shape the community's context by speaking and acting (intentionally or unintentionally) outside the expectations of the congregation. The community's response reinforces or changes aspects of parish culture.

Congregational culture is not theologically neutral. Some congregational cultures foster values and practices that are inimical to the gospel. Other cultures contain elements that witness to the gospel. One of the important callings of the preacher is to reflect on the degree to which congregational culture is theologically appropriate or inappropriate. One trick is for the preacher to do so in a way that maintains a positive ethos during sermons so that members will remain open to the preacher's analysis.

To explore the roles of congregational culture and ethos in the event of preaching, we asked the following questions. Questions 1–7 uncover wider aspects of congregational culture–of how the listener perceives the nature of the congregation as a community, especially qualities of community life that are more and less important to the interviewee and to the community. Questions 8–9 focus especially on ethos as traditionally understood, that is, on the appeal of the character of the preacher. Questions 1–7 call for responses that reveal much about preaching in the culture of the congregation and/or in the life of the listener as an individual Christian.

1. Tell me about how you became a part of this congregation.
2. What are the most important things that happen in this congregation?
3. Describe a typical Sunday morning in this congregation.
4. Tell me what preaching does in this congregation that other things do not do.
5. What would be missing if there were no sermon?
6. Tell me about how preaching shapes your congregation–who you are as a community. Can you give an example?
7. Tell me about your history as a person listening to sermons. What are some high points? What are some low points? Was there ever a time when you almost walked out?
8. Talk a little bit about your relationship with the pastors and preachers that you have had.
9. Tell me about a pastor you have had who was also a good preacher. What did you like about that person?

In the case studies in chapters 2 through 7, comments about the preacher in listener responses to these questions often reveal much about how the relationship between the preacher and the congregation influences the receptivity of the congregation or the individual to the sermon.

Logos

Logos refers to the preacher's appeal to the listener through varying forms of argument. Logos has reference to the reasons and other kinds of material that a preacher uses within the sermon to help the congregation want to adopt the position advocated in the speech or to experience the world or act in the way portrayed in the sermon. "Logos, in rhetoric, is concerned with actively thinking about and reflecting on the situation, and then making appropriate choices of words and arguments, given the situation, the listeners, and God's call to bold proclamation."[15] The preacher seeks to offer the congregation responsible motivation for the position or action the sermon invites the congregation to adopt.

While *logos* in Aristotle's dictionary narrowly refers to the arguments that a speaker uses to persuade listeners to support a position, many rhetoricians point out that public speakers today need to broaden their understanding of the kind of material that helps listeners enlarge, refocus, and otherwise reinforce and change their ideas, commitments, life orientations, and world views. At the most obvious level, logos in the expanded view includes using formal logic and data to help a congregation accept the invitation of the sermon. Beyond that, preachers employ both deductive and inductive patterns of reasoning and also use examples, illustrations, and other modes of bringing the central message of the sermon to life. [16] Furthermore, the content of some sermons can be an imaginative experience; hearing the sermon can be less like paying attention to a lawyer's brief or a debater's arguments and more like entering into the world of a novel or movie. The message of the sermon comes through participating in the experience created in the sermon.[17]

Logos places a premium on contextual thinking. A sensitive preacher seeks to make appeals in the sermon that will be taken seriously by a particular congregation in a particular context. Our study shows that persons and congregations differ with respect to the values, pieces of data, lines of reasoning, and experiences that they find authoritative. The preacher needs to know the patterns of reasoning and data that a congregation finds convincing and unconvincing. The methodology in this book could help preachers discover how these things are particular to their own congregations.

Our questions below give listeners a chance to identify the sources of authority that they find most compelling in sermons. Because the Bible is central to so many schools of Christian preaching, we focus particularly on it and give listeners opportunity to call attention to other materials in the sermon that they find important.

The rhetorical tradition reminds us that different kinds of public address have different purposes. Significant communication has a greater opportunity to take place when the speaker and audience share a common understanding of the purpose of the speech than when they differ. Books and authorities in the field of preaching offer various understandings of the purpose(s) of the sermon. However, we do not know of any studies prior to this one that asked significant numbers of listeners how *they* understand the purposes of a sermon. We believe preachers will find it instructive to compare their understandings of the purposes of preaching with those articulated by interviewees in the case studies below. How do the understandings of preaching posited by these listeners compare and contrast with your own? In some congregations, the actual assumptions regarding the aims of preaching could suggest that the preacher needs to educate the congregation in deeper and more theologically adequate understandings of the sermon.

Because Christian preaching aims to help the congregation interpret the world from God's perspective while also helping the congregation arrive at an adequate interpretation of God, we asked listeners what they would most like to know about God. Because most Christian communities believe that God is present in the world, interviewees were also asked how they think God is active *in the sermon.*

Contemporary theologians as well as preachers and writers in the field of preaching sometimes speak of preaching as an event of transformation. However, relatively little attention is given in the literature of homiletics to dynamics in the sermon that can contribute to an atmosphere in which transformation (or more modest forms of change) can take place. This concern is a focus in the interviews. We think it is revealing to hear listeners themselves indicate those qualities in preaching that help bring about a change of mind and heart, and those qualities that do not encourage change.

To explore the role of logos we asked the following questions:

1. What do you think your pastor is doing when she or he preaches?
2. Tell me about a sermon that you really found engaging.
3. What was it about that sermon that engaged you?
4. Tell me about a sermon that did not interest you. What left you cold?
5. What was it about that sermon that left you cold or put you off?
6. What role does/should the Bible have in preaching?
7. When does a sermon have authority for you?
8. What do you most want to know about God when you hear a sermon?
9. What do you think God is doing during the sermon itself?
10. I'll bet you have heard a sermon that caused you to think or act differently, maybe about some big issue, maybe about a smaller issue. Would you tell me about that sermon?
11. What did the pastor say or do that prompted you to act differently?

Pathos

Pathos has multiple dimensions. At the most obvious level, it refers to the role that emotions play when a hearer receives a public address. "The orator persuades" when the hearers "are roused to emotions by" the speech. "For the judgments we deliver are not the same when we are influenced by joy or sorrow, love or hate."[18] In some circumstances, a congregation may be profoundly swayed by emotional dimensions in the sermon. A group may also be moved by emotional factors in the wider environment. The setting may stir the congregation's emotions so as to orient the congregation to be receptive (or resistant) to the speech.

The role of pathos in coming to a decision leads the preacher to recognize that while Christians often take into account "abstract, rational demonstrations" in arriving at significant conclusions, they also make "judgments in cumulative, associative, and practical ways" including the fact of being moved at the level of feeling or intuition by the sermon.[19] People often adopt ideas because of the emotional associations we have with those ideas. Indeed, at times factors in a person's life of feeling may bring about changes in perspectives, values, and behaviors about which the person never thinks critically, or even becomes conscious. A change can occur deeply within the self without the person even becoming aware of it.

Lucy Lind Hogan and Robert Reid note that, with respect to reinforcing or changing the ways that people are oriented to the world, pathos must do more than simply stir emotions and release feelings in the listener. They point out that at its best pathos helps people care about the viewpoint the preacher advocates. "The most effective use of emotion in a speech occurs when it helps listeners understand why you, as the preacher, *care* in a way that helps them, as listeners, *care* as well."[20]

Toward finding out more about the phenomenon of pathos in the sermon, we asked listeners what moves them both as individuals and as congregations. While pathos includes more than emotion, emotions can have quite powerful effects. Consequently, we did ask the listeners how they react to emotion in the sermon and to cite instances when they were moved both positively and negatively by emotional elements in preaching. Indeed, we wanted to know whether the interviewees think that some subjects are simply too explosive for the preacher to discuss in a sermon.

To explore the role of pathos in the sermon, we asked the following questions:

1. When the pastor stands up to preach, what do you hope will happen to you as a result of listening to that sermon?
2. I'm going to ask you a question about you personally and then a similar question about the congregation. Can you tell me about a sermon that stirred your own emotions?
3. What in the sermon stirred you?
4. I would like for you to describe a sermon that seemed to move the congregation as a whole, as a community.

5. What was it about that sermon that seemed to move the congregation?
6. Would you describe a time when the sermon stirred emotions that made you feel uncomfortable?
7. When the sermon stirs the emotions of the congregation, what happens after worship?
8. Do you think there are some issues that are just too explosive, too dangerous, for the preacher to deal with in the pulpit? Would you name some of them for me and tell me why you think they are dangerous?

Embodiment

Embodiment refers to the moment when the sermon comes to life in the pulpit. Preachers and scholars used to speak of this aspect of preaching as "delivery." However, the term "delivery" could imply no more relationship between congregation and preacher than the parcel service delivery person has with the householders who receive the parcel. "Embodiment" is intended to suggest that the sermon comes alive through the complete self of the preacher.

Aristotle does not discuss embodiment as a separate category. However, our research team wanted to investigate what listeners had to say about embodiment because leaders in the preaching community have long thought that congregations are typically more engaged by certain types of embodiment than others. Indeed, to our eyes some modes of embodiment appear to be energizing to the congregation while others have anesthetizing properties. We wanted to know what the listeners would describe as engaging (and disengaging) qualities in the preacher's use of the voice, eye contact, face, gestures, movement, and other aspects of speaking the sermon.

We asked the listeners to identify traits in embodiment that help them participate in the sermon, and traits that put them off with the following questions:

1. Would you please describe for me a preacher whose physical presence in the pulpit was really good—whose delivery was really engaging?
2. What are some physical things a preacher does (while delivering the sermon) that help you to want to pay attention?
3. Can you think of a time when you could not hear or see the preacher well? How did that affect you?
4. What difference does it make to you when you can see the facial features of the preacher and hear distinctly?

Wanting to give the subjects of the study a chance to say something that the previous queries may not have called forth, we concluded each interview with this general question:

If you had one or two things you could tell preachers that would help them energize you when you are listening to a sermon, what would they be?

Whether the listener introduced new information into the discussion by responding to this question, or reinforced earlier themes, the responses to this last question revealed things that are important to that listener.

Identification

From time to time in our writing we use the terms "identification" and "identifies" to speak of the relationship between the preacher and the congregation. Of an interviewee's response to a question, for instance, we might say, "This remark shows that the listener identifies with the preacher's appeal to logos."

Contemporary rhetorician Kenneth Burke, who urges speakers to pay attention to the social and cultural dimensions that are present in every rhetorical situation, writes of the speaker establishing a sense of identification with the listener. This identification can occur through the presentation of one's personality or character in the pulpit in a way that hearers can easily identify as "preacher" (ethos), through the use of identifiable language and forms of reasoning (logos), and through appeals to an allowable range of emotions (pathos). Burke himself notes, "Only those voices from without are effective which can speak in the language of a voice within."[21] Karlyn Kohrs Campbell expands, "At its simplest, this statement recognizes that we are most influenced by those whose voices are most like the voices we use in talking to ourselves, and the more the rhetor shares with the audience, the greater the chance he or she will have of being able to speak in ways the audience will hear and understand and feel."[22]

Through various strategies of identification, the preacher is responding to, supporting, and in some ways creating the culture of listening in a congregation. In other words, the preacher seeks a variety of identifications with the congregation so that the congregation feels at one with the speaker, but also to build up members' relationship with one another as listeners. Another way to say this is that the preacher is "negotiating a hearing" over a period of time in the congregation.[23] The speaker seeks to stand on common ground with the audience so that the audience will be disposed to feel the conclusion of the speaker as its own. According to this theory, when identification is established, listeners tend to persuade themselves.[24]

Identification occurs in every type of rhetorical appeal: to ethos, logos, pathos, and embodiment. The minister seeks for the community to identify with her or his character (ethos). The preacher prepares the content of the sermon in the hope that the congregation will identify with the types of arguments or imaginative experiences that are at the center of the sermon (logos). The preacher wants to stir the congregation's feelings so that listeners are moved to care about the subject of the sermon and to act on it (pathos). The pastor intends to speak the sermon in ways that the congregation will embrace (embodiment).

The emphasis on congregational culture (above) reminds preachers that the preacher needs to pay careful attention to qualities in ethos, logos, pathos, and embodiment with which people *in the congregation* will identify. The preacher needs to know what qualities of character the local community respects, the forms of argument that they find persuasive, the feelings that they regard as authentic and that move them, as well as uses of the voice and the body that will welcome the congregation into the sermon (and not put them off).

Listening to the Case Studies that Follow

We can hear the themes of ethos, logos, pathos, embodiment, congregational culture, and identification in the case studies that follow. Each chapter presents a transcript from an interview with one person (chapters 2–6) or a transcript of a small-group interview (chapter 7). Each transcript gives us a sketch of how that listener (or group) interprets good preaching. While most of the interviews lasted about an hour, some were longer and some shorter—facts that account for the differences in length in the transcripts that follow.

For this book we selected transcripts that are roughly representative of the persons in the study but that also represent the variety of listener responses to the questions. We discuss the following cases:

> **Anthony,** a fifty-year-old African American man in a large, predominantly African American, urban congregation (chapter 2)[25]
> **Helen,** a sixty-year-old Caucasian woman in a medium-sized, urban congregation (chapter 3)
> **Cassandra,** a forty-five-year-old African American woman in a medium-sized, urban, predominantly African American congregation (chapter 4)
> **Jim,** a thirty-two-year-old Caucasian male in a suburban, mega congregation that is made up primarily (though not exclusively) of Caucasians (chapter 5)
> **Jane,** a Caucasian woman in a small, rural congregation (chapter 6)
> **A small-group** interview with five people in a medium-sized, racially mixed, urban congregation (chapter 7)

In addition, Appendix A contains two transcripts that are not annotated so that you can read and think about what you learn about the listener without interference from our commentary. One transcript is of a thirty-two-year-old African American male from a medium-sized congregation comprised of both African Americans and Caucasians, while the other is a group of six people in an African American congregation. Both congregations are in urban settings.

We do not include complete transcripts because space is prohibitive and because some of the exchanges do not help us understand the listener's perceptions of preaching in that congregational setting.[26] For instance, one of the listeners described, in some detail, what this person had for lunch at a nearby café. The generous excerpts from each transcript included in this book present the main themes that relate to preaching from each listener or group. In connection with each transcript, we provide basic information about the person or persons being interviewed as well as about the congregation and its context.

Each chapter contains three parts: an annotated transcript, notes alongside the transcript that comment on implications for preaching in the listener's remarks, and an essay interpreting implications for preaching and theology derived from the interview.

Excerpts from the Transcripts

The largest parts of chapters are the selections from the transcript annotated with comments that call attention to things that might help preachers understand how that listener's participation in the sermon is affected by relationship with the pastor, by the content of the sermon, by the feelings that are engendered by the sermon, and by the way the sermon is embodied.

A preacher wants to know what *the listeners say* about how they process sermons. A preacher who prepares a sermon constructs a picture of what the preacher thinks the congregation is like and of how the congregation will react to the sermon. Talking with congregants can help preachers construct a realistic picture of how the individuals in the congregation process sermons. Without such listening, a preacher may create a picture of the congregation that is more a projection of how the preacher wishes the congregation would respond to sermons than of how the congregation is likely to respond. Even when the congregants do not process sermons in ways the preacher wishes, we need to respect their processes as *their* processes.

The annotations appear in notes alongside the text of the transcripts on which they comment. When the words of the interviewee in the transcript are in italics, that indicates a connection between those remarks and the comments in the notes. The numbers at the beginning of the italicized remarks signal the reader that the remark is discussed in the note of the same number on the right side of the page.

In the notes, we try not simply to note the appearance of ethos, logos, pathos, and embodiment concerns in the transcript, but to comment on how those concerns appear to function for the particular listener in focus. In these notes we try to call attention to qualities that help sermons engage the listeners. These notes are also numbered so that the interpreter can refer to them in the essay that follows.

Listening for Preaching

The second part of each chapter is a brief essay in which the commentator attempts to describe what the listeners say they think and feel about preaching and the event of hearing the sermon. This essay calls attention to distinctive qualities in the listener's responses. Many listeners state their perspectives explicitly, but some of the congregants' responses to preaching are implicit and must be drawn out as fully as their remarks or our knowledge of the context will allow.

The essay further provides an interpretive frame for understanding what the respondent has said from the perspective of classical and current thinking about the nature and purpose of preaching, and about what communicates and what does not. Does the listener reinforce the preacher's presuppositions, add to them, reframe them, call attention to neglected aspects, or challenge them? Each commentator states some payoffs for the preacher of listening to this listener. The writer of the essay states straightforwardly how preachers might take the listener's responses into account in order to communicate more effectively with this listener.

Listening for Theology

The third part of each chapter is a short commentary in which the writer attempts to interpret the theological perspectives that seem to come to expression in the listeners' observations about preaching. As much as allowed by the data from the transcript and from awareness of the congregation and its setting, the commentator seeks to identify the theological ideas that are most important to the listener. Responses to some of the following questions come to the surface in these remarks:

- What are the listener's deepest convictions concerning God and God's purposes in the world?
- What is most important about the nature and purpose of the church for this listener? What does the listener hope will happen in the congregation, and more specifically in the service of worship and the sermon?
- Based on this interview, what seem to be the theological concepts that are most important to this listener?
- How do the listener's theological convictions lead the individual and the community to act in the church and in the world? What are the implications of the theological commitments voiced in the interview for the behavior of church and wider community?
- How is God active in the different phases of the sermon for the listener?
- How do the listener's comments help us understand the ways that authority and theological meaning are constituted in and by sermons?
- How will members of the community know that they are being faithful to the divine intentions in the common life?
- How will the community recognize a faithful sermon?

One part of this project is simply to name what listeners explicitly say they believe and what they imply. Another part is to reflect on the degree to which their remarks are internally consistent with one another. Still another part is to consider what listeners' remarks say about the ways that theology and rhetoric interact in sermons.

In addition to commenting on how the listener perceives these and other matters, the writer will explore how the perspectives of the interviewees relate to larger theological discussions in the past and in the present. For example, does a listener's understanding of sin correlate with a classical understanding of sin in Christian tradition? Do listeners in a congregation in the Wesleyan tradition exhibit understandings of God, persons, and community that are typically Wesleyan? If not, what are the understandings that come to expression in the interview?

With such knowledge, a preacher can reflect on the degree to which the theology of the listener is consistent with the formal theology of the congregation (or denomination, or Christian movement with which the congregation is affiliated) as well as with the actual theology of the preacher.

The result of this reflection can be helpful in two ways. For one, when the preacher and the listener use different vocabulary for similar theological ideas, the preacher may be able to use some of the listeners' language and concepts in the sermon. When the preacher makes such a change it increases the likelihood that the minister and community are on the same wavelength. When a preacher discovers that certain things are important to the congregation, the preacher may be able to include such things in the sermon (when they are theologically appropriate).

For the other, preachers cannot simply assume that parishioner likes and dislikes prescribe approaches for the preacher to take in the sermon. Listeners may seek qualities in preaching (or may imagine God and the purpose of life in ways) that are inconsistent with the deepest understandings of God for the preacher and the church. A pastor may conclude, in the prophetic tradition, that aspects of the theology of the listener (and, hence, aspects of how the listener needs to listen) need to be clarified, amplified, refocused, corrected, or replaced. Such a discovery would suggest that the preacher needs to work with the listening community in the sermon and in other settings in the congregation to nurture a theological viewpoint that is more faithful.

We recognize that the deepest and most appropriate convictions about God, the world, and the church are often a matter of discussion, and even debate, in the Christian community. Indeed, the six writers of this book (and their differing theological traditions) understand these matters with different nuances. In the theological commentary of each chapter, the writer notes the theological convictions that she or he uses to gauge the appropriateness of statements about God, the world, preaching, and other things. For instance, Dale Andrews approaches this evaluative task from the perspective of the theology of the African Methodist Episcopal Zion Church calibrated to liberation theology, while John McClure thinks in terms of Reformed theology in a revisionary theological mode. These differences lead us to slightly different norms, questions, and issues in reflecting theologically on the interviews. [27] The process is precisely what we hope preachers who read this book will do: reflect on the listeners in their congregations from the perspectives of their preachers' theological visions and norms. We aim to foster critical self-awareness.

The aim of this book is not to present demographic typologies or generalizations such as, "Certain kinds of listening are due to race and ethnicity, gender, size of the congregation, or location." Instead, our hope is that preacher-readers will use these cases as fruitful starting points for listening more attentively to their own listeners in their own contexts.

Challenges for Preaching

Each case study concludes with questions for reflection. While these questions invite further consideration of the material in the transcript and the interpreter's remarks, they are more aimed toward prompting preachers to compare and contrast their own perceptions of preaching with those expressed in the interviews, and to reflect more broadly and deeply about preaching in each preacher's own congregational setting.

CHAPTER 2

"Like I'm Dancing Right There without Dancing"

Anthony: Urban African American Male

L. SUSAN BOND

The following is an interview with Anthony, a fifty-year-old African American male in a Midwestern city. He attends church in a large congregation, part of an historically African American denomination in the Wesleyan tradition, with an average Sunday morning worship attendance of 300. This largely middle-aged, middle-income to upper-middle-income congregation is seeking larger facilities not only to accommodate growing attendance but also to provide facilities for mission in the immediate neighborhood. The congregation is friendly and has a high degree of consciousness of Afrocentrism as well as its affiliation with its historically African American denomination.

The congregations that belong to this tradition (African Methodist Episcopal Church or AME, African Methodist Episcopal Church of Zion or AMEZ, and Christian Methodist Episcopal Church or CME) are characterized by their struggles with racism, slavery, and the emergence of an independent Black Church. Not only were African Americans attracted to the anti-slavery message of prominent Caucasian Methodist preachers, but they were also attracted to a livelier style of worship and the straightforward claims of evangelical Christianity and general commitments to social justice.[1] The African American Wesleyan denominations have a history of more formal liturgical elements than their Baptist siblings, by virtue of the Anglican history, but a significant amount of local adaptation is common. At Anthony's church we see posters on the wall and circulars throughout the building that provide historical and doctrinal information about the denomination. The congregation makes extensive use of Afrocentric names and symbols.

The service of worship has a combination of lively music, spontaneity, formal liturgical moments, and Afrocentric cultural elements. The service begins with a fairly formal processional and ends with a formal recessional (including acolytes and traditional hymns). Between these "bookends," the service is often spontaneous, with the pastor or other worship leaders departing from the printed order of worship. The congregation is particularly vocally interactive during the several musical selections and during the sermon. The congregation focuses more intently on the pastor during the sermon than on the other worship leaders in the service. The preacher tends to stay behind the central pulpit for the sermon, using a hand-held microphone that not only helps the congregation hear but gives the preacher freedom of expression and movement.

Anthony joined a congregation at a young age, with roots in the same denomination, but had a period of young adult inactivity. He's returned to the church; he's been attending this particular church for over ten years. It was important to Anthony to locate a congregation within his denomination and the tradition of his youth. He's married, well-educated, and has a household earning in the upper part of the middle-income range, as do many of his fellow-congregants. His personal demeanor is dignified and thoughtful; in fact, he reports that he gave a great deal of thought to his ideas of preaching before the interview. He chooses his words carefully, and his answers demonstrate a strong desire to express ideas with clarity and precision. Anthony particularly enjoys the music, the friendliness of the people, and the scriptural content of preaching.

Anthony's interview is reproduced here almost in its entirety (one of the shorter interviews in the collection); introductory and concluding remarks have been removed. In this transcript and in subsequent chapters the italicized words correspond to the comments beside them.

Excerpts from the Transcript

INTERVIEWER: What are the more important things that happen in this congregation that help you stay?

ANTHONY: The people. (1) *The people are very nice here to you. They speak to you. They ask. If you look concerned about something, they just say if you'd like to talk, just give them a call. Like I said, they're being nice. They ask you out, or they ask to get together and go to a ball game. Or stop by the house and talk about certain things. The fellowship is very strong here in general.*

1. Anthony places positive emphasis on the authenticity of members' behaviors and attitudes. Preachers who focus entirely on their own character or personality to gather credibility may not make an impression on Anthony. Notice that he has to be prompted to discuss the preacher's own character or personality. As the interview continues, we'll see that listeners like Anthony are not as impressed with the preacher's own character as we

INTERVIEWER: What is your relationship with the pastor or previous pastors and how did that affect your membership here?

ANTHONY: My membership is experienced… Actually, the pastor that was here when I joined (2) *gave me an outlook of looking at the life perspective as seeing in the right direction. He gave me a better perspective to see what Church is all about. But his sermons particularly touched my heart and put me back in the right perspective of what I should have been, instead of what I was when I strayed away for about ten years.* As for the present pastor, like I said, all the pastors we've had at the church, you continue to listen to the sermons on Sunday. You continue [to] listen to the teachings in the Bible study. Particularly, what I'm concerned with is what I get out of those two sessions. That's what keeps me here…Sure, I've visited other churches for teachings, but since I am a member of [African American denomination] faith, then I continue to come to this church.

INTERVIEWER: You mentioned an interesting term when you said that the pastor touched your heart. In what ways do sermons touch your heart most often?

ANTHONY: (3) *Generally, it touches your heart… It touches my heart when it touches my inner self, my inner feelings. That's when that's going to have…The pastor that can do that to me, I feel that he can get to anybody. I consider myself a strong person, but also an emotional person to the degree of letting someone else say something which will touch me. You grow up. You're out there between streets and church and activity outside of church that you have to grow up in. I just don't let everybody touch my feelings. It's very important to me when the pastor has the ability to do that. It's almost like the words that he says, he just touched your hand and go right through you.*

might assume. The congregational context or culture seems to have more authority for him.

2. Anthony doesn't comment on his personal relationship to the preacher, but to the emotional and intellectual impact of the preacher's sermons. The use of "heart" language usually indicates pathos elements. The language of "outlook" and "perspective" refer to logos categories of sermon content. It's curious that he answers an ethos question with a combined pathos and logos answer. We'll want to listen carefully to the kind of language listeners use, since they may not be answering the question we've posed.

3. This is another pathos comment, expanding on the "heart" language to include "inner self" and "inner feelings" as part of the total pathos package. Anthony qualifies his pathos experiences by insisting that his emotional response does not indicate lack of "strength." He indicates that he is selective (in command?) about when he allows his emotions to be affected, which could be a logos comment. We see the use of bodily imagery ("It's almost like . . . he just touched your hand . . ."). We'll also see the use of bodily imagery later in the interview. Anthony seems to guard his emotional responses. Would he be uncomfortable or suspicious with a purely emotional appeal? Preachers need to remember that some folks will not be satisfied with appeals to emotion.

INTERVIEWER: What kinds of things actually touch you in a sermon?

ANTHONY: I look at basically the stories that he tells, biblically, that transcribe… (4) *how things are directed to you out of the scriptures and interpreted to one sitting in the congregation.* That touches my heart. That's the best way I can describe that.

INTERVIEWER: Can you think of story that you've heard in a sermon that would be a good example?

ANTHONY: As I wrote on the paper, (5) *that one about Ishmael and Isaac, the two sons of Abraham and how they perceive and how God directed that each son will have* his own per se kingdom. They will be kings of other…how do you say it?…communities or tribes, that they each would have their own in the promise, and it did come true.

INTERVIEWER: Do you find that in your congregation that the same types of things that stir your emotions in a sermon or stir your heart do so also for other persons in the community, in the congregation?

ANTHONY: Yes. Definitely. Definitely, because you have other people react the same way that I do to it. Basically, yes. I've always thought of asking one, how (6) *did the sermon touch you today like it touched me? To see if there has been any difference on how I feel and how you feel.*

INTERVIEWER: What have you discovered in asking people that?

4. Anthony uses the metaphor of "direction" to speak of scripture's relationship to the hearer. It's unclear whether the preacher directs scripture or the scripture contains its own directing abilities. Scripture or preaching as "directive" could be either a logos or an ethos element. Anthony wants the sermon to do more than please him or excite him. He wants a sermon with serious content, and especially content that offers him cues for critical thinking and ethical living. Again, Anthony's intellectual and ethical interests are primary; he is only "touched" by sermons that meet these standards.

5. The specific story, whether part of the preached text or a biblical illustration used by the preacher, is of male characters in competition. It's particularly interesting that Anthony has connected a story to a logos or propositional idea (God keeps promises) instead of a feeling or an ethical directive. And we should note that it's a story of male power and success that he has remembered. We can't know, but it would be interesting to see if female listeners also remembered this story. Would this illustration exclude people with different identifications? If Anthony were not a successful male professional, would he remember this story?

6. Maybe Anthony has emotional responses after he has a certain intellectual experience in the sermon? The pattern seems to be that he reacts emotionally after he understands something better, which would be the reverse of some preachers' assumptions. At least, it calls into question the idea that emotional responses generate intellectual agreement. Let's also notice that Anthony wants to check out his reactions to see what others felt, almost in a "scientific" model

ANTHONY: Well, I found out that (7) *it makes me grow to be a better person.* Any two sides… coming from someone else, if they like to talk about it. Because everybody has their own story to tell, either that you was brought up in the church or brought up to understand what our Lord says Jesus Christ is all about. Or whether or not you had joined the church to the point where what you have done that you want to *get rid of your transgressions* that you have and what you've done in the past to make you a better person. I've seen both sides of it, personally. I've seen both sides of it. *I've always known what direction I should go, or get back to. It's helped me a whole lot.*

INTERVIEWER: What kind of things do you feel ought to be in sermons?

ANTHONY: Oh, definitely, most definitely (8) *descriptions of what the Bible has to offer individuals and how to put in perspective better. How I can use it today. You use operative and speculative. Operative being what is done in the past; speculative, what you can use today. That generally is what I get out of the sermons.* Did you ask a question about what you want to put into it?

INTERVIEWER: What ought to be?

ANTHONY: Ought to be in it? That too. Mainly that. (9) *If the pastor is giving you the ideas of what the Holy Bible has to say to you or to me, then that's what I'm there for, to be fed. God gave us our own intelligence, each man his own type of intelligence.*

INTERVIEWER: Interesting.

of gathering data. Different listeners may have different ways of dealing with emotional and intellectual elements.

7. This is a logos appeal, signaling that one purpose of preaching is to have an ethical content. He doesn't respond to simplistic rules, but wants to reason about Christian life. So far, it seems like Anthony's mode of listening demands an intellectual argument, an ethical direction, and then a glorious "amen!" emotional reaction. We should also note that Anthony's understanding of repentance and mercy are somewhat demanding. Faith requires changed behavior. Such a perspective is consistent with Wesleyan understandings of "growing in grace" or growth in both personal and social holiness.

8. The language of this response (operative and speculative) is strongly logos. Anthony values description and uses fairly technical language to discuss different kinds of description. It's clear that he places a great value on sermon content: on biblical interpretation and its daily usefulness.

9. Anthony uses another overt appeal to logos here. The Bible contains ideas, the sermon explains those ideas, and human intelligence is an appropriate concern for preaching. He makes a strong theological claim about intelligence as a valuable and God-given attribute. How can we prepare sermons that address Anthony's desire to honor the intelligence of the listeners? Preachers are challenged to think theologically themselves, to make sure their sermon claims are clear, and to make sure the ethical implications of preaching are clearly spelled out. Listeners like Anthony won't tolerate sloppy thinking or vague sentiment.

ANTHONY: You see? I would say (10) *some pastors get too extreme, maybe for an extreme person. Or you can say, well, everybody don't think that way. I'll take it… Well, from one to fifty, I'll take it about thirty percent of that fifty, because I have to use it and judge it the way my life is.* I know that I'm getting something out of it if he is giving over half of that percentage that I'm taking home with me.

INTERVIEWER: Do you feel that the preachers you most often have heard recognize [what] occurs in your decisions of what to take with you?

ANTHONY: At least I hope so. While they're preparing their sermon for that Sunday or (11) *when they're preparing the sermon period, that they open their mind up enough to where they can deliver to that point where I perceive it. Then I can dissect the way I like to.*

INTERVIEWER: What do you think people come to hear from the sermon, or expect to hear?

ANTHONY: You're asking "people," not my thoughts about it?

INTERVIEWER: Well, you, being one of those persons.

ANTHONY: Me being one of those persons, (12) *what I come to hear is a minister that is prepared to give me insight on what the Bible has to say and…directing what it has personally in lives today. We get the political side. We get different sides of his view on how it's delivered to me and how it's delivered to others. You did ask what I liked about it?*

INTERVIEWER: Yes.

ANTHONY: That's probably about what I like about it from a minister. That you can tell if he was prepared to deliver that sermon for that Sunday. Even though he might be busy all week. Well, I can get this sermon prepared in a few hours, but when he gets through, I should have taken another day.

10. Anthony distinguishes pathos (emotional response) from logos (an intellectual activity), and seems to trust logos appeals more than pathos appeals. Once again, with his appeal to statistics, this listener is strongly influenced by the intellectual activity of quantifying and categorizing. To get Anthony's attention, a preacher needs to make more of a rational argument than an emotional appeal.

11. Anthony may be referring to inspiration in logos categories, as "mind-opening." It's an interesting comment, since he clearly distinguishes himself from those who find evidence of the Holy Spirit in emotional responses. Anthony assumes that the Holy Spirit is operating in the preacher's own preparation and in the hearers' ability to think. In traditional terms, this would be the "teaching" function of the Holy Spirit. He also refers to the listening process as involving "dissection," a particularly scientific logos term. This is a claim with some strong theological implications about the activity of the Spirit in preaching. How do preachers think about the activity of the Spirit in their own preparation? In the listeners' reception? Do we expect serious thought or just emotional reactions?

12. Anthony gives a logos answer when he says he expects to receive "insight" from the preacher. He also refers to different perspectives or views presented in a sermon. His comments about "the political side" may indicate that he expects the preacher to consider all sides and implications of sermon claims. His reference to delivery is not the oral delivery by the preacher, but to the delivery of some content within the sermon. He might be asking, "Does the preacher deliver me some serious ideas? Has he or she thought

INTERVIEWER: Do you think other people come with other expectations?

ANTHONY: Other expectations from other people are for themselves that if they have burdens, (13) *if they have feelings about home, health wise, someone else being sick, they come to be comforted in a way so they can feel full.* How to preserve those who are sick or your child that is not doing right at home to you in your perspective measures. Our pastor, he or she gives you an insight on that. So that's what they come to hear.

INTERVIEWER: Very good. What do you think God is doing during the sermon?

ANTHONY: God is, to me, the light that is lit. When I say that is what a preacher preaches, that he reaches in. His hand is inside of me, helping me understand, to feel about what has been said and how I perceived as far as me inside, my mind and myself.

INTERVIEWER: How do you perceive that?

ANTHONY: Well, with myself, like I said at the beginning, (14) *I can be an emotional person. So I reach out enough to feel what I feel that I…not should feel but what I feel that is there at that present time.*

INTERVIEWER: Can you think of a sermon that you've heard that has caused you to act differently in some way or to do something in particular?

ANTHONY: No more than just stand up and no more than just say, backing the preacher on what he says, knowing that those things are right. To me, saying…Not saying I say the right things, but (15) *what comes from my heart, saying "Hallelujah," "Praise the Lord." Those things to me make me feel good. Those things entirely, I can stand up and say it. I'm never been that…person to feel that I'm going to go dance out in the aisle, but I seem like I'm dancing right there without dancing.*

hard about it?" Anthony is more interested in the "what" than the "how" of delivery.

13. Even when referring to pathos issues (feeling language) our listener uses logos categories. For Anthony, feelings seem to be something to "deal" with, almost as problems. The pastor doesn't generate those feelings, but gives insight on ways to deal with feelings. It's possible that Anthony's preference for logos or sermon content leads him to be suspicious of uninterpreted feelings. His earlier comments bear this out when he makes a clear distinction between emotional and intellectual reactions.

14. Here's another powerful reference to bodily imagery and to logos imagery. The use of "light" metaphors is typical logos language referring to intellectual understanding. What's fascinating is that Anthony doesn't suggest that this enlightenment occurs mind to mind, but that the preacher's own enlightenment becomes embodied and touches the hearer's inside thoughts. The more Anthony discusses preaching, the more his categories converge and interpret each other. We may want to pay close attention to this fusion of categories. It's the messiest part of an interview, but may be the most revealing.

15. Anthony attempts to describe the pathos and logos reactions as integrated, and does so in the bodily language of reaching out, as if a hand is extended. This is particularly interesting given his earlier attempts to distinguish between the two.

INTERVIEWER: Can you describe what in a preacher makes you dance? Describe a preacher for example whose presence in the pulpit while preaching you identify as engaging?

ANTHONY: Well, let's start at the part where you said "dance." Like I said before, I only dance within myself without exposing the dancing out in the aisle. Can you repeat that?

INTERVIEWER: What about a preacher's presence do you find engaging while preaching?

ANTHONY: I find that (16) *I have the insight of looking to see a glow on the preacher* that's preaching. I can say that's something that's been with me for years, even with pictures that I've taken that things are there that shouldn't be there. (17) *A bright glow around his head to appear, but to me I visualize that it's there because that's the way I'm feeling at the moment.*

INTERVIEWER: Is there anything a preacher does or can do during the preaching event itself that will help you listen more attentively or more closely?

ANTHONY: Well, I'm not…That's a tough one. I'm not going to say the preacher should act out a little bit more or put a little act or activity into his preaching. Of course, that's what some do, and that's what gets your attention. That's just about it. That gets your attention. Me, (18) *what gets my attention, is how well I perceive the sermon. So whether they're standing still or jumping up or running out in the aisle, that doesn't faze me too much, but to others, it gives them emotional feeling* because he's interacting with what he's saying.

16. Anthony describes his own understanding (a logos element) as having an emotional (pathos) dimension, and he uses bodily language to describe it. His emotional response confirms what he's learned, and it makes him feel like he's dancing. He reminds us that strong emotional responses don't always show physically. Notice that he doesn't reduce his experience to just one dimension, but at the very best, the elements of logos and pathos come together. Anthony continues to operate on two dimensions, without even mentioning the ethos issue of preacher personality or character.

17. Anthony's attempts to explain what engages him become even more complex at this point. He uses logos language again to describe inspiration as a bodily phenomenon. *Insight, looking,* and *picture* are all logos words referring to cognitive activities, or maybe to the function of imagination. But, to make his comments even more complex, Anthony adds the dimension of his own feeling, which is related to his imagination. It's as if he's saying, *"When I understand something, and consider it to be true, I imagine that the preacher has a glow and it's all related to how I feel I'm being touched by the truth of what he's saying."*

18. Anthony carefully distinguishes again between a purely emotional (pathos) element and an intellectual (logos) element. He admits that some listeners may be impressed with emotional appeals, but he is more interested in the logos dimension of perception or how he "sees" the sermon. Maybe he's talking about imagination, holding images and pictures in his mind. This would be an interesting convergence between logos and pathos.

INTERVIEWER: What would be missing on Sunday worship, or in the church worship for that matter, if there were no sermon?

ANTHONY: Now that's a tough one, if there was no… (19) *You're missing it if there were no sermon, period. Even though if you have a nice choir or the choir just sings, it can also…Songs make you emotional before even the preacher preaches. So without a sermon and no other church, just the choir or the songs that you sing before the sermon, if you open up your heart, you'll be involved and be prepared to intake what the preacher has to say in his sermon…* (20) *I don't think anything would be missing to me,* because I think my faith is strong enough to understand exactly what I perceive to being in…the sanctuary itself, giving praise. Even my prayers, I have walked up and gone to the altar myself and just knelt for prayer. People are sitting in the congregation and their thoughts about, "Why is he doing it?" instead of understanding why I'm there. There's only one reason why, because what I'm thinking and what I'm either asking or thanking God for.

INTERVIEWER: Very good. We're going to need to actually close out our interview, but before doing so, are there any ideas or issues or even questions that you can think of which you feel I should ask?

ANTHONY: Oh, I wasn't prepared for that question. No. (21) *I feel that what I've come here for the interview that I was preparing myself for questions that I thought might be asked, but in general, the ones that you have asked have enlightened me to understand myself better, because I'm hearing myself telling you the inner…*about what's expected of pastors and what I expect out of myself.

19. Anthony makes a pathos comment about the music, but sets this in distinction to the sermon. Does the responder assume that different parts of the service have different purposes? Even without the sermon, Anthony himself would not feel slighted. Is this a contradiction of his earlier comments? This comment is surprising, given the careful attention he's given to preaching up to this point. Since it's unlikely that he's suggesting preaching doesn't matter, he may be referring to the difference between any particular Sunday and the overall cumulative effect of preaching. What does it suggest to worship leaders to discover the disconnect between the different parts of the service? How is preaching related to other parts of the service?

20. Anthony's comment suggests that there may be some relationship between the role of praise and the role of preaching. How do preachers and listeners understand this relationship? What are the theological issues at stake?

21. As a final confirmation, Anthony evaluates the success of the interview in the logos terms of *enlightenment* and *understanding.* He uses the word *feel* but seems to be commenting on an aspect of logos, or understanding. We could easily substitute the word *think* and Anthony's narrative would not be compromised. Should we pay more attention to the use of these particular words?

Listening for Preaching

Anthony presents us with some serious practical challenges. Contemporary preaching books recommend that preachers either go for the gusto or go for ancient biblical meanings, while Anthony challenges us to make a rational argument for pursuing the Christian life as it relates to his daily life. He's a complex character, not easily swayed by pretty stories and not convinced by mere commands to be a better Christian. While this individual shows a range of reactions to preaching, Anthony expects preachers to brood over the sermon text, to invite the Holy Spirit in interpretation, and to present some message that is simultaneously rational, ethical, and emotional. He is more impressed by logos categories of intellect and understanding, but these categories don't stand alone. For Anthony, a rational sermon will be true, and will also find some correspondence with the preacher's character, delivery, and ethical directives. Notice, Anthony doesn't base his agreement on either pastoral character or emotional reaction, but seems to expect that the sermon be reasonable, ethical, and congruent with emotional responses. He seems to suggest that if it's true, it will generate ethical promptings and make the listener respond with some joyful reaction.

Some of his ethos comments relate to his appreciation of the ethos of the congregation (we might also call this congregational culture) and to his own ethical interests in preaching as moral direction, but he places little emphasis on the ethos of the preacher. His strongest pathos comments relate to other people who have emotional responses to sermons, but he doesn't comment much on the preacher's own emotional engagement. The responder's strongest pathos reactions are not related to the sermon at all, but to the music in the service.

By far his strongest category is logos, with his comments about the sermon as a teaching tool, his comments about being enlightened and learning, his own continued use of "light" and "enlightenment" metaphors to discuss what happens during a sermon. He also uses an interesting combination of somatic imagery ("touching," and "dancing") to describe the intellectual assent to the sermon. A good sermon "touches" his mind; in fact, the mind of the preacher seems to become embodied and touch the mind of the hearer. A sermon that connects this way can cause him to have an embodied response: to "dance inside himself." What's particularly interesting for preachers is to recognize that Anthony expects some mind/body integration as opposed to a mind/body separation. All his language strains toward that of the mind and the intellect, but he can only do it in the language of the senses.[2] Instead of saying "I understand," Anthony says, "I see." When it all comes together, it is like that fully coordinated activity of dancing. Of course, Anthony dances in his mind, and not with his body. His own intellectual dance of joy is described in the image of a real dancing in the aisles, "like I'm dancing right there without dancing." We know, by the time he explains it, what the difference is.

Anthony also gives us some tiny clues about how listeners remember sermon illustrations. The only one he cites is an extremely masculine story of competition and authority over others. While we can't know how the preacher used this story (whether it was simply a biblical example supporting the Sunday text, or whether it was a whole sermon about Ishmael and Isaac), we know that this story had a tremendous impact on the listener. At the very least, we know that stories can have a profound impact on listeners, and we may want to give more attention to their selection and interpretation.

Listening for Theology

Even though Anthony doesn't discuss the sermon in terms of inspiration or the activity of the Holy Spirit, some of his comments suggest that he's indirectly dealing with precisely such issues. In much contemporary homiletic theory, especially in homiletic theories of African American academics, it's not uncommon to claim inspiration or the activity of the Spirit by an appeal to the pathos categories of emotional response.[3] More specifically, within African American theories of preaching and within the Wesleyan evangelical tradition (and most of the American frontier religious experiences), there is some expectation that the Holy Spirit can be discerned through physical and emotional responses. The African American pulpit tradition is marked by those preachers who can get folks to respond, to shout, to cry, to express themselves through bodily exertions.

Anthony, in a move contrary to much contemporary African American preaching theory, distinguishes very cautiously between emotional impact and intellectual confirmations.[4] He discusses this in terms of the preacher's own emotional delivery as well as the listeners' emotional responses. He seems suspicious of sermons that depend upon the generation of emotion, saying that some pastors get too extreme and that he weighs (in careful percentages!) how much impact he'll allot to emotion. Anthony also comments on his own emotional reactions to sermons, and claims that he doesn't just let everybody touch his emotions, even if he thinks good preaching can accomplish that. In fact, what "touches" Anthony most is a sermon that feeds his intellect and offers specific behavioral direction for living the Christian life.

In this regard, Anthony shares some assumptions about preaching with respected African American homileticians. Like the late Samuel Proctor, Anthony is somewhat indifferent to matters of spirited delivery and emotional impact. Proctor's own method of "dialectical" preaching attempted to show the discrepancy between actual situations and ideal situations, calling for sermons to project specific remedies for personal and ethical problems.[5] Proctor's method was straightforward and down-to-earth, but full of direction for daily life. Proctor frequently used sermon material drawn from the world of education, politics, and science; his was a self-consciously rational model.

Anthony's language of "glow" or light on the preacher also sounds similar to James Forbes' discussion of anointing by the Holy Spirit. Forbes' work is singular for its "logos" approach to discerning the Spirit. He describes his approach as "progressive Pentecostalism [with] a strong emphasis on spirit but deep commitment to transformative social action."[6] Forbes discusses the "marks" of the Spirit as beyond amorphous inner feelings or emotions; the Spirit directs people toward humility, honesty and social justice. In Forbes' own work, we see an intriguing combination of logos "content" with language that is traditionally reserved to describe emotional or pathos elements.

Henry Mitchell's work in preaching theory argues more strongly than either Proctor or Forbes for that dimension we've called "pathos." Mitchell certainly acknowledges the logos elements of intellectual content, but argues that the various elements of preaching are activated and unified by emotional response. For this reason, Mitchell urges that sermons move toward a celebration or cathartic moment. "However much the details seem intellectually important, they gain their spiritual impact primarily from the way they move the hearer toward *feelings* of bonding with protagonists and problems and potentials, to the end of growth for the hearer…"[7] Mitchell's perspective is strikingly different from Anthony's. Even though this listener demonstrates some convergence of logos and pathos, he doesn't seem to identify pathos as either the primary motivation or the final arbiter of the sermon's appeal.

Another related issue that surfaces is Anthony's theological anthropology: his understanding of human beings. In one of his strongest logos statements, Anthony argues that intelligence is God-given, a gift to be embraced and respected. Not only does he value this for himself as a listener, he expects other listeners to exercise their own intellectual gifts in discerning (separating) what is true and worthy from what is false and unworthy. We might want to conjecture that Anthony considers this discerning activity as part of the Holy Spirit's work. He doesn't quite make that leap in terms of listener responses, but he certainly expects that the Holy Spirit is working hard on the preacher's brain.

What's at stake in any discussion of human nature is the degree to which we assume something positive or negative about human possibilities.[8] Are human beings fundamentally good, or are they fundamentally flawed? Is it possible for humans to exercise their morality or will or intelligence in ways that are reliable and trustworthy? As Lee Ramsey notes, "How we see the human being unavoidably shapes our approach to care in the sermon. For instance, the theological anthropology of the sermon may define the human problem as individual sin, understood as disobedience to God's laws. What is needed, therefore, is for the disobedient one to come down to the altar, confess his or her sin either privately or to the preacher, and receive the forgiveness of God."[9] Ramsey identifies other models, and shows how such assumptions shape preaching decisions. We might also conclude that listener assumptions have similar power. Anthony assumes that human beings have been granted intelligence by God, and that they should employ it in making rational decisions and commitments.

Anthony also indicates something about his understanding of scripture. Scripture offers individuals (there's a strong sense of human autonomy operating here) insights into how God has acted in the past and how God will act in contemporary lives. We see this in his discussion of "operative" and "speculative" modes of interpretation, but also in his discussion of the Isaac and Ishmael story. If God was faithful to the sons of Abraham in the past, God will be faithful in the present. But, even beyond what the scripture teaches us about God, it also teaches us how to act in the present. Scripture (and therefore preaching) should direct us in our understandings of God and in how we direct our own lives. Anthony assumes a strong teaching function for scripture, and he expects good preaching to have a strong teaching function as well. Since we can assume that Anthony has been formed by some version of Wesleyan theology, we might recognize his approach as very similar to the Wesleyan quadrilateral, or the four-fold approach to interpreting and understanding faith. The Wesleyan quadrilateral grants equal authority to Scripture, Tradition, Reason, and Experience.[10] The quadrilateral requires serious discerning functions by ordinary Christians to weigh the various claims of scripture, history/ tradition, reason, and regular experience. One of our questions should be whether or not this discerning, weighing function occurs within an individual or as part of some community conversation. Anthony hints that he checks his interpretations with other listeners.

Another theological issue for preachers and worship leaders is the way Anthony distinguishes between the purpose of preaching and other parts of the service, particularly the music. As much emphasis as Anthony places on preaching, and he clearly considers it important, he almost trivializes its importance when he says he wouldn't be missing anything if the sermon was absent. He's already claimed that music is important for creating an emotional context for preaching, and then seems to say that music would be enough for him. Anthony's particular congregation combines a strong formal liturgical tradition (use of creeds and a printed liturgy) with a more evangelical preaching and music tradition, creating an eclectic approach to worship. The theological issue at stake for preachers is to consider a whole theology of worship (not just a theology of preaching), and whether or not *we* expect all the elements of a service to be integrated into one purpose or a variety of purposes. What method of theological discernment operates when worship leaders combine different elements in a service? What is the impact on preaching? on the rest of the service?[11]

Challenges to Preaching

1. How do we understand the logos activity of the Holy Spirit in sermon *preparation*? Do we think about this most in terms of emotional delivery, or do we consciously seek the guiding and teaching functions that Anthony assumes before we ever take the pulpit?

2. What kinds of illustrations are we using? Even if we have several illustrations in a sermon, are there some that appeal only to certain populations? If so, what behaviors or values do these illustrations promote?

3. Does our preaching take a stand on ethical behaviors, or those that involve inter-group dynamics? Does our preaching take a stand on personal piety or individual moral "tests"? Are we specific enough for listeners to know how to organize their lives?

4. Are we depending on emotional responses to carry preaching? If so, why be content with this limited response?

5. How carefully do we think about preaching with regard to the demands of reason? How much time do we spend preparing a sermon that will meet the intellectual and ethical demands of someone like Anthony?

CHAPTER 3

"All of a Sudden, I've Got to Concentrate on the Sermon"

Helen: Urban Caucasian Woman

G. Lee Ramsey, Jr.

This chapter explores a conversation with Helen, a sixty-year-old member of a medium-sized Anabaptist congregation located in a large metropolitan area of the Midwest. Helen has been a member of this church for over twenty years. The congregation is predominantly Caucasian with several African American and Asian members. Most are middle-income and highly educated, and the average age of all members is under sixty. Many young children participate in the life of the congregation and its corporate worship. Some members live within close proximity to this urban parish, and others commute from a distance to participate in the gatherings of the congregation.

The sanctuary is simply appointed with movable chairs arranged in a horseshoe pattern around a slightly elevated platform. A central pulpit is the focal point for the space with a table behind the pulpit and an organ and piano against one wall. A number of banners hang along the walls of the sanctuary emphasizing peace, one of the central theological and social commitments of this denomination. As a historic peace church within the wider Anabaptist tradition, the congregation shares a history of active social concern and gives priority to matters of social justice. Some of these concerns are mentioned in the interview, indicating a tension among members on issues such as race relations and human sexuality.

Worship in this congregation can be characterized as relatively informal, though well-planned and coordinated. Various lay members take active leadership roles in the worship service. Communion occurs with participants of all ages gathering around two different prepared tables to share bread, wine, grapes, and pretzels (for the children). Though only celebrated four times a year in many Anabaptist congregations, communion functions for the congregation as a service of reconciliation and renewal of the spiritual bonds between the members of the congregation.

The most significant element of the worship service not only for Helen but for many Anabaptists is the congregational response to the preaching of the Word. In keeping with historic Anabaptist practices, the congregation places high priority upon the community as a location of authority. Following the sermon, it is customary for the congregation to share its response to the reading and interpretation of the scripture. People may offer comments about their own understanding and application of the sermon. They may give testimonials, share concerns about events in their own lives or in the world, or they may seek congregational support, guidance, and prayer. This sharing in response to the Word is not a critique or evaluation of the sermon. Rather it is a communal appropriation and extension of the meaning of the gospel among the congregation. The congregation shares responsibility with the preacher for the interpretation of the gospel and for discovering the gospel's call upon their lives.[1] In keeping with the Reformers' understanding of preaching, especially Calvin and Zwingli, the congregational members must apply their own reason and understanding to the sermon's interpretation in order to discern the revelation of the gospel.[2] This community response to the proclamation takes as much time in the worship service as needed. In the interview below, we will hear how this dynamic of shared preaching and listening actually impacts Helen and the life decisions that she makes.

Excerpts from the Transcript

INTERVIEWER: Let's think a little bit about pastors you've had over your lifetime. What kind of relationships have you had with your pastors or preachers?

HELEN: Let's see. When that little church started up down the street from me, that's how I got involved. (1) *It's probably more the pastor's wife that sort of took me in. I would say I was welcomed into the Kingdom, I really was. They sort of adopted me, not officially, of course. I was a little in awe. That particular pastor's personality was a little grand.* He would come down from the pulpit and pinch the ear of one of his kids that was misbehaving. That was the first one.

1. Helen is making a response to ethos, the character of the pastor and, in this case, the pastor's wife. Significantly, the character of the pastor does not seem to create a positive association for Helen, whereas the personal relationship with the pastor's spouse does. This could be a comment about gender relations, but it is also a reminder to preachers that others often do the work of pastoral care as well as or better than the preacher. Notice the early reference to "adoption" for Helen, because the theme is both personally and theologically significant as the interview unfolds.

(2) *The next one, there again, it was the pastor's wife that really shepherded.* Basically, probably, I remember her saying, and I still keep in touch with them now. She encouraged me to go to Bible school in Canada. She wanted me to get to know the larger Anabaptist tradition, rather than just this little, conservative, mostly from the Amish background kind of thing. Lionel, (3) *that was her husband, the pastor, he was the one who baptized me when I was nineteen. He's the one that baptized me. There again, I think it was a personality thing more. He was a caring person and a good person. I just didn't feel close...Probably when I was that young, a teenager, I probably wasn't into sermons so much as the rest of it.* We'd have everyone...Most of our people were rural people coming into the city. So everyone would bring their own lunch just to save time. They would fight over who got to have me with them. Then as I went along, I got to know more about theology and became convinced that this was for me.

(4) *One pastor I really didn't care for too well. It wasn't that I didn't like him so much. I didn't think he had any people skills or particularly a whole lot. He would just get awkward and didn't know how to talk to you. I'm a strong person. I tend to come off pretty strong. But his sermons were good. They were fine. I talked about them on that paper how great they were. I guess they were all great. Basically, what he did from the pulpit was a good thing. Administratively, there were some people who actually left the church, and I don't know why. It was stupid stuff. It wasn't anything he really did. I don't know. I don't remember. That was kind of sad. At the time I remember I could see that's probably important, but then...I'm thinking over the years.* When I first came here, the pastor here was really a warm person and just really, really good, but I always had the feeling he didn't like me too well. You know how you sense that. He

2. Here again, Helen connects her own spiritual nurture to the pastoral care that she received from the preacher's spouse. But when it comes to preaching, the personal traits of the preacher, his ethos, do not seem as important. In fact, the preacher's sermons hardly registered with Helen at all.

3. Helen makes it clear that she is responding to something other than the preacher's ethos when she weighs the importance of preaching.

4. Notice that the preacher can be "awkward" interpersonally, but his sermons are still "good, fine." By now we know that Helen is looking for something other than a pastoral relationship with the preacher in order for the sermon to be significant for her. Preachers sometimes overestimate the importance of pastoral relationships when they step into the pulpit. Many listeners do attend to the content of the sermon whether or not they know the preacher or think that he or she is an effective pastor.

didn't feel comfortable with me. He didn't have a lot to say when I would try to talk with him. (5) *Basically, from the pastor's point of view, I never looked for the nurturing part of it. I'm trying to figure out what I can do about that. Mostly it's from the leadership from the pulpit part of it, worship leader kind of thing and planning and providing for that worship time. That's a real important thing to me. I don't expect any one person to be all and everything.* I think that's stupid. In fact, I think in the past we as a congregation have acknowledged that.

We had a pastoral couple for a while. She was somebody that I had known in college. That was real interesting. She did most of the preaching. He saw himself as a teacher. He did a lot of that kind of stuff and the nurturing stuff. (6) *We really grieved when they left. They just felt it was time to move on. They were here for twelve years or something. We really grieved.* It was hard. So we did an interim kind of thing. That pastor, he was there just for two years. I am still in touch with him because he went to another congregation nearby. I did do a couple counseling sessions with him, but he was a social worker turned pastor.

INTERVIEWER: You felt an affinity there.

HELEN: Maybe so. I don't know. Then Pastor Swanson, when he first came I felt this kind of discomfort. I felt like once again, he didn't quite know what to do with me. But then so many people don't. But that has grown. I feel he's been real supportive. There again, and I told him this: (7) *I really believe his sermons make a difference in my life. Not wonderful, grand, major effects, but the ones that did make a major difference in my life were*

5. Helen makes a distinction between what she expects or does not expect from the pastor in terms of pastoral care, and what she expects from him as preacher and worship leader. The preacher must provide organization and leadership in worship even if the pastoral relationship is absent. These ordering functions that she associates with the preacher and preaching suggest the importance of logos for Helen as listener.

6. Notice that when Helen does make a comment about pastoral relationship, she talks about the entire congregation's grief over the clergy couple's departure. This suggests that congregational culture is important for Helen as a listener. What sort of preaching helps strengthen congregational identity and pastoral bonds with the congregation as whole?

7. Helen points out that some preaching has a gradual and positive effect while other single sermons can make a "major difference." Logos contributes to these varying effects of preaching. As preachers, do we trust the work of proclamation to both build up and transform the believer?

not done by him. (8) *Over the summer we had a student from one of the denominational colleges who was exploring the pastorate. His delivery was not real great, but the sermon was about what God is calling you to do. It got me thinking about [my life] because* things are changing now. During that sermon it became clear what I had to do. The next morning I called the Special Needs Adoption program and started the process. I had a thirteen-year-old a little over a year later.

INTERVIEWER: What do you think preaching does in this congregation that no other thing does?

HELEN: I'd say probably it's the main source of—(9) *this sounds hokey, but—spiritual enlightenment, if you will. What the Bible says. I think we really look to our pastor for that, because he's the one that does the Bible study and has time for that and knows. What does the Bible say? What should we be thinking about?* (10) *Even if I don't always agree, which often I do with my pastor, what should I be thinking about in terms of what's going on in the world, in terms of what's going on in this city or this congregation? What should I be thinking about?* Sometimes he gives opinions and that's fine. There's probably sometimes where I don't always agree.

8. The sermon causes her to *think* about what is changing in her life. This is a reference to the logos appeals of the sermon that make it "clear what [she] had to do." Notice that even a mediocre delivery (embodiment) does not interfere with the sermon's impact upon the listener. Appealed to at the center of her self, she "knows" what to do. A timely word, logos, brings into sharp focus her life before God and motivates Helen to take action. Here the adoption theme has come full circle, as the one who was "adopted" by the congregation adopts her own daughter.

9. The reference to biblical authority shows that Helen views the sermon as instructive, teaching the listeners what we "should be thinking about." The sermon is logo-centric. By preacher and listener thinking together, Helen sorts out how to live the Christian life in the city and the world. In this way, the sermon makes another kind of logos appeal to Helen as "enlightenment." Helen informs us that listeners want clarity of expression in preaching that is biblically sound.

10. Here Helen is pointing out the importance of the preacher as a public person to name crucial social concerns that the church confronts in the world. This, too, is a logos function within preaching. Many listeners *want* to hear preaching that engages the larger social world, even if they disagree with the sermon. Preachers who, for fear of disapproval, are reluctant to name the gospel in the world can take heart.

(11) *I really think people get up, like I said, during sharing time and talk about the sermons from that point of view. "I needed to hear that right now," they'll say. Sometimes they're more specific and sometimes not. Our people are not... I've been in a lot of different kinds of congregations. Our people are very well-educated, sophisticated people, so it's not like it's a fundamentalist, very simple view of Christianity. So when people from here stand up and say those things, I think, "Oh wow." I'm just real impressed.* It does. You're able to make it real personal, because we don't have a lot of time together to do that as intensely as some groups might.

INTERVIEWER: What would be missing if there were no sermon at all?

HELEN: That's the part that would be missing. My daughter would like it, because the services would be shorter. The sermons are often real meaningful for her, too. It just wouldn't be complete. There would be a piece missing, like a puzzle. You're all done, but there's still one piece missing. I think it would be that way. It's all part of a unit. (12) *We've had some where we've done a little different version of the sermon, and that's nice or different, but I don't think I'd want to do that all the time. I like that input. I need that input.*

INTERVIEWER: You mentioned one sermon that really spoke to you, but thinking back over your lifetime, your history of listening to sermons, what are some high points?

HELEN: I don't have any, except that one.

INTERVIEWER: That was the only one?

HELEN: (13) *I don't even remember what the sermon was...*I remember a lot of stuff, but when I actually made my first Christian commitment. I know there was a visiting preacher there at my little church back home. I remember we prayed together afterward. The only other person I remember is our pastor's wife. Obviously,

11. Notice, the sharing in response to the sermon is another indicator of Helen's logos preferences, but the preference is enhanced by congregational culture. A sermon for her is something that is enriched by discussion among a community of "educated, sophisticated people," who give honest response to the content of the sermon. Such responses allow her to make the sermon personal. At the same time, communal life impacts the way Helen and the other hearers respond to the sermon. This congregation has a certain character that values community discussion of the sermon and its implications for Christian living. Such emphasis upon the community of hearers grows, in part, out of Helen's Anabaptist tradition. It highlights the way that ethos and logos interact in the preaching and hearing event. How can preachers encourage such community response to the preached Word?

12. The sermon provides "input" for Helen. It is a distinctive content that she says would be missing if the sermon were not present. As a listener with logos preferences, she needs the reliability of clear preaching; otherwise, worship is incomplete. Preachers can be encouraged that listeners like Helen do expect a weekly sermon with depth and a sermon that offers challenge for the hearer.

13. Helen does not place much value upon a sermon's memorability. Even though she is a listener who thinks about the content of sermons, they do not have to be memorable in order to be important. This telling comment indicates that listeners respond to a sermon's immediacy, the Word spoken here and now. Some sermons may become memorable for the congregation, but preachers need not fret over preparing

something was said. I was ready. At least the man did that one good thing. He did many others, but I wish that I could have… If I had known, I could have maybe said that to him, and maybe it would have helped. (14) *Other than that, I really don't remember specific sermons. I don't remember specific sermons. I don't even remember specific pastors in the way they preach…a little bit, but that's not important to me.*

INTERVIEWER: How about some low points?

HELEN: (15) *Low points? I suppose there have been people who preach who put you to sleep because they have this monotone… I think it's important to be…*

INTERVIEWER: …a little bit more animated…

HELEN: …*a little animated or at least conversational.* (16) *I remember that one was certainly not well presented, but the idea was. I was trying real hard, because he was trying real hard. So I was trying real hard to get into it. So that may have been part of it, too. I really believe that's more than 50 percent of it, is what I bring into it. Even somebody who is really, really boring in their presentation, I still can learn from. I don't like it, but I will still listen, because I feel like this is what God is giving me right at this moment. I will benefit from it.*

INTERVIEWER: Is there something that you hope will happen to you as a result of listening to sermons?

HELEN: (17) *Just a little bit more of a germ of an idea of what is going on. I don't expect big things from any one sermon. I'm always kind of overwhelmed if it happens, kind of surprised if it happens. Just steady growth. The sermons that I really think when I go away from here thinking are really good are the ones that during the time I made a decision, "Okay, I'm going to change things by doing such and such." I don't always pull it off totally, but the result is there. Then the next time a little bit more.*

sermons that hearers cannot recall, nor should we evaluate the effectiveness of our preaching upon the basis of memorability.

14. This fascinating comment suggests that there is an overall impact of preaching that transcends the specific content and the person of the preacher. Helen is suggesting to us that neither the rhetorical category of logos nor ethos is ultimately important. She is reaching for something beyond the content of the sermon and the person of the preacher. Faithful preachers know that she is speaking of God.

15. These are comments about the rhetorical effects of delivery or embodiment of the sermon. She values animation and conversational style in delivery.

16. Notice that Helen adds as criteria her own willingness to hear the sermon. She notes again that "embodiment" on the part of the preacher is not the primary factor. She can still learn from a boring sermon. God is speaking to her through the sermon and her job is to be ready to listen. Helen's comments offer encouragement to preachers. Listeners want to hear a word from God through the sermon, and many come to worship prepared to listen despite the preacher's shortcomings.

17. The sermon plants ideas for this listener that are like seeds that slowly grow and one day surprisingly push her toward change. Then the cycle begins again. She values the decisive sermons as "really good," but she recognizes the importance of regular preaching that leads up to a moment of conviction.

INTERVIEWER: Can you think of a time when the sermon may have really stirred the emotions of the entire congregation as a whole?

HELEN: There have been times when... Well, right after Sept. 11, a lot of what he had to say...Now he didn't talk about that directly, but a lot of what he had to say fit. Either that or it was an amazing coincidence. (18) *An awful lot of people, because a lot of people were emotional already. Sharing time during that day was just interminable, because people just kept talking about it and talking about it. Times like that probably more than just the sermon itself.* People would be emotional anyhow, and the sermon kind of helped.

INTERVIEWER: It sounds like that's the same kind of situation that it was when the sermon really impacted you. It was more your state of...

HELEN: Oh, my, my, my. Yes. I had been doing the junior high program for a long time. I was in that program. We hired a part-time pastor who was going to be doing youth stuff. So I was being phased out. I was thinking I need to get out of here so they can do it their way. I'm not totally happy with that, but I had been thinking what should I be doing with my life now? (19) *That morning I had read the Sunday paper, and Sunday's Child was in there, a little girl. I thought, hmmm...There were a couple of things about it that moved me. I come here and I'm hearing this. All of a sudden I've got to concentrate on the sermon. I said, "Okay, God. I will. I'll call tomorrow."*

So yes. It was. It was the timing. I see these kinds of things as God. God made the call, and during sharing time I got up and shared what happened. People were just really responsive to me. So I went through the whole process, and two days before Christmas, I got a child. The

18. This is one of Helen's rare comments that suggest the rhetorical category of pathos. But the emotion of the worship service is generated by outside events (Sept. 11). The sermon is responsive to the existing pathos rather than generative of or dependent upon it for effect. It is also significant for Helen that pathos is shared among the community. Communal culture and pathos join together in the hearing of a sermon. How can preaching grow out of the genuine feelings that are always present within the congregation?

19. Helen reflects upon how a particular sermon intersects with her own life and with what she believes God is calling her to do. In this case she receives a clear call to begin preparing for an adoption. She recognizes that the impact of the sermon depends upon "where I am." But the sermon has a content (logos), a meaning of its own that has intersected with her own story. The situation urges her to "concentrate on the sermon" because through it God is making a call to her. Her call, however, comes within the Christian community at worship. Congregational culture as well as logos play into Helen's hearing and responding to God's call. The sermon evokes a response from the listener, in part, because of the congregational life that helps Helen to discern this call. Through preaching, for Helen, God does issue life-changing calls to individuals, but such calls are always to individuals within communities.

adoption was final...she wanted to be baptized here, because she had already made a commitment. That's been a really good thing.

INTERVIEWER: Do you think that there are any issues that are too explosive for a pastor to talk about from the pulpit?

HELEN: (20) *Not if it's done well. I think a pastor shouldn't get up and start berating people or really being mean and hard on people. It would be more style than the topic. I think a pastor should approach most any topic. I think it needs to be done well and carefully. The smart thing is if you want people to hear and not shut you out, you do it in a way that's going to be [acceptable to the people].*

INTERVIEWER: What kind of issues do you have to be careful about like that?

HELEN: (21) *Not too long ago we were dealing with the issue of homosexuality. I felt like during the church service time, the preacher did a good job. There were some that felt like he could be a little too liberal. Some of the people in my small group are a little older, and it was a little harder for them to deal with. In our small group we couldn't talk about it...I really felt the need to process more.*

I'm going to renege a little bit here in that (22) *I certainly hope a pastor would not preach about an individual, against an individual in a sermon. I don't know that anyone ever does that, but I suppose in some places they do. I would hope they wouldn't do that. I think that would be totally inappropriate.*

Of course, in the Anabaptist tradition peace is not a controversial thing, but some of our pastors in the past have had a more radical view on that than some of our parishioners. I worked for a number of years with a church-related social service and still work for them sometimes. That's been a good thing. Anabaptists like to think our pastor is a real activist. This is good for

20. Both style (embodiment) and organization of the sermon's content (logos) are important for Helen when sermons are preached on controversial topics. Attention to both will help the listeners hear the sermon.

21. Again, even though addressing a controversial topic, Helen determines that a sermon that is carefully developed (logos) and well-delivered (embodiment) is "good." But what she needs to complete the sermon is the opportunity to respond to the sermon among the congregation. When we preach on controversial topics, we should not be surprised that the congregation wants to respond. The content is worth engaging, and doing so may be the first step toward congregational action for the sake of the gospel.

22. Helen does not want to hear sermons that are either condemning (a logos concern) or insensitive to another's humanity and dignity (a pathos and ethos concern). Such sermons are "inappropriate." Helen reminds preachers that the gospel may "scandalize" church or society with its tough love, but it will never demean.

him. (23) *We have one woman in our church right now who is a mediator on a peacemaking team. Everyone just thinks it's wonderful what she's doing, and we all want to be part of that. Like everyone wants to be part of me and my adoption project. We all want to be a part of that. What we couldn't do ourselves, and I'm not sure I am ready, but it's nice to know we have someone out there representing us in that way.*

I don't know. I think definitely one that should be [preached about] but is often kind of touchy is the whole race relations thing. (24) *I think the pulpit is where some of that stuff belongs...in the leadership. If it can't be talked about there, where can it be talked about?*

INTERVIEWER: What do you think that the preacher is doing when he stands up to preach?

HELEN: I've never gotten the feeling from him...that he sat down that week and said, "Oh, no. I've got to do another sermon. I've got to just have something to say. So I'll come up with this." (25) *I more get the feeling like, I really think God lays these things on this heart. Basically, giving him this message, and it's kind of like he just goes for it, and he really likes doing it. He really likes it. He has all of this information. I notice right away he puts on the lapel mike on so he can move around. He gets into it. He obviously likes what he does. So what he's doing up there is sharing. I think that's probably it, if you had to say it in one word.* (26) *He's sharing what he believes and what he thinks and what he's read. He doesn't sit there and read what other people said, but he puts it together.*

23. Preaching occurs within a congregation that has a distinctive communal identity. The sermon contributes to the shared commitments of the congregation in such a way that everyone participates or wants to be "a part of" what others are doing. This congregation reminds preachers that listeners are eager to know how they belong to the whole body of Christ.

24. Helen wants the preacher to address crucial social concerns such as race relations from the pulpit. It is not only a question of justice but of leadership. Preachers learn from Helen that some within the congregation want to hear the prophetic voice of preaching. Preaching would not be complete without it.

25. This comment shows how Helen listens to sermons on multiple levels. The sermon is a message from God (logos) laid on the preacher's heart that he likes to preach with enthusiasm (pathos, embodiment). The sermon is also a "sharing" with the congregation of what the preacher believes and has been given by God to tell. Sharing points toward *ethos* as the preacher connects with the congregation and helps build up community identity. In this summary statement from Helen, preachers can hear an appeal to preach thoughtfully with passion, and to offer the sermon as a gift within the community.

26. Notice Helen's identification of preaching as something other than strict biblical interpretation. The preacher is making sense for the hearers out of all that he has read and thought. She does not use the term, but Helen appears to be saying that preaching is, at least in part, the doing of theology (a logos orientation that blends the distinction between preaching as proclamation and teaching).

Insights for Preaching

The clearest sound that we hear from this listener is a steady note about the integrity of preaching's content, its logos. Several times in the conversation she distinguishes between the pastoral relationship (ethos) and the content and purpose of preaching (see sidebars 1, 3, 5). She recognizes the need for pastoral nurture outside of the worship service, but listening to a sermon is about hearing and responding to the call of God. Preachers who are also pastors often think that the quality of the pastoral relationship determines the degree to which listeners engage the sermon. For many listeners this is true. But Helen indicates a different understanding. She listens to a sermon for the content that it conveys, the biblical authority from which it is derived, and the possibility of hearing the voice of God speaking through the sermon. The pastoral relationship for listeners like Helen is secondary. In Helen's comments, preachers can find relief from weighing too heavily the importance of a pastoral relationship when stepping into the pulpit.[3] Some listeners, like Helen, will find the personal care that they need from other members of the congregation, but in the sermon they want to hear a word from God.

Helen offers to us a second insight about preaching. She thinks of preaching and listening as a gathering of thoughtful, responsive Christians who want to engage God through the preaching and hearing of a sermon that is based upon biblical authority (11, 19, 21). This emphasis upon the congregation as co-interpreters of the gospel points us toward the category of congregational character. Specifically, because it is a congregation that values the community as a community of interpreters, each sermon has the potential to shape members and the congregation as a whole. Listeners test out their own hearing of the gospel with each other in and beyond worship. There is no assumption that all hearers will agree with the content and implications of the sermon. Rather, the sermon works incrementally among the hearers who respond to the proclaimed word through conversation with the preacher and one another.[4] Occasionally, such communal sermon listening will result in discernment of God's call and a decision to do something as life-altering as adopting a child in the late middle years of life. Helen deems such moments as stemming from good preaching, but preachers should not attempt to orchestrate such moments.

Helen raises some potentially fruitful questions for preachers when she links preaching's logos appeals to communal character. Within one's own given tradition, how does the community as a whole participate in the interpretation of the gospel? Is the sermon complete without an acknowledged congregational response? What is gained or lost when the response to the word is the same week after week, whether that response is a discussion, a hymn, a creed, a testimonial, or an offering? Some preachers might want to find specific ways of opening up conversation in worship following their sermons. Others might want to think carefully about the ways in which they do or do not invite communal interpretation of the sermon. Helen's candid comments suggest that since we value the gospel so highly, we should not leave its interpretation up to chance or the individual alone.

Helen also has a word of instruction about sermon delivery. She, like many listeners in this study, reports that she values clarity of expression and an animated yet conversational style in the pulpit (15, 16, 21). Nevertheless, even poor embodiment of the sermon by the preacher should not interfere with the hearer's ability to discern the call of God, which requires listener preparation, concentration, and a willingness to respond (8, 13, 16). In other words, given the choice as a sermon listener, Helen prefers substance over style, a thoughtful gift rather than a pretty package. For her, the preacher's job is to prepare well, speak as clearly as possible, and from a biblically sound authority instruct the hearers on God's direction for the congregation (9, 10, 12). As long as these aims for the sermon are in place, she is willing to overlook less than stellar delivery. Preachers need not take these comments as license to ignore matters of sermon delivery; shoddy embodiment may, in some cases, indicate poor sermon preparation or an unwillingness to serve the gospel. But Helen reminds preachers that the gospel speaks in many forms. The vessels that God has, for the time being, are the broken ones who answer the call to preach. If we remain focused upon the content of the gospel in our preaching, a modest attention to matters of delivery will be sufficient to get the job done.

Listening for Theology

Helen expresses strong conviction about the power of the preached word to call and instruct the hearer (7, 8, 16, 19). The logos is indeed "with God" (John 1), and through the preached word God summons the hearer into new and faithful response. Luther, Zwingli, and Calvin might all be more than a little pleased to hear, in this age of acculturated Christianity and linguistic fragmentation, a faithful believer say that she is listening to the sermon for a "call from God." Yet this astute listener for the Word is no naïve biblicist, waiting for an authoritarian interpretation of scripture to guide her every step. She wants to engage with the logos among a community of thinking believers to discern God's direction for herself and the congregation (11). As this listener expresses it, the sermon is also about "what I bring into it." Such receptivity on the part of the listener should not be underestimated by the preacher. It can cause people to give away all that they have to the poor and draw widows and orphans into relationship with the church. Preachers always run the risk of underestimating the congregations' readiness to hear the good news. Helen shows us the face and posture of a hearer sitting on the edge of the pew eager to hear in community the voice of God in the words of the sermon (8, 14, 16).

Helen makes striking comments about how preaching contributes to the edification of the listener. She has a keen ear for how preaching challenges the hearer to growth and maturity in the faith. She reminds preachers that each sermon is part of a larger whole, like planting the "germ of an idea of what is going on" (7, 17). We can distinguish Helen's understanding of preaching from those who claim that it must always emphasize decision. Listeners expect "steady growth" from preaching that has instructional content. Such theological planting and watering of the word can usher in moments of intense flourishing in which the believer chooses life over death, risk over hoarding the fruits of faith.

When, in faithfulness to the Word, one believer risks a response of great consequence, it is both a sign of the work of God within the Christian community and a call to the community to accept its responsibility for this act of faithfulness to God (19, 23). In Helen's case we see how the congregation assists her in interpreting the word of God, then as her "adoptive family" shares the obligations that her adoption of a daughter entails. The preacher may shudder when seeing such a harvest, knowing the cost that will yet be required. But as Helen perceives, preaching is not about the preacher; it's God's call.

For the purposes of our study, it is noteworthy that such an immediate, corporate response to weekly preaching heightens listeners' engagement with the sermon. Congregational members "complete" the sermon that the preacher initiates. They carry out the response to the Word in worship and on into the active small group life of the congregation.

This leads to an observation about the effect of preaching. Preachers recognize that the effect of any given sermon upon the hearers is impossible to anticipate. So many factors come together in the preaching moment–the work of the Holy Spirit, the situation of the hearer and the preacher, congregational context, community and world events, etc.–that any attempt by the preacher to predict a sermon's impact is futile. Logos, ethos, pathos, and embodiment of the sermon all contribute toward but are not determinative of, a sermon's effect. Helen wisely notes that sermons have both a gradual and a transformative effect upon her (7).[5] Sermons shape congregations over time through ethos, pathos, and logos, and they provoke moments of profound awakening that cause the hearer to say, "All of a sudden I've got to concentrate on the sermon." Preachers can trust the cumulative impact of faithful preaching within a congregation while remaining open to the particular moments when the hearer arrives at a startlingly fresh encounter with the gospel.

Finally, Helen challenges preachers to widen the scope of our preaching to incorporate church and world. While the Anabaptists of her congregation would expect a prophetic word from the pulpit, there is probably no more agreement on controversial topics among Anabaptists than among

Wesleyans or Lutherans. Theological disagreement should not cause us to shy away from a faithful interpretation of the gospel in the world (21). Helen reminds us that listeners expect preachers to give attention to how the gospel addresses our social lives–from war and economics to race and sexuality (20, 21, 24). What will gain the preacher a hearing on controversial subjects is respect for the listener as a child of God (22) and as co-interpreters of the gospel and world (21, 26). Approached in this fashion, listeners will eagerly hear a sermon that ranges across the whole social landscape, and they will join with the pastor to discern where God is leading the church in the world.

Challenges to Preaching

1. Recognizing that the pastoral relationship with the congregation is important for preaching, do we also give sufficient emphasis to the content of the sermon to engage listeners like Helen?

2. What opportunities are available in and beyond worship for the congregation to share the completion of the sermon? Is our preaching respectful of the hearers' desire and ability to add their own interpretations to the sermon?

3. How does our preaching contribute to both a gradual and transformative effect in the life of the congregation? Do we trust both of these aspects of preaching?

4. Does our preaching faithfully respond to the many listeners who, like Helen, want to hear how the gospel interprets the wider social world? If not, why not?

CHAPTER 4

"I Told You, It's about Relationship"

Cassandra: Urban African American Woman

DALE P. ANDREWS

This interview is with Cassandra, an African American woman in her mid-forties. Her professional life includes a consultant position at a small corporation and starting her own small business in partnership with a friend. She has extensive experience with public communication, as her work requires presentations. Cassandra reports that she has been quite reflective on several interests in preaching even prior to her interview. Cassandra expresses a strong desire to share her feelings in an ongoing effort to work through her questions.

Cassandra's church is a medium-sized, largely African American, urban congregation within a Methodist tradition in a Midwestern city. The members appear to be predominantly middle-aged and middle class. Participants in worship dress simply but somewhat formally. The contemporary church building is furnished well. Between the several announcement boards and table material regarding community events and congregational activities, information is readily available in the church. Art work reflects the cultural identity of the congregation, with a range of expressions between Afrocentric art and actual pictures of church events.

Preaching appears to have a prominent place in the worship life. The pulpit is at the center of the chancel, in a forward location with other important liturgical furnishings to each side. Music and prayer prepare for the preaching event. The sermon is central in the service even when the sacraments are involved. Quite consistent with the prominence of preaching in the worship life of the church and with Cassandra's own interests, her pastor expresses an open and deliberate effort to develop his preaching ministry.

Excerpts from the Transcript

INTERVIEWER: Tell me a little bit about what seem to be the most important things that happen in this congregation?

CASSANDRA: Probably the most important things that are happening right now is (1) *our reaching out more into the community, our focus and emphasis on the sick and shut-in.* Visiting the sick and shut-in. (2) *The pastor and our communion stewards and others will visit the sick and shut-in. We all send cards. We make sure that all the sick and shut-in receive some communication from the church.* We do that on first Sundays. There's usually a basket with the names of everybody sick and shut-in. People take cards from there, and then they take ownership, responsibility, and become partners with a sick and shut-in person for the month. I have a grandmother in Cleveland in a nursing home, and I know what it's like when they get a card from somebody or a call from somebody, and they know they're not forgotten. I think that's real important. (3) *It's important that our church is inclusive to the point that if you're not a member of the church, but you have a need of this church, this church will be responsive.* There are some churches, if you died, and you weren't a member, your funeral wouldn't have been there. Or it would be some additional cost or things of that nature. That is not the case here.

INTERVIEWER: Describe a typical Sunday morning in this congregation.

CASSANDRA: For a while I was so busy, I just felt like, "I don't need to go to church, because they'll work me to death." That in

1. Immediately, Cassandra weighs heavily congregational culture as communal care and social ministry.

2. Strong associations are drawn early between the preacher's pastoral care (a form of ethos that originates outside the sermon, but becomes part of the preaching event itself) and the members' cooperative care of each other (congregational culture). Working as "partners" is vital for Cassandra in her sense of communal life and ministry.

3. Here, congregational life forms or reflects communal identity and meaning. Consider how our week-to-week preaching may shape this "need-response" aspect of a congregation's theological culture or identity.

itself can be an issue at some churches, that (4) *you become so caught up in the mechanics of stuff going on, you don't get to enjoy church.* I have found myself in that situation, probably more times than I would need to be in that situation. But a typical Sunday morning here, (5) *we have a lot of people that attend early morning service, which is led by our laity, our lay speakers. Pastor always attends those, but he doesn't preach those. The laity does a very good job with those.* There are some people that like that 8:00 a.m. I actually grew up with an early service. I like them, but it's too early for me from where I live. Yes. After that there are a lot of people that attend our church school of various ages.

INTERVIEWER: Describe the worship service.

CASSANDRA: Our worship service, I would say, (6) *generally for most people is a fairly uplifting time.* My personal opinion, I think, *sometimes the sermons are too long, but people like the music. People like music. I think people like the format.* We don't spend a whole lot of time on a whole lot of announcements. We try to get to the *important things* done there. Depending on what Sunday it is, there can be more music, and in summer we cut it back a little bit, because it shortens the length of time, but there's usually more music throughout. I think the sermons can get too long. I think…

INTERVIEWER: What makes them too long?

CASSANDRA: When you've said what you had to say, and you've made the point, and you've reiterated the point, then that's when you need to let it go, because if you keep trying to go somewhere else, you're going to lose people. (7) *Because sometimes the point in our sermon gets made right around the time that it should be made, and you're there, and he takes another road. Then you wind up, "Where was I? Where did we just go?* What's the path here?" when you thought you were where

4. The listener relates a heavy work ethic to a congregational culture that disrupts potential enjoyment or engagement in the worship life of the church (an ethos-pathos association).

5. For Cassandra, sharing leadership is an ideal for pastoral ethos, along with a congregational culture that tackles the work of the church. As we will see, a pastoral ethos within the sermon or preaching event itself works best for Cassandra when her expectations of partnership in the life of the congregation are met. As Cassandra describes the activities of this church, the ecclesiology is very relational. This ecclesiology indicates values in pastoral leadership and how preaching may shape congregational life, if nurtured.

6. Perhaps Cassandra's emphasis on uplift, music, and "the important things" points to the roles of emotion and affect (pathos) in shaping the congregation's responsiveness to preaching and worship; but notice also the tie into potential issues of logos (too long?).

7. The listener identifies clarity of points and directions taken (logos), which reflects strong concern for argument and the sermon's contextual content. However, the listener returns to pathos language to communicate the connection or disconnection.

you were. That's why I say sometimes he *needs to figure out where's the point that you leave people, and people feel good.* Not that people don't enjoy the sermon, his messages. I think they do. I have sensed, and people have told us that sometimes he's there, and then he goes on too many different paths.

INTERVIEWER: So, it sounds like it's not just number of minutes, but it has to do with the content and the focus. Is that right?

CASSANDRA: Yes, the content and the focus. (8) *The reason I only said it goes on too long is because when you asked me what makes it feel too long,* it's not that somebody's watching the clock, because it's forty minutes. *It's that people become disengaged.* You will become disengaged. Or I can speak for myself. *I will become disengaged once you start going down multiple trails, and I can't follow these trails.* Then I become... "Well, you know what? This could have been done, because I've got what I needed to get." *Often times I don't see the connection where,* "Okay. I've got it. Now is he going to take it so somebody can get it?" Maybe that's what happened. I don't sense that. *I don't feel it.*

INTERVIEWER: You talk about going down different roads and not being able to follow. What helps you to follow a sermon? To be able to keep up with what's going on?

CASSANDRA: All of his sermons, and most people's (9) *sermons, have a theme.* When you're within the realm of that theme, I think I can hang with you. *If you tell a story in a sermon, you have to make sure that people connect* as to what in that story belonged where it was. Whether it's a personal story, whether it's a story that you've heard, *if I don't understand why that story has been told in the context of what you're saying, that's a disconnect.* You've just gone down another road, or "disconnect" may be a better word.

8. The disengaged feeling-response in "too long" expresses concern for logos development, but again relies on the sense of pathos indicators ("I don't feel it"). Attention is lost wherein the preaching lacks appropriate identifications or does not sustain connections with the listeners.

9. Notice the language of theme and story; again we see the demands of logos through the needs of pathos. Cassandra weighs clarity, understanding, and context by some determination of connecting or disconnecting, which is her chosen language to communicate the role of "feeling" responses to preaching (see above).

INTERVIEWER: Talk a little bit about your relationship with the pastors and the preachers that you've had.

CASSANDRA: They've all been different. The relationship I have with this pastor is very different than relationships I've had with some of the previous pastors. (10) *Preaching styles have been different.* One of our pastors, Pastor [Former Preacher 1], I called him our Sleepy-Eyed Pastor, because he wasn't an energetic kind of person, *but had such a poignant way of making his point and making his story.* You look at him and go, "Can he preach?" but then *there was just something about his style that made the point.* He was very, *very open, very humble, very gentle.* I really liked him. He was the pastor here when I joined the church.

INTERVIEWER: What was your relationship like with him?

CASSANDRA: I had a good relationship, but I'm going to say it like this, I also wasn't as ingrained in the church, which will tell you (11) *that when you're outside looking in, you will know less about the family than when you start to live there. Now, when you start walking in the church, and you start finding out the rest of the story, as I like to say it, it makes your relationship change, because you're in a different kind of interaction with the church.*

Concerning my current relationship, (12) *I am probably more disconnected with this pastor than any other pastors I've had. Part of that is his style and my style. He's a loner.* He will admittedly tell you he's a loner. That's how he is, and that is the total opposite to how I operate. This is what you need from me. This is what you want from me. I used to tell him. I said, (13) *"You're the visionary of this church. You need to put the vision out there, so that those of us know what the vision is."...Just tell me what you need, and let me meet your needs in the best way that I can.* It's a different kind

10. Assess the "connection" between preaching style or presence (delivery or embodiment) and the former pastor's ability to make a poignant point (the preacher's manner of communication in the sermon). When Cassandra is asked to talk about relationships with preachers, she refers to preaching style and ethos directly.

11. The role of the preacher's leadership style (pastoral ethos) is perceived in degrees. The language of "family" functions as a window or fulcrum, although one could question if Cassandra is referring to the preacher's family or the church family; the latter seems likely. Relationships change in response to familiarity and roles within the church (congregational culture).

12. The preacher's leadership style is captured in the impressions of going at it alone or being more directing with others. This ethos affects the sermon in various perceptions of partnership and contributes to the work ethic of this community's culture of engagement.

13. The dialectic between the preacher's ethos, which here is the nature of his pastoral leadership, and the congregational culture is strong. The preacher's gifts as a visionary work closely with Cassandra's response to preaching and her desire to share in mission. A particular kind of ethos weighs heavily for this church, or at least for this listener.

of relationship. I do know if I need anything, I could call him, and he would respond, but he's just such a loner. I'm such the opposite that I work best with people with whom I develop relationships. For my growth is learning to accept people where they are, why I am who I am, and knowing that both are okay. That's what I'm trying to do.

INTERVIEWER: In thinking of your relationship with various pastors and thinking about their preaching... (14) *Thinking about one that may have been a good preacher...What especially did you like about that person and how they preached?*

CASSANDRA: *They make contact with you.* They looked at you. Well, they appeared to look at you, and I say they "appeared to" because I've stood in front of groups, and I look out, and maybe I'd see you, yet it's not that I see you, but I looked at you or for you. That would make sense for me, "*... because I told you, it's about relationship*" and therefore it's very *difficult to have a "relationship" or connection for me if I don't think you can see me.* I think they've made that initial kind of effort, always like they're right there reaching out and touching. The *style that somehow can make a point resonate*, make it so real that it just resonates with you and creates one of those "Aha!" moments as I call it, because the language is such that it has to be scripturally based for me, *but it's turned into something that it really works.* It really works. I really need to think about that. (15) *That's piercing. Our current pastor, he doesn't look at people. He does not look at you the whole time he's doing his sermon.* I asked myself, now why does that bother me? And I don't mean this the way it's going to come out, but that's the only way I can think to say it. We could be a distraction to him. Some people cannot look out without

14. Emphasis on connections seems to reflect directly the correlation between caring and visionary leadership (pastoral ethos) and the congregational culture based in a mutuality clearly desired by this listener. Notice the language of "contact, relationship, connection, and see[ing]." Even the embodiment of a good preacher in efforts to look at Cassandra, or even to appear to do so, affects hearing the sermon and relating to her.

15. Notice the strong correlation between embodiment and identification, which becomes relational.

getting distracted. So they choose to look above or to one way or the other. I don't know if you've seen ministers do that. But he doesn't. He doesn't.

(16) *But I still sense that you're not really making a connection. It's almost like…to whom am I speaking? Am I speaking to you all here that are gathered with me, or am I speaking somewhere else?* Sometimes I think that. There are times when he's very clear that the message is for us, but sometimes my sense is, "Who is he really speaking to?" I wouldn't want him to be distracted. But I think when I'm sitting out in the sanctuary, gee, it would be nice to see his eyes every once in a while. I've struggled with that personally, because I keep asking myself, "All right; why do I not connect?"

INTERVIEWER: How does it make you feel?

CASSANDRA: You know that's a difficult question, and (17) *it's a difficult question because I'm linking the fact that I don't have a relationship with him to the fact that I definitely don't connect as well with his sermons either.* One or two of his sermons will resonate with me. The majority of his sermons, they don't. I look at that as maybe this is where I am right now. Maybe it's something in my life that's preventing me from having some of these connections, but I don't connect with a lot of them. I don't connect with the majority of his sermons, but lately, a couple more than others. (18) *I used to be in the sermon,* and I'm the one with the notebook, and I will write it out, and I will go back and look at it. *I sometimes can get inspired to write. I write short poetry.* From sermons in the past, I have been inspired to write. I haven't been inspired lately.

INTERVIEWER: Now I want you to think back over the sermons you have heard over time, not necessarily this pastor at this church. When you talk about the ones that inspire

16. Here embodiment becomes an example of how a preacher may fail to communicate or how one may convey even unintended meanings or an inadvertent ethos.

17. Cassandra links the relational ethos of the preacher, in and beyond the sermon, with her ability to connect with his sermons. To what extent should preachers then weigh their congregational relationships in evaluating the effectiveness of their sermons?

18. While it appears that the listener is referring to her ability to focus within the sermon and become inspired to create her own interpretations, the point that she "used to be *in* the sermon" may reflect more than her attention span. In what ways do listeners expect to be *in* our sermons?

you, (19) *what is it about those sermons that inspired you?*

CASSANDRA: *They were piercing. They evoked some kind of emotion out of me,* whether it was happy or sad. On the questionnaire you asked me about a sermon I might remember. I was at another church, and there was a sermon about *"Don't block your blessings because of who may bring them to you."* The essence of that sermon has stayed in my head, which is why I struggle to have a conversation with you about that, because I keep asking myself, (20) *"Am I blocking because I have made some judgment about the person in front of me? In other words, we can make judgments about people that can prevent us from being all that we can be and doing God's work.*

INTERVIEWER: Tell me about that sermon.

CASSANDRA: I was trying to remember where was I in the time that sermon happened, and if there was something going on in my life that made it personal, because we've all heard, "Boy, he must have been talking about me today." (21) *There was a passion and energy about the sermon.* The flipside of that is as I told you about the other pastor, who, when you look at him, *you would not necessarily say that he was energetic, but there was a passion he could inject in his sermons. Yet it was like a quiet, powerful passion*—not always the whooping and the hollering. People can get up and whoop and holler and have nothing to say. So it's not simply that whooping *gets me motivated.*

Ever since I knew that you were working on this project, I was trying to decide: (22) *What is engaging me? When am I engaged? When am I disengaged? But when the issue is something real and relevant, I think I get pulled into it. I think there's a lot of truth... Maybe that's what it was about this sermon.* For whatever reason, that has stayed with me.

19. The sermons that inspired Cassandra were both in-breaking and evocative (pathos). And still these responses emerge from her evaluation of a preacher's ethos and connections with the congregation.

20. Listeners are indeed responsible for listening. It is helpful to hear that Cassandra struggles with her own integrity in listening. Listeners raise ethos questions within the preaching event as well as ethos questions shaped by interactions or relations outside of the sermon. To what extent can preachers enable hearing when judgments do "block"?

21. Cassandra's memory illustrates that a variety of styles in preaching are possible, but the integrity of energy is an important characteristic of ethos. Pathos (motivation) grows out of that integrity.

22. We often ask, "Just what will be engaging?" Cassandra points to being pulled in by the relevance of a message or issue. We are reminded then to ask, "What is the actual relevance of the immediate sermon to the lives of our expected hearers?"

INTERVIEWER: How long ago was that sermon?

CASSANDRA: Over a year! Over a year!

INTERVIEWER: Do you remember what made that sermon relate to you? What did the preacher do, or how did the preacher present it in such a way that it became real to you?

CASSANDRA: (23) *He asked some question. That's probably a key. He posed some question. I couldn't tell you what the question was, but I know if you ask the right question it will make you…It will stop you dead in your tracks, because you cannot deny it.* It's not accusatory. It's not like, "You are God awful!" No, it was some question that got answered, and you go, "Am I doing that? Is that what's going on here?"

INTERVIEWER: When you think about preaching in general, and think about in this congregation over a period of time, over several pastors, what do you think the preaching does in this congregation that other things do not do?

CASSANDRA: (24) *Preaching and singing to me are very close. Preaching raises an awareness and brings about a clarity* of some issue, some quaint, *something that I need to know* for me. Maybe that's what I've come to expect. *Preaching to me should also inspire me to do something better* than I did when I came in here, or to be much more focused and aware of something I can do better than when I came in here. *Songs emotionally inspire me. It is the songs and the rhythms and the words and the energy behind songs that can do that. Prayer deepens your spiritual connection to God, and I don't know that preaching deepens my spiritual connection with God. It may open the door for me to move in that direction.*

INTERVIEWER: You're in a position in the choir to see the congregation. During the

23. Here, Cassandra discovers a key in "relevance" via posing ideas as questions. Do questions focus logos? When do questions within sermons imply something about ethos or the congregational culture? For Cassandra, posing questions or even being called into question need not be accusatory or judgmental. However, she does seem to suggest that an important role of sermons and an important tool of preaching may be found in questioning. Our further reflections may explore the implications of ethos and relationship in this key for Cassandra.

24. Pathos and logos are almost indistinguishable for Cassandra when she attempts to describe the things that "happen" in preaching, singing, and praying. They become even more difficult to decipher when she is asked what do these things "do" or "do not do." Moreover, notice that Cassandra is not sure if preaching deepens her spirituality like singing or praying does. What can the preacher do in sermons that may help to deepen spirituality in listeners? How is spirituality affected by ethos, pathos, or logos?

sermon, what is going on with the congregation in relationship to preaching or the preacher?

CASSANDRA: When I look out, I know the people whom I will call—I shouldn't say this, but this is how I'm going to term it for lack of a better way— (25) *people whom I will call automatic responders.* That says to me, no matter who's up there, no matter what they say, you're going to get an "Amen" or a "Uh-huh" or something out of them. *There are other people who take in sermons and when it really resonates with them, you will hear from them. That's a way that you can gauge.* Our congregation is very interesting, and I never paid attention to this until I recently read an article about clapping after sermons or if somebody does a presentation. There were some pros and cons about it, and the thing was if you do it consistently and all the time, that's fine. If you don't do it all the time, then you have not acknowledged at least the attempt that somebody was trying to make. As I watched our congregation, and I never paid attention to this. (26) *We respond with clapping when we are really there or something has really happened.* I don't care whether it's singing or preaching. That's what I have noticed. *When the prior minister was here people clapped for that man almost every single Sunday. Since the current pastor has been here, I want to say it took almost a year before I heard that.* I never really connected this until I had read that article, and I go, "There's some truth to that," because it is a symbol of affirmation. *It has become a symbol of affirmation whether we've intended that to happen or not.*

INTERVIEWER: Has there been a time when you wanted to walk out?

CASSANDRA: Yes, there have been times I've wanted to walk out. I'll share a story with you, and I didn't understand this story until

25. Listeners observe levels of connections during sermons in terms of meaningfulness and emotions (pathos). When Cassandra "gauges" responses she also relies on relationships or knowledge of persons, which implies that even ethos among listeners shapes congregational culture between them. Other listeners' responses are part of our listening to the preacher or the sermon itself.

26. Affirmation is part of ethos and congregational culture. Cassandra discovers an unanticipated symbol of affirmation in clapping. Learning how one's congregation expresses affirmation of a sermon, or within a sermon, may not only offer insight to the congregation's development but also may offer insight to what has become so important to Cassandra—different ways (logos) and levels (pathos) of connecting with different people as well as a community.

it happened to me. We had a change of pastors before. A lady and her family had been coming to church for a long time. She came to me and said, "I want you to know I'm leaving the church." I go, "Why?" She said, "I'm not getting anything out of the sermons. I sit here Sunday after Sunday, and it's not doing anything for me." (27) *She said, "Now I want to be clear with you. It's not that I don't like the pastor. I'm not getting anything out of these sermons. I cannot continue to come."* I told her, "Okay." I appreciated the conversation and wished her well, and said in the back of my mind, "*Gee, how do you get there?" It can happen that the sermons don't engage you,* and if you're not engaged, then you don't get anything out of it. Then you go, "I need to go somewhere else. I need to seek." I can only speak for myself; (28) *I do come seeking some sense of fulfillment, and I guess my expectation is I'm coming with my cup empty now and I need a little something in my cup.* Quite frankly, it's something I've wrestled with.

INTERVIEWER: It's interesting because you talked about not understanding what happened with that other person, but you were listening to the same preacher. What was the difference?

CASSANDRA: (29) *That's what I haven't figured out yet...Is it preaching style? Is it how we relate and connect to people? And I'm starting to think that's what it is.* I'm starting to think that's what it is. I have been in other churches, and go, "This is okay," or, "This was really great." *I'm starting to think the problem for me is that I haven't made a connection with the person delivering the message.* Until I can make that kind of connection, I don't think it does

27. "Gee, how do you get there?" More difficult than asking what a listener may "get" from your preaching is to ask: When do you sense listeners may *not* be getting anything out of your sermons? How can you sense it? Why?

28. Cassandra appears to correlate engagement or fulfillment with pathos. Being "filled" is something more than content.

29. It may come as no surprise that listeners are not always clear on what creates a difference in feeling fulfilled. However, Cassandra returns to ethos between a preacher's communication style in the sermon and how the preacher relates otherwise to people.

a whole lot for me. (30) *I'm not looking for a whole long relationship, because I have been in a church as a visitor and something has connected.* So it's not like…I don't know anything more about that person. *Maybe it helps when you know less about a person.* I don't know.

INTERVIEWER: Let me ask this, do you believe [your pastor] when he preaches?

CASSANDRA: Do I believe him? I think so. I haven't given it much thought. I say it that way, because (31) *I don't know that he's said anything that's so disputable.* The reason I say it that way is *because he reads a lot from the scripture, and he draws a lot from the scripture,* and given that, what he usually says has not been disputable. *What can be disputable is how it manifests itself in your real life example. The examples that he gives and how he ties it, … some of those disconnect for me.* Some of those definitely disconnect for me. But at the same time, he will tell you the stories about when he wasn't something, and how he's grown to a different point. So he's very open about "I've been there. And I've done these things, and then I look back…" That shows his learning to me. (32) *He's very open about where he's been and where he's going. So that shows some learning to me…It's helpful [to me] in that it helps to establish a sense of credibility.*

INTERVIEWER: Do you think he understands your condition? Your human condition? Or the congregation's?

CASSANDRA: Yes and no. (33) *I think he understands people's trials and tribulations. But I don't know that he always understands our whole work and home life.* See, church for this pastor is twenty-four/seven and his expectation, I think, is for it to be twenty-four/seven for everybody else. So, I think, sometimes we have to remind him, "Pastor, we own houses. We pay our mortgages. We cut our grass. We do all the things we have done for you. We can't necessarily extend

30. Cassandra points out that a sense of connectedness can be communicated within the preaching event itself. Her reference to a visiting experience illustrates that affective ethos is not only enhanced by context but is also shaped in how one is introduced or presents oneself.

31. For Cassandra, scripture is authoritative and gives the preacher added credibility. Logos therefore can enhance ethos. When a preacher steps outside of trusted logos, Cassandra struggles to trust the preacher's ability to connect or relate to her life. We know from earlier comments that a preacher's ethos can play a significant role in this distrust.

32. The preacher reaches across the chasm that separates him and Cassandra when he is able to show his own vulnerability or growth. Notice how this revelation corresponds to the strong ties between personality or character (ethos) and the congregational culture discussed earlier.

33. Cassandra helps us to understand different strengths and weaknesses in relating to persons in the congregation. Preaching can detach from the lives of our listeners much like character relations can become detached in the daily demands and interactions with congregants. The dynamics of ethos therefore suffer as well. The larger context directly influences the preaching event in the ongoing worship life of the church.

ourselves to the same level and depth as you do. You have to remember there are services we pay to have done for you, but the rest of us, we're doing those things ourselves."

...Does he understand pain and suffering from illnesses and death? Oh, I think so. We've experienced a lot of illnesses, and we continue to experience a lot of illnesses and deaths in this church—tragic ones. We've had a lot of funerals. So, yes, I do think he clearly understands those needs. I also think he understands, ... no, let me say it differently. (34) *He's most comfortable, I'd say, with old people and young people. Those of us in between, I don't think he knows what to do with us. He's very comfortable in the male arena. I think he's learned how to deal with strong women.* That's his learning curve. In most black churches, you've got strong black women. Like it or not! That's how the church became what it is. *I think he's learning how to work with us. I think it's different, because he's such a controlling person, and to do that you have to relinquish some of your control.* That's what you have to do, if you really want the people on board. Then it's going to have to be a "give and take" on the control. He's learning that.

INTERVIEWER: What do you think a preacher is doing when he or she is preaching? What's the purpose there?

CASSANDRA: I think for different preachers, there are different things. I think some preachers take an intellectual point of view, and that they're there to...let me say it differently. (35) *All preachers, I think, should be about delivering the message of God in such a way that we can all grasp it and understand it.* I think there are different *styles in doing that. There can be an intellectual take* on that. There can be what I call *the real "down home" take* on that. It could be the old, *fire and brimstone*

34. Age and gender play significant roles in Cassandra's assessment of her pastor's relational strengths and comfort areas. Quite important to her insights are questions of power and control in relating to the very people to whom we seek to minister or preach. How do power dynamics and control affect a preacher's ethos and the congregational culture? How are power and control experienced through our sermons? From whose perspective do we normally answer these questions?

35. Cassandra sees logos understanding as the preacher's goal in sermons. Her "grasping" language heightens the goal of understanding the message. However, she does identify different styles that may point beyond logos ("the intellectual") to include ethos ("the real 'down home'") and pathos ("fire and brimstone...the fear in you so that you can understand"). In what ways do our styles open up our understanding or goals in preaching?

that almost puts the fear in you so that you can understand the message. I think that (36) *they're there to deliver that message. I choose to believe that many times the Spirit can manifest itself through the minister, but I don't know if that happens every Sunday.* I know I have seen that happen.

INTERVIEWER: Does that also answer the question, "What do you think God is doing during the sermon?"

CASSANDRA: What do I think God is doing during the sermon? The other question was just directly related to the preacher. See, *I think God is trying to move in all of us during the sermon if we open our hearts to do so. Again, that's why I have that struggle about, "Is it me?* Lord, let me hear something here. Give me a clue." I think that God is trying to reach all of us through the messages of the ministers who deliver them in the pulpit.

INTERVIEWER: What do you want to know about God in the sermon?

CASSANDRA: I think what I want most is to know *how I might prepare myself to hear God.*

INTERVIEWER: When you hear a sermon?

CASSANDRA: I don't know if it's most about God. (37) *I want to know my purpose, my being, how I live out that purpose and that being. How do I become a better steward of God?* I finally came to a point in my life of tithing and I've been there for a few years now, but I can tell you when I wasn't. *It has been through sermons, through testimonial, through spiritual growth that I have come to accept, understand and do that.* That's been a journey. *Sermons help to take people on journeys toward something else.* What am I looking for right now? I hope one day to come to church and really know what my true purpose is. *What am I really called to do in this church or somewhere in God's ministry?*

36. Cassandra is unsure that the Spirit is manifest through every sermon. How do we understand the roles of style and ethos within the sermon event itself? In what ways is the Spirit manifest in the congregational context? What are our theological claims on the Spirit in preaching?

37. Preparation, purpose, being, and stewardship weigh heavily in this listener's encounter with sermons and preachers. Even when asked what she wants to know about God, Cassandra is concerned with identity, character, and mission. Yet, her language points to the content of the sermon (logos). For Cassandra, developing relations, faith, and purpose are central to the content of sermon. She includes in her concept of journey the functional roles that pathos and logos play. Clearly for her, sermons do not work above all other events in the life of the church. Even her emphases on ethos-oriented goals of preaching conflate with testimony (experience—or pathos) and spiritual growth (understanding—or logos) on a pilgrimage in which functioning and one's purpose are the primary goals.

INTERVIEWER: What makes a sermon authoritative for you?

CASSANDRA: I would think (38) *what makes a sermon authoritative is that it is grounded in the Scripture*, and it doesn't have to be grounded in ten scriptures for me to get it or to believe it. *I don't need ten different ones, because to be honest with you, when I'm given ten I don't resonate as much as when I'm given one or two that I can really go back and pay attention to.* Ten is too many for me. You know you give me one or two, and I can stay with those.

INTERVIEWER: A couple questions about delivery. You've already talked about some of these things. Could you describe a preacher whose physical presence in the pulpit was really good?

CASSANDRA: I don't know what our expectations are sometimes with ministers and preachers. (39) *Someone who usually stands in one position in a pulpit and delivers a sermon is less engaging sometimes than one who— they don't have to be dancing or jumping—but who has some movement, some expression, either with their hands or vocal expressions, I think, are more impacting and more engaging at least to me.* At least to me, because there's some movement there. There's some energy there. There's some passion. Some people walk. Some people just walk. I remember a lady who was here. She was just a walker. She didn't do anything, but just that movement. (40) *Actually what she did, is when she really wanted to make a point hit home, she stopped. Her activity was walking, but when she stopped, it's like…then you're like…You're right there.* Now that you've made me think about it, this is an interesting technique. I don't know whether she intentionally does it or not, but that's exactly what she did.

INTERVIEWER: Can you think of a time in which you could not see or hear a preacher?

38. The authority behind sermons is scripture; however, logos is better aided by a single content or focus than it is by "proof-texting" topics or scrolling through multiple points of scripture.

39. Cassandra emphasizes that embodiment makes a significant difference in connecting with people. Embodiment can be physical, facial, or even tonal. Delivery accents meaning.

40. Here again through embodiment, Cassandra weighs another preacher's ability to accent a point with her presence and movement. This preacher helps listeners to hear—to be present themselves.

CASSANDRA: I'm not one who listens to sermons on the radio. I could, but I wouldn't want that to be my sole basis of preaching. (41) *I think my most preferred method, the method that would probably connect with me the most, would be when I can see and I know they can see, and do see, and recognize me.*

INTERVIEWER: Recognize you? Recognize you as Cassandra sitting in the congregation or recognizing what?

CASSANDRA: Now the *recognition of people in the congregation,* not that it's me or it's you, but it's the same when I go back and say, you look out and it appears that you're looking at me and maybe you really haven't, but I think you are. Therefore, it makes that kind of connection. Yes. Then you know what happens whether someone is looking at you, Pastor [Interviewer], or somebody else sitting there. (42) *The moment that person glances at you, there's a momentary whatever, and as that person is actually glancing toward you, that same glance is going around you, but for each of you. It's that momentary connection. It's about you for the moment.*

INTERVIEWER: If you had one or two things you could tell preachers that would help them energize you when you are listening to a sermon, what would it be?

CASSANDRA: (43) *Be authentic. Be who you are.* Don't try to become whoever the latest, greatest preacher is on TV. Just be authentic. Be who you are, because that's what's going to add the credibility. *That's what's going to add the credibility.* Be authentic. Just from my own background, I know that (44) *you must be factual,* which means *you must have the Bible as your base of authority* because there is no other base of authority when it comes to ministry; *you must be very symbolic and as visual as you possibly can be with people,* because most of us visualize. The symbolism comes through stories that are quite *relevant. There*

41. To hear and see is not enough! The pastoral ethos in "recognition" of listeners breaks in upon Cassandra's understanding of significant embodiment.

42. The moment of connection makes all the difference. In Cassandra's purview, ethos and embodiment come together here. In what ways can we embody or develop recognition of listeners in the preaching event?

43. Authenticity and credibility certainly appear to be vital values throughout Cassandra's understanding of preaching and the integrity of the preacher. But being "who you are" still falls within the integrity and need of "relationship."

44. Cassandra makes a case for the interdependence between each and every one of our categories in rhetoric for preaching ...you must be factual, symbolic, and relevant—logos...visual, with a degree of emotion, passion, and energy—pathos and embodiment; yet for this listener, a lens—ethos—brings the confluence into focus through authenticity and credibility.

needs to be some degree of emotion, passion, and energy from them if you're going to energize me. I don't know how I get energy from anyone who doesn't radiate or emit something.

INTERVIEWER: Let me ask you one more question. When you have been in a congregation where there's been a really dynamic sermon, what happens after the service?

CASSANDRA: (45) *They all want to mingle around the pastor.* They really do. They all just want to get close. It's almost like *they want to draw more energy, and they want to acknowledge him or her. They want to acknowledge the pastor for what experience they just had,* and you hear people going, "Oh, wasn't that great? *Didn't you really get into that?"*

45. Consider what happens in Cassandra's congregation when hearing a dynamic sermon: "Mingling, drawing energy, acknowledging, experiencing, getting into that." Cassandra seems to end her interview as she began it, "...because I told you, it's about relationship!"

Listening for Preaching

Cassandra believes the exchanges in preaching's ethos, congregational culture, and embodiment are equally dynamic. When one's embodiment or a style in preaching accents particular points or movements we begin to see ways in which ethos engages listeners during the sermon event (10, 15, 16, 39, 40). At the same time, we may observe ethos functioning through the preacher's relational character as it affects listeners in connecting or disconnecting within the congregational context (11, 12, 13, 14). This dialectic between the preacher's character or personality and the congregational culture becomes integral to the ethos of the preaching event. This interview reveals a particular, strong influence of the preacher's ethos in the congregational culture and the preaching event. Cassandra notes that the "loner" style of her pastor not only creates a chasm in the preaching event, it alienates her. For her, values in the congregational culture of partnership suffer substantively and affectively. When the preacher's relational style moves beyond personal character into pastoral leadership qualities, the conflict between ethos and congregational culture takes over the preaching event, which can hardly withstand disorientation. Contact, engagement, and relationship through the sermon do not occur independently or by happenstance for Cassandra. A strong correlation exists. It follows, then, that unintended embodiment may communicate unintended meanings. And lack of attention to one's ethos may result in lack of address.

Often in the effort to describe the role or impact of one of our categories, this listener would use language from another category to gain clarity. Cassandra weaves between pathos and logos language in trying to describe the worship services and preaching in her church (6, 7). Worship is generally uplifting, but the format is attentive to getting the "important things done." And in speaking about getting the important things done, the sermons are too long.

The logos and pathos dialectic continues in concern for knowing what point to make, when to make it, and how to remain focused on it. The authority of a sermon is scripture, but even its use needs the clarity of a singular focus in logos (38). A disruption in the continuity or flow of the sermon results in a disruption of "feeling good" or actually "feeling it" (8, 9). When stories and themes are not immediately relevant to context or meaning, Cassandra again uses pathos language to communicate her discontent. This tendency suggests that some of our hearers may ultimately make sense of sermons based more upon continuity between our classical categories of rhetoric than simply the weight granted predominately to a particular category. However, the weight of a particular category still functions as a lens or filter—as ethos does for Cassandra. We may also glimpse a dominant category in a listener's preference for a preacher, selecting a church, or deciding whether to stay in a church that has changed or not changed to one's liking.

This interview reflects the interdependence of these categories of rhetoric that permeates the traditions of African American preaching. Ethos and delivery play vital roles in the preaching event. Likewise, their dynamic interplay with the pathos and logos of a sermon affects listeners and makes the message accessible. Perceived character and charisma weigh in the balance. The preacher's call narrative lends spiritual authority to the preaching event in a sense of anointing for preaching's very purpose—to reach listeners. Persuasion by ethos, logos, or pathos is structured only to discern and communicate the Word. Pathos has often been mistaken as the principal element of black preaching. Notwithstanding its distinctiveness, pathos is difficult to evaluate aside from meanings that pervade logos and the integrity that it receives from ethos. Embodiment breathes life into the meanings, feelings, and an actual encounter. Within the encounter of the preaching event one "experiences" a transforming message.[1]

Cassandra implicates relational ethos amongst the preacher, the congregation, and herself as a problem. We are reminded accordingly that we do not preach simply to individuals, but to persons in community, or at the very least to persons who find themselves in an encounter with a community (17). The predominance of ethos here offers an opportunity to recognize how theological and cultural worldviews of listeners or preachers often function. Even the strong interdependence of our rhetorical categories in this case gains clarity as the listener's worldview is focused both by and through a preaching lens (ethos) that deciphers what the listener likes in a sermon, as well as those things with which she struggles in response to her pastor's "style." Similarly, the listeners' wants and needs encompass the congregational context. In response to the sermon, the repeated language of (dis)connection and (dis)engagement may refer to actual content or structural continuity within the sermon; but the listener "explains" her difficulties under the weight of relating the preacher's style and relations (ethos) as they impinge upon the sermon's message (logos), as well as how logos impinges upon ethos (31), along with the listening styles (30) within congregational life (ethos) and feelings (pathos) (29). Cassandra's critical self-questioning reveals an important dynamic involving both pastoral ethos and congregational culture in the preaching event. Questions of power, control, and separation are dominant themes (34). A weak or broken relationship (ethos) itself is the probable culprit. When relations or worldviews constitute dissimilar visions, our preaching lens refracts more light than it sheds in communication.

Some of the more vibrant parts of Cassandra's interview involved revelations of what has been engaging in her listening experiences. The sermons that have inspired her were relational (ethos) (17), as well as piercing and evocative (pathos) (19). Pathos emanated from energy within the sermon even when she described a preacher as subdued (21). Cassandra eventually credits the preacher's method–posing some question (logos) as key. She finds in the question at once a relevance, inquiry, and an invitation that connects her and the preacher relationally (ethos) and becomes a lens of engagement (22, 23). Herein, ethos and experience seem to have come together for her. When Cassandra moves on to describe what preaching does, she resorts to describing the preaching event (24). Her key insights entail awareness, clarity, emotions, inspiration, rhythms, energy, and affirmation (25, 26). In short, she describes the domain of experience in the preaching event, which she characterizes in qualities of relationship. Ultimately, fulfillment is best experienced in a sense of purpose and mutual enterprise (28, 37).

Cassandra reminds us that there are levels of experience in preaching that demand our attention. African American women in particular continue to wrestle with a cultural history in lack of recognition, dismissal, or exploitation.[2] It may prove helpful to restate one's level of experience in preaching as a sense of participation. What elicits participation among listeners? What is the aim of the preaching event? Cassandra desires participation. The preacher attempts to create opportunities to participate in the preaching encounter and response. As we move into listening for theology in Cassandra's participation in this study, her homiletic insights drive us to reflect on her experiences in view of her gender, social location, and church culture–where her experiences, reason, and feelings engage her sense of being, needs, or desires.[3]

Listening for Theology

This listener identifies repeatedly her concerns for relatedness. Cassandra begins with shared forms of ministry and mission that constitute the most important things that happen in the congregation. In an interview that has been contextualized for her as research regarding preaching and listening to sermons, Cassandra weighs heavily the impact of her church community and the role of the preacher and his preaching in terms of mutual engagement in communal care (mission) (2, 3, 5) and later in functions of vision (13). She names the congregational culture of her church in terms of care for those in need. Her church is not only responsive and inclusive, but sees ministry in partnership. Lay leadership is part of this shared ministry. In fact, part of the struggle she feels with her pastor stems from divergent styles of mature functioning between pastor and congregant. Theologically, Cassandra shapes and unfolds the impact of ecclesiology in her desire for shared ministry.

Cassandra's emphasis on connectedness and engagement in listening to sermons is consistent with her sense of ecclesiology. Her views on partnership or mutuality in ministry may reflect strong influences from Methodist theology in the doctrine of the church. While John Wesley urged that the church is continually formed by a living faith that emerges from "pure" preaching of the Word and in continuity with the sacraments, the role of this "living faith" hardly could be overstated. The church takes shape in the fellowship, communion, accountability, and work of believers and seekers. The worship life of faith involves partnership in service. The congregational ethos of Methodist ecclesiology is therefore held together in the unity of shared mission and mutual nurture.[4]

Interestingly enough, Cassandra appears somewhat conflicted in her affirmation of and resistance to the prevailing work ethic in the congregational culture (4). Her caution reminds us that our work ethic can become problematic when it loses sight of the living faith that draws us together. Still, her frustrations with how her pastor's leadership style affects preaching (ethos) are also characterized by a disrupted sense of mutual service that appears to struggle with respecting or trusting the congregant's independent functions even in partnership (12). Cassandra offers up a healthy theological reminder (33) for both preacher and congregant: The demands of daily living and living in partnership within a faith community are indeed parts of discerning a living faith.

Cassandra interprets the preacher's ability to develop sermons with thematic and structural clarity in terms of knowing how to connect with people. Herein she evaluates both his preaching style and pastoral leadership. For example, her account of an effective preacher she has experienced makes reference to the preacher's openness and humility. Her struggles with the current preacher emerge in making contact with persons (embodiment and ethos) and having a vision, but with particular emphasis on pastoral leadership style (logos and ethos). Cassandra's ecclesiological understanding of community and shared ministry places strong relational expectations on her preacher as well as the sermon's content and role in the life of his listeners.

The integrity of recognition is interpersonally and theologically a vital factor in Cassandra's encounter in the preaching event (ethos). Her sense of being recognized in the actual preaching moments seems to take on multiple theological meanings (15). The preacher must pay direct attention to listeners, stretching across their daily lives and living faith (33), but to do so one must seek an encounter with them. Even embodiment is thus adorned theologically. The listener discovers meaning in being recognized (14, 41), much like in the notion of prevenient grace. Grace seeks us out; grace recognizes us in our condition, in who we are, and in where we are. To recognize that we are recognized is to experience grace. And in being recognized, we are empowered to enter relationship.[5] Moreover, recognition in preaching bears the burden of integrity in relationship. Cassandra looks for authenticity and credibility in the preacher (43). Many listeners look for relationship with their preachers, in who they are. Preachers can impede the encounter when we fail "to recognize." We can violate the encounter when our leadership ethos or preaching ethos does not recognize the power and control dynamics that pervade even our mutual service (34). Cassandra seems "to hear" the relationship in listening to sermons.

One of the wonderfully stark queries raised in this interview questioned whether the Spirit is manifest through every sermon (36). Cassandra is even unsure if preaching deepens her spiritual connection with God (24). Singing inspires her and praying deepens her spiritual connection. Listening to others in the worship service resonates with a reliance on relationship to understand (25). Theologically, preaching operates among the ordinary means of grace.[6] Yet, in both Wesleyan and African American church traditions, praying and conferring between co-worshipers also share in the means of grace.[7] While we may groan over the possibility that our preaching does not always manifest the Spirit, it is in the Spirit that we groan with creation[8] in prayer, testimony, and—in those times—even in our preaching.

Cassandra laments when she is not *in* the sermon (18). She desires sermons to be sources of inspiration even if she is unsure that they deepen her spiritual connection with God. She relates her lack of connection with the sermons of late with her lack of connection with the preacher. Relationship becomes a theological factor in preaching. The notion of being *in* a sermon is intriguing. Could the lack of connection reflect that she cannot find herself in the preacher's vision or in the sermon's focus? Clearly, this question pushes beyond Cassandra's words, yet perhaps not beyond her understanding of preaching, relationship, and sermon composition. When asked what has engaged her in the past, Cassandra finds a key in posing questions in the sermon (23). A question can be probing. A question can elicit response. A question can generate reflection. In all, questions place the listener *in* the sermon.

What does Cassandra want from preaching? She wants to know her purpose, her being, her stewardship, and even her journey (37). Preaching shares in a discerning process. But it is also a developmental process. In the truest sense of sanctification, the gift of preaching calls forth a response of faith and nurtures or continually transforms that response into a living faith.[9] In the language of Cassandra's ecclesial tradition, sanctification seeks to live in the perfect unbroken presence of Christ. That relationship educes an increasing desire and sensitivity to live in God's purpose.[10] Preaching shares in that relationship. A preacher cannot evade such a calling.

It is interesting that Cassandra needs to know her purpose, being, stewardship, and journey when asked what she needs to know about God. Her relationship with and experience in Christ is what she needs to know in the sermon. Cassandra's relationship to the preacher is part of her relationship to the preaching event. This listener needs to hear herself in the sermon and needs to hear the preacher in the sermon, but in dialogue together in a living faith. Whether in mission, stewardship, leadership, purpose, or, yes, even being, the preaching event may be just as Cassandra tells us, "…it's about relationship."

Challenges for Our Preaching

1. How do we address listeners in our sermons? By direct or indirect address? Are our listeners *in* our sermons? Who is *not in* our sermons? How are *we in* our sermons?

2. What do our listeners affirm about our sermons? What questions arise from our sermons? What potential problems or complaints may these questions reflect?

3. What are our preferred styles in pastoral leadership? How do they meet the needs of our listeners? How do they meet our needs? How do we function within our congregations? In what ways do our congregations function without our intrusions?

4. What is (are) our purpose(s) in preaching? Do our listeners have others? How do our listeners experience preaching? How do they respond? How do they participate?

CHAPTER 5

"It's a God Thing"

Jim: Suburban Caucasian Male

JOHN S. McCLURE

The interview in this chapter takes place with Jim, a thirty-two-year-old Caucasian member of a megachurch, where he has been a member for thirteen years. Jim came into this church largely because of the memorable and relevant preaching he heard. He, his wife, and two children are very active. Jim especially appreciates the sincerity, authenticity, and passion of his preachers. He is also attracted by the preparation, novelty, biblical focus, and relevance of their preaching. Although the senior pastor, Fred, does most of the preaching, a younger associate pastor, Tom, is also an important, regular preacher.

The church has well over ten thousand members, primarily Caucasian, and is located near a freeway in an upper-middle-class suburban area approximately ten miles from a larger city. The congregation tends to be theologically, socially, and politically conservative, and has grown steadily over the past twenty years. The new building is very large, and the sanctuary resembles a coliseum surrounded by many acres of parking lot. A high percentage of members are involved in a wide variety of educational, small group, and mission opportunities. Worship services occur on Saturday evening and twice on Sunday morning. There is a more informal service on Sunday evening.

The sanctuary has theater seating encircling a large stage where the worship band is situated. Large television screens are suspended above the stage and television cameras are located on platforms around the sanctuary. The movable pulpit is small and clear acrylic plastic, and the preachers are dressed in suits rather than robes. Sermons are often accompanied by dramatic presentations or videos designed to help bring home the message. Communion is served weekly, reflecting the tradition from which the church originated. Baptisms in a large baptismal pool are frequent.

Excerpts from the Transcript

INTERVIEWER: Talk to me a little bit about Tom [the associate pastor]. I know Tom's a little different than Fred [the senior pastor].

JIM: When he came, I was in college. I was in my freshman year in college. In the summer, we had the college class. The college class was decent size, but not very big...I got to know him real well. (1) *When Tom is... I don't want to say when he's unprepared, he's better than when he's prepared. That's not the truth, but when he's off the cuff, he's just unbelievable. He comes up with things, just "How does he come up with that stuff off the cuff?" He's just an entertaining, fun guy to be around.* I got to know him. Some people haven't been here long enough that they get to know the ministers here on a one-to-one basis so much. I've been privileged to be around when it was small enough that you did get to know them. I know Tom very well. The only thing about Tom, and he's gotten a lot better about this. I think when he first became the associate minister that was going to take Fred's place, he almost tried to be Fred in the pulpit. It just wasn't Tom. Not that he wasn't any good, but (2) *when Tom's Tom, he's the best.* When he gets up there...I think he couldn't be himself and take over, but yet he had to learn how to mesh his style with Fred's. He's done a great job at that. He'll get better because of it.

INTERVIEWER: What in particular...? How is his style different from Fred's?

1. One aspect of the logos of preaching is rhetorical "invention," or, in Jim's words, "coming up with stuff" to say. Jim links this positive logos-quality of inventiveness with the preacher's character – "he's just an entertaining, fun guy" (ethos). Notice, however, that Jim carefully distinguishes between being "unprepared," a negative logos-quality and "off the cuff," a positive ethos-quality. This raises an important question for consideration. How can preachers appear spontaneous and at the same time deliver well-prepared sermons?

2. Jim articulates an important ethos-value here: *authenticity*. It is very important that the associate minister *be himself,* and not attempt to become the senior pastor.

JIM: (3) *Tom's more willing to get out and move around out of the pulpit. He doesn't necessarily do this very often, but he's more willing to move around. I think some of that's even worn off on Fred a little bit. Since we've been here, every now and then, Fred will do a sermon where his illustrations will go beyond just standing there at the pulpit.*

INTERVIEWER: He'll move a little more?

JIM: (4) *A little bit, but not much. Not much. I don't mind it. I think it's great. I kinda like knowing that you're going to get a well-prepared sermon.* So many preachers that I've heard in the past, the reason I didn't get anything out of it is [it's] almost like they got up there, they had their verses they were going through, and they talked and talked and talked and talked, but (5) *it's not really anything that you haven't heard or anything different or anything new.* Even if what they're speaking is the truth, there's nothing that (6) *you can relate with.* The difference between Fred and Tom...the biggest difference is their voice. That's the thing. There's nothing you can do about that. In my case, you wouldn't want me to be a preacher unless it was in the middle of Kentucky somewhere. I've got a...My voice is not a radio voice or television voice. (7) *Tom, his voice is not as pleasant as Fred's is. Fred has one of the voices, it's not threatening, but it's very smooth.* Tom's gotten a lot better. (8) *Before when Tom was first starting, he'd get so into so many different things, you'd almost lose some of it, because he wasn't as fluid with what he was talking about. But he's gotten a lot better.*

INTERVIEWER: What I'm hearing is one thing that's really important to you, and maybe you didn't have in your past, was well-planned, well-organized sermons, and you think that Tom's picking up on doing better at that now.

3. Here is a fascinating linkage between the preacher's mobility "out of the pulpit" (an embodiment concern) and sermon illustration (a logos concern). Rendering illustrations out of the pulpit seems to be valued positively, since the senior pastor is learning to do it by watching the associate. What is it about sermon illustrations that make their delivery a good time to get away from one's notes?

4. One reason that movement out of the pulpit is good is that it indicates to Jim that the sermon is "well-prepared."

5. Jim moves on to articulate a new value for preaching: *novelty.* This is another logos issue. Sermons should not always have the same message. Well-prepared sermons will have something new to say week to week.

6. Here he shifts to the idea of identification, being able to identify or "relate with" something in the pastor's sermons.

7. He comes back to embodiment, this time accentuating the importance of the preacher's voice. It should be "not threatening" but "smooth."

8. Jim draws a connection between personality (ethos), vocal quality (embodiment), and tendencies toward more or less organization in a sermon's message (logos). It seems that the associate minister's spontaneous personality and accompanying vocal quality can undo or overshadow the organization of his message, leading him to pursue "so many different things." The senior minister, on the other hand, demonstrates a more fluid, smooth, and nonthreatening vocal quality that contributes to a well-prepared, organized, message-centered (logos) approach to preaching.

JIM: The thing about Tom though, he's got a gift. Not everybody's *gifted* to be…I particularly learned to believe that a minister is a public speaker. They really are. (9) *I think you want to have a minister that's gifted at public speaking, but at the same time, they have to carry whatever they preach over into their everyday lives.* One thing about Tom and Fred is, I know them well enough personally to know that these guys are full of integrity. When they say something from the pulpit, you can believe it. You can relate to it, because (10) *they're no different than you except they hold themselves to a higher standard.* Tom has gotten to be where he's extremely well prepared as well, but you can tell…The last sermon series we had here that Tom did was on Christians in the workplace, and it was one of the best series he'd ever done. I think you could tell he was more well prepared for that than he'd been in some other ones. (11) *When Tom is challenged with a tough topic, he's always well prepared. I think if it's a topic that he's covered before, he may not be as inclined to go out and be as prepared for it.* Not that he won't give a good sermon, but sometimes those of us who have been at church for a long time and have heard a lot of the stories and a lot of the illustrations before, you know…we're wanting him to come up with new stuff. Fred's the same way. You'll hear Fred tell a story that you've heard before. Doesn't mean they're not any good the second time or third time that you've heard them. (12) *I think it's important that they continue to try to come up with fresh stories and fresh illustrations and things like that. Most of the time they do. Sometimes you can almost tell that they weren't as prepared when you start hearing things you've heard before.* Especially a church this size, you get so many first time visitors or people who haven't been here before who haven't heard that, to them it's all fresh and new. You don't want them not

9. This is an abrupt shift to ethos. Jim is looking for *charisma* in his preacher—a "gift." At the same time, he is looking for *integrity*, that the preacher practices what he preaches in everyday life.

10. According to this listener, he is looking for a preacher who communicates a shared humanity with the listener. As we will see, this is more than ethos-identification or the kind of self-deprecation that implies good character. This is something more—identification at the level of pathos or *real* shared needs, problems, fears, passions, aspirations, etc. At the same time, the preacher must communicate a standard of personal conduct and self-expectations that are ideal—"a higher standard" (ethos). In other words, Jim's preachers communicate that they are deeply *real* (appealing to human pathos) and loftily *ideal* (appealing to exemplary ethos)—at the same time.

11. Jim connects being "well-prepared" to preaching tough new topics. The implication is that preachers may rely on previous research that may not be fresh. This lack of original, timely preparation comes through in the pulpit, draining energy from the logos of the sermon.

12. Another sign of poor preparation is the practice of reusing sermon illustrations and stories. Jim lets us know that listeners are aware of this and can feel slighted when they hear illustrations recycled.

to ever get to hear some of this stuff. You don't want to lose some of that either.

INTERVIEWER: Let's focus a little bit more on the sermons themselves and preaching. Talk to me a little bit about what you think Fred and/or Tom are trying to do when they preach? What are they up to when they're preaching?

JIM: That's a pretty good question. I would think…From my point of view, when I'm watching them preach, you never get the sense that they're struggling for what they're going to say next. You never get the sense that they're searching for, "Is what I'm talking about hitting people?" I guess because when you've heard a few sermons here, you realize (13) *they've had that sermon prepared for a while, and they've gone over it several times on their own.* The thing flows really well. When you're listening to especially Fred…I think it comes across with Tom too, but with Fred I really get the sense that (14) *he's just got a passion to try to explain this stuff to people. You get the feeling that it's like a mission for him for this to get across to people, and to have an effect on people. He wants…You can really tell that he loves Christ, he loves the word of God, and he's really trying to get it across to everybody else, too.* At the same time, when you hear either one of them speak, you also don't get the sense that, "Hey, I'm better than you, and you need to be like me." (15) *You get the sense that, "I'm imperfect just like you are. We all need this."* I think that's an important thing, too. You don't feel like you can't relate to the guy up there talking, because he doesn't seem to be any different than you are.

INTERVIEWER: You feel like they're standing with people, rather than barking at them from a distance?

JIM: Oh, yes. I've never felt like here that they've been trying to lean over people or

13. Another positive *logos* value for Jim is sermon *rehearsal.* Listeners can tell if a sermon has been practiced or not. Rehearsal contributes to the perception that a sermon is well-prepared and organized.

14. Notice the close relationship that Jim draws between message (logos) and affect (pathos) when he thinks about the purpose of preaching. He links the desire to "explain this stuff" to the desire to "have an effect on people." What the preacher wants to "get across" to the people is both a *message* and an *experience.*

15. Once again, Jim accentuates the importance of relating with one's listeners, creating a sense of shared *need* (a feeling) in the process of communication. The message should not be communicated from "on high" but from the midst of a shared feelings of struggle and common need.

boss people around. It's always a, "I'm here with you in this. We're all working together to try to achieve this."

INTERVIEWER: Go back to the thing you were saying a little bit earlier, that you could feel some kind of passion to explain things. How does that come across to you in the preaching? Is there a physical manifestation, some kind of urgency, or what?

JIM: When you listen to them, their tone is not always loud. Their tone is not always soft. Tom's good at this, too. They both will speak normally during normal events they're talking about, but when they get to points that they want to emphasize, either their voice gets lower or you almost have to lean in and listen, or they get louder and drive it home. I think, because of that change of tone and the fact that they're not always yelling and screaming or always so low that you can't hear them, not only does it keep your attention, (16) *but it helps you to feel what they're feeling. Which I don't think they necessarily train themselves...I don't necessarily think that they sit in their office and say, "At this point, I want to be loud. And at this point..." I think they do it because they themselves feel the passion...*It comes through in what they're saying. I'm not saying they're not prepared, and they're not trying to consciously do that, but that's what it comes across as.

INTERVIEWER: You feel like in the moment, in the room, they are really standing in their own feelings? They're really feeling the things that they're saying?

JIM: (17) *Right. I don't ever get the feeling they're saying something because they know it's the thing to say. Obviously, when they speak from the Bible, they're just trying to relay whatever the Bible says.* Tom's been really good at this, I think, even more so than Fred, when he sometimes goes through a story of the Bible and breaking

16. Here Jim points out that passion in communication is not so much a function of artificially manipulating one's volume and pitch, but of maintaining a real connection to the message—feeling the reality, depth, and importance of each word and sentence preached. Embodiment must be in service to logos.

17. Jim now articulates the main purpose of preaching: communicating the message of the Bible. What Jim's preachers so passionately want to "get across" or "relay" is "whatever the Bible says" as opposed to saying what people want to hear. Excitement about preaching emanates from a sermon's connection to special, counter-intuitive, and counter-cultural information and knowledge from the Bible. For Jim, this seems to be a very important logos-value in preaching.

down the characters of the Bible and trying to put you in their shoes. When you hear a story, and it may be a story you've heard a hundred times, whether it's the Good Samaritan or somebody else. You've heard it, and you know what it is. But sometimes you'll get, especially with Tom where he almost puts you in one of their character's positions and try to look at it through their eyes. Sometimes it's very humorous in the way he does it. Sometimes it's very serious. I like that. Don't try to preach it just the way it's always been preached, but think of it from a different perspective, whether it's as an outsider looking in or through the eyes of somebody in the story that you never really paid much attention to. (18) *Historically, it seems like they tend to have a lot of information that you haven't heard before, whether it's historical data that somebody's drummed up or whatever that makes the story more meaningful. They always have...It just seems like most of the time they always have a purpose for how they put you into the story.*

INTERVIEWER: You get the feeling like they're looking for new perspectives on stories that people may have heard of a couple of times?

JIM: How else can you spend every Easter on the same topic and every Christmas on the same topic and now make it fresh and new? I've been to thirteen Easter services or more here and the same thing at Christmas, and they never sound the same to me. Wow, I got something different out of that. (19) *I know you might get it one year from one person's perspective and the next year from someone else, but it's really... It's a gift to be able to creatively change things and not to change the story.*

INTERVIEWER: It is.

JIM: There is, I think, something that may be more important than everything put together: the fact that they don't waver in

18. Here Jim seems to be aware that, beyond "relaying" the Bible in a simple and direct way, preachers can feel free to use historical information to make the Bible more meaningful. Preachers also intervene with their own agendas or "different perspective(s)." Each preacher brings "a purpose for how they put you into the story." As we will soon see, however, Jim does not believe that these other agendas should "add anything" to the biblical message. The logos of preaching can be supported, but should not be overwhelmed, by non-biblical resources.

19. Remember that Jim desires novel messages and illustrations each week. We see here that he does not believe that newness each week needs to change the core message of scripture. He continues to locate the authoritative norms for correct interpretation and invention in the Bible itself, rather than in the theology or agendas of the preacher.

what they teach. It's the Bible, nothing else. They don't take anything out of the Bible and say, "Well, that's not important." If it's in there, it's important. (20) *They never add anything to it that's not there. It's straight biblical teaching. I think some people may not want to hear that, but they appreciate it. I think that they learn to appreciate it and respect it.*

INTERVIEWER: What I hear you saying is that one of the really important things in their preaching is a fidelity to the Bible—that they just stand on that.

JIM: They're not ashamed of it. If this is what the Bible says, then we're going to preach it. I appreciate the fact that they're not afraid to tackle any topic. If the Bible has something to say about it, then we're going to talk about it. It doesn't matter if it's a topic that's controversial or not, they're going to talk about it. It was at the old building, and I don't remember what the sermon series was, but every week it was a new…It was like a five- or six-week thing, and Fred and Tom were doing every other week, each other. It seemed like every other week, when Tom did it, it was the controversial subject. Tom really got the hard part of that, but he really did a good job, because one time it might be the subject of homosexuality. I think one time he did it was on divorce. (21) *These are all subjects people don't want to talk about or the worldview is so much different from yours.* They just do a good job.

INTERVIEWER: I think that's an important thing that they don't dodge the tough issues at all.

JIM: Most people would think, too, if your church is going to grow and be large, you've got to pander to the audience, so to speak. They've never done that. They don't water it down to try to get more people in here. I

20. Again, Jim asserts a simple trust that, in spite of his preachers' much desired inventive creativity, they "never add anything to [the Bible] that's not there." This is an important value for the logos of preaching. How does Jim know that nothing is added? In part because people hear what they "may not want to hear." In other words, part of what creates a sense of straightforward biblical authority in preaching is treating the Bible as a counter-intuitive and counter-cultural authority.

21. Again, the Bible and the preacher gain authority when they articulate words that some people may not want to hear about topics that many would rather not address. For Jim it is important that the biblical worldview, as expressed by his preachers, is *different* from the worldview of other people on issues of sexuality or marriage. This difference seems to add to his perception of the persuasiveness and authority of the logos and ethos of preaching.

think because (22) *they've stuck so hard to their guns,* that's why some people are attracted to it. There's probably a thousand different reasons why people would come, especially now, but from the very beginning, why would Fred be the one to grow [this church]? I think it's a God thing, and everybody here would say that...I do think one of the reasons for the growth has been because Fred, and now Tom, are both willing to stick to their guns on the issues and say it how the Bible says it, versus trying to water it down.

INTERVIEWER: I think that's really a strong, strong point. Let's flip it a little bit. What's the stuff that you *don't* want to see in sermons?

JIM: My personal thing, what I personally don't want to see, and I've seen it...is when I see these (23) *people wearing the robes and the purple gowns and all that kind of stuff.* Not that there's anything wrong with it, I guess. From my own standpoint, I get the feeling that people are up there dressed like that, that they're holier than I am. It makes it immediately harder for me to relate to that person. I know that's one thing that I never liked is that "holier than thou" appearance, even if it wasn't the case. The thing about it is I know a lot of that is probably just judging a book by its cover, but at the same time if you can't get past that...

INTERVIEWER: It's a barrier.

JIM: Yet for other people, it may be that they like that. Maybe that's what they like, but to me, it's something that's always turned me off. Another thing that's turned me off is someone that can't ever say anything without yelling. It's not that I don't appreciate when you've got something you're passionate about, and you've got a section of your sermon where you really

22. Notice that Jim attributes the growth of his church to this unwavering, consistent, oppositional, and even stubborn ("sticking to their guns") quality of the ethos and logos of preaching. This is part of what it means to live within God's revelation—"it's a God thing."

23. For Jim, vestments, an embodiment option, create a fundamental pathos-problem. They create a negative feeling of broken identification between speaker and listener.

get passionate. Speaking of passion, I think it was the first year we were in here, and they did the pulpit exchange, and Mike preached a sermon on Jesus. It was strictly Jesus and that was it. It wasn't, "I'm trying to get across any special notion. I just want to tell you about how I feel about Jesus." His sermon, and I bought the tape, that was the most impassioned sermon I think I've ever heard. He's got a way of...He's not always loud, (24) *but he has a way of getting loud and getting passionate about something where you get into it with him. But I've heard other people that when they get loud, that's all they are is loud, and they're not saying anything.* Yet, I understand that it takes all kinds to reach all kinds and that you're going to have some ministers who preach a certain way because of their congregation. That's the way they want to hear it.

INTERVIEWER: Sounds like out of your background...there may have been some other things that don't connect with you.

JIM: Yes, it never connected. It's not that I didn't understand...From my parents and grandparents and the people around me, it's not that I didn't know most of the Bible stories from growing up, but it just seemed to have no effect on me from my own personal standpoint. I knew right and wrong and all that, but when I was in there listening to the sermons at the old church, it was just like nails on a chalkboard, because nothing was really being said. They just rambled on and on about...Let's say they would go into...Let's say we're going to study the book of Matthew today, and we're just going to start reading here. I'm going to tell you a little bit about what's said.

24. Indiscriminate loudness is another embodiment issue that has negative implications for a sermon's pathos for Jim. Jim encourages preachers to use volume purposefully to communicate passion in a way that helps the listener to "get into it with" the preacher.

(25) *It was all monotone and no substance, and there was no illustrations to go with it. There was just nothing there from a… You might have got the story, but it just seemed like that, just a story. Just a story from long ago that has no relevance to you today, and it was never put in a way that showed how relevant it is to you today.*

I think that's important, because the Bible has been around for so long that most people tend to think of it as no different than picking up a Dr. Seuss book or Walt Disney movie or something. It's just another story, so how do you…? You see that even on movies where the television has done it or somebody has tried to do a movie about a story in the Bible, and it's presented that same way. It's just kind of a bigger-than-life story. (26) *There's nothing there. Nothing that says: This is how it is now. This relates to you now. In the old church, I think the biggest problem was there was nothing in the sermon. No passion in the sermon. No way of relating the Bible to how it was relevant to you today. From a sermon standpoint, that was just frustrating.*

25. Again, Jim dislikes preaching in which both embodiment and logos communicate monotony, lack of preparation, and irrelevance.

26. Notice, Jim is very frustrated when preachers simply retell the Bible story, perhaps with a little exposition along the way. For the logos of preaching to persuade Jim, it has to show the relevance of the Bible for life *now*. This is crucial to "passion" in preaching (a positive pathos-value).

Listening for Preaching

Our interview with Jim reveals a unique configuration of rhetorical elements he believes are essential to good preaching for himself and for others who are attracted to this megachurch. Because of his past in a church where sermons were monotonous and poorly prepared, Jim places a high premium on sermon preparation and rehearsal, important values for both sermon logos and embodiment. He steers us to several very important rhetorical indicators that communicate to the listener the preacher has not spent enough time preparing the message. These indicators include not having a new topic each week (5, 11), the tendency to re-use sermon illustrations (12), no "flow," which indicates that the sermon is poorly planned and un-rehearsed (13), and the tendency to consume an inordinate amount of sermon time retelling the biblical story with little or no reference to everyday life (26). Jim even indicates that certain vocal characteristics betray a lack of adequate preparation, especially a voice that fails to communicate any sense of continuity or fluidity (8). He believes that listeners expect and deserve well-prepared sermons relevant to everyday issues. He indicates that a prepared preacher can be spontaneous, "off-the-cuff," and free from the use of a manuscript, especially during the telling of stories or illustrations (1, 3). He is aware, however, that this strategy can backfire. Throughout this interview, he provides us with a negative subtext about extemporaneous preachers who: (a) ramble, retelling biblical stories with no topical unity; (b) use monotonous, loud voices; (c) are unable to move small units of thought toward a broader, relevant topic; and (d) preach the same thing over and over again (24–26).

Jim's comments are very instructive when he speaks about what he thinks listeners are looking for in the areas of ethos and pathos. Regarding the ethos of preaching, Jim desires a preacher who is "gifted" or charismatic, and who possesses the highest standards of personal and spiritual integrity (2, 9, 10). Although the preacher must "be himself," this "self" must be someone who practices what is preached and who holds to a higher moral and spiritual standard than the listener. At the same time, the preacher is to establish some emotional identification with the listener. The preacher must communicate a shared, needy, and struggling humanity (6, 15). Jim is very put off when preachers communicate from an ivory tower. For him, this is the problem with vestments. They create a faulty or contrived distance between the speaker and the listener, placing the speaker on a pedestal that is not necessarily earned in the school of hard knocks. According to Jim, preachers must find small ways to communicate that "I'm imperfect just like you are" (15), while simultaneously demonstrating that this imperfection can be overcome. In short, the preacher must communicate both an *ideal* ethos and a very *real* pathos in preaching.

It is this tension that is at the heart of authoritative preaching for Jim. On the one hand, the preacher must represent both an ideal, or higher standard, as the chosen and gifted representative of an ideal gospel message (logos). This message stands over and against culture and cannot be compromised. On the other hand, the preacher must find a way to present that message as something which meets the deepest needs of all persons in their common humanity, including the preacher. When Jim thinks about the embodiment of the sermon, this same dynamic is at work. Instead of distancing oneself from one's listeners and communcating in loud, monotonous tones, Jim wants preachers to speak in a straightforward, non-threatening way (7, 8, 25). The "passion" of preaching is found not in making a lot of noise and strutting about in front of people. Rather, passion is communicated by connecting deeply with both the urgency of the gospel message and the very real needs of the listeners represented (16). In the last analysis, preaching must communicate both the *message* and the *experience* of the gospel (14).

Listening for Theology

Aristotle, in his treatise *The "Art" of Rhetoric,* identifies two feelings that are fundamental to creating pathos in communication: feeling *friendly* toward those who are like us (2.4) and feeling *pity* towards those who have experienced similar evils in the past but have escaped. (2.8).[1] As we have seen, one of the things that Jim values in the preaching at his church is that the preachers present themselves as "imperfect just like you are" (15). This comes through in the ways that his preachers place themselves in situations and struggles that seem to be very similar to those of the congregation. Instead of wearing the hero hat constantly, his preachers humble themselves and demonstrate how it is that the gospel is a redemptive word in their own potentially broken and sinful lives. At the same time, however, the preachers represent themselves as persons who somehow manage to live by "a higher standard."

In the background of any preacher's identification with the imperfections and needs of listeners is the theological idea of *participation.* Participation, in the works of Augustine, Luther, and Calvin, is the idea that all humanity stands before God tainted *equally* by sin. The classical doctrine of participation wraps together the inclination toward sin and sin itself (cf. Calvin's "*total* depravity"). Regardless of the nature of one's actual sins, or whether one acts on one's sinful nature or not, our "original" sinful nature is a painful reminder that, as the apostle Paul puts it in Romans 3:23, "*all* have sinned and fall short of the glory of God." The doctrine of participation is the great leveler. It reminds us that all persons are *ontologically* sinners (sinners in their *being*) and therefore *equal* in the sight of God. This protects Christians from creating hierarchies of sin in which some sins (and sinners) can be unduly stigmatized.

Pelagius, arguing against this doctrine, asserted that although we share a common struggle with sin, "humanity has the capacity to choose sin or righteousness."[2] Pelagius, therefore, elevated the ability to resist and overcome sin. Full participation in a sinful nature is reserved for those who are lost in sin and not choosing a higher road in life. Over time, this idea results in a heightening of distinctions between sinners. As theologian Stephen Ray demonstrates, Pelagian theology asserts a deep, unconscious message of "ontological difference" (a difference in *being*) between individuals or classes of human beings who choose rightly and wrongly.[3]

Jim's responses to our questions indicate that he understands his preachers, like many similar preachers, to make good use of this Pelagian model as a part of the pathos of preaching. He perceives his preachers to communicate *identification* with the felt *needs* of imperfect sinners, while avoiding communicating full *participation* on a level playing field of sin. As Jim presents it, the preservation of an ideal form of ethos in the rhetorical situation implies that it is possible for the preachers at this church, and for those who emulate them as ideal character types, to rise above a fundamental equality in sin before God. This indicates that, to Jim, there is a hierarchy of sin and redemption in the rhetorical situation moving downward and outward from the preacher to imperfect listeners, and then via the logos of preaching to those with "different worldviews" who don't want to hear and respond to tough, biblical words about sexuality, marriage, etc. (21).

At the same time, the emphasis on particular life-choices that lead to the preacher's higher standard makes it possible to identify clearly those who are on the pathway to redemption, and those who are not. A clear line emerges within the rhetorical situation between those who are choosing to follow errant church leaders who, in Jim's words "pander to their (sinful) audience," and those who are choosing to follow those who "say it how the Bible says it" (22). This emphasis on a particular type of biblically based church leadership from the pulpit brings us to a second theological consideration: the construction of authority through the assertion of biblical-moral *difference.*

As we have seen, for Jim, the Bible, sermon message, and preacher all represent a higher standard that contradicts the culture in which we live (17–22). All three of these elements of preaching are presented within the rhetorical situation as if they run counter to a particular model of sinful experience. In fact, they gain authority for Jim inasmuch as they seem to contradict this experience (21, 22). This perception of authority as a function of *difference* from the prevailing worldview is reinforced as Jim's preachers work to identify a certain prevailing individual, social, and cultural worldview that must be contradicted and redeemed (21–23). As we have seen, this sinful worldview belongs to all actual or potential listeners who don't want to hear the tough words that biblical preachers proclaim. The Bible and the sermon's message (logos), and the preacher's character (ethos), represent God's answers to controversial issues (homosexuality, divorce, etc.) that are left unchallenged by those with the culture's prevailing worldview.

For Jim, therefore, the authority of the sermon is created in a self-contained way within the rhetorical situation itself. Because of Jim's commitment to the authoritative difference of the Bible, preacher, and preaching, there can be no allowance for the preacher to have a cultural or experiential perspective that might "add anything to the Bible" (20). Nothing outside of the rhetorical situation is allowed to authorize the sermon. It would be inappropriate and unnecessary to grant authority to the testimony of anyone, including the preacher, who might live and hold a worldview outside of, or in contradiction to, this situation. Authority for preaching is created as a function of the assumed *difference* of the Bible, preacher, and preached message from the worldview of a broad group of others within and beyond the rhetorical situation itself. Authority increases inasmuch as each week's sermon expresses new ways to live differently from those who hold this worldview.

Rhetorically, therefore, authority seems to be established in the following way. People enter the rhetorical situation via the preacher's partial identification with their sinful humanity at the level of their struggles and needs (identification at the level of pathos). For Jim, the preacher's words gain authority because of the preacher's ability to find ever-new messages that contradict the sinful humanity of each listener (logos), presenting choices that can lead listeners away from a sinful worldview toward the preacher's higher, biblical standards for life (ethos).

Undergirding this rhetorical process is an understanding of biblical authority and, by extension, the authority of the preacher and the sermon, which assumes a theology of revelation that attempts to separate the authority of God's revealed Word from the authority of human experience and reason.[4] Jim also indicates that there exists, within his church, a theological ethic in which the church can and should be distinct from the culture in which it lives.[5] These counter-experiential and counter-cultural assumptions are supported rhetorically by preached messages expressing that the biblical witness is being co-opted and suppressed by certain experiential, cultural, social, and/or political forces. In this way, a kind of theological and ethical separatism bolsters the authority of the church and its leaders for persons like Jim who are in search of a firm and frankly authoritative theological voice in a culture that he perceives as largely at odds with the biblical witness. This is borne out in Jim's references to the importance of having preachers who "stick to their guns on the issues" without trying to "water it down" (22). This, as he sees it, is the key to his church's growth. For Jim, his preachers are providing a stubborn, undiluted, oppositional Word of absolute *revealed* authority (difference) in a culture of relatively like-minded, wrong-headed people whose trust of their own reason and experience, instead of this revealed Word, is leading them astray.

Challenges for Preaching

1. How can we communicate that we are well-prepared and organized? Can we leave notes behind and render illustrations in an extemporaneous way? Are we able to insure that each sermon communicates something new and relevant? Can we come up with fresh illustrations each week? How can we make the time to adequately rehearse each sermon?
2. How can we learn from good preaching models and mentors while remaining true to ourselves in the pulpit?
3. How can we use a voice that is nonthreatening and communicates only the passion called for by the words we are speaking?
4. How can we communicate an authentic identification with our listeners' life struggles? Can we lead them toward a higher ethical standard by being someone who practices what we preach?
5. How should we establish authority in and for our preaching?
6. How can we communicate an honest and consistent understanding of the relationship between our church and culture?

CHAPTER 6

"It Was like Jesus Himself Was Coming. I Kept Saying, 'It's Our Preacher.'"

Jane: Caucasian Rural Woman in a Community Church

Dan P. Moseley

The following is an interview with Jane, a thirty-year-old Caucasian mother of two who lives in the rural Midwest. She attends a small, rural, nondenominational church with about forty in attendance on Sunday morning. Half of those in attendance are under fifty years of age and there are a few more adult women than men. Most of the people drive ten to twenty miles to church.

The sanctuary is a relatively new, one-story, brick building with about twenty pews divided by a center aisle. The wooden pulpit is at the center of the front of the sanctuary on a slightly raised platform. It is flanked by a piano on one side and an electronic organ on the other. On the wall behind the pulpit is a large wooden cross, draped with purple cloth with a white dove on it. The cross is topped by a crown of thorns. Artificial plants cover the altar and the tops of the organ and the piano. The congregation is friendly and the service itself is very informal with warm greetings and attention to the birthdays and personal lives of the congregants.

This is Jane's first real experience with church. She was encouraged to attend by her oldest daughter and her husband's family also attends this church. She attends worship once or twice a week with her husband and daughter. She is in her thirties, but information about her social formation and educational background is not revealed in the interview. Jane enjoys the personal relationships and likes having direct contact with her minister, Bob. In many ways, Jane is part of the oral culture that Tex Sample refers to in his book, *Ministry in an Oral Culture: Living with Will Rogers, Uncle Remus, and Minnie Pearl.*[1] While she gives the preacher some authority based on his ability to explicate the Bible, she is suspicious of experts who don't live among the people. Frequently, those in more rural settings tend to trust the folklore of the community rather than the "wisdom" of some expert they do not know.

Excerpts from the Transcript

INTERVIEWER: Does it make a difference to you that you know Bob when you listen to him preach?

JANE: Yes, definitely. At first when Bob came here, we didn't know him, because he hadn't attended here before. I guess he did years ago when he was little. (1) *But yes, it does, because you got to know him and you knew he lived what he preached, but it makes him more accessible.* You don't mind going to him if you've got a problem or just want to talk or whatever. I like it.

1. Jane feels good about being in a church where she knows those around her and the minister who speaks to her. This congregational context and pastoral ethos give her confidence in what she is hearing. Notice the ambiguity in Jane's perception of Bob.

INTERVIEWER: So that personal relationship is important to you?

JANE: Yes. Oh, definitely. Having him over for dinner a month or so after he started preaching here, and I'm running around the house. (2) *It was like Jesus himself was coming. I kept saying, "It's our preacher. It's our preacher. I've got to have the house clean. It's no big deal."* Once he came and sat down and we got to talking, I'm like, "What did I worry about cleaning the house for?" Yes. They're much more accessible, I guess.

2. Jane likes knowing Bob as someone like her, but she also wants him to be different. Her personal relationship is important to her, but she also had some sense that he was like "Jesus Christ himself." Jane had expectations that the minister would be distant but discovered him to be very accessible.

INTERVIEWER: When you think about preaching in the church, what does preaching do that nothing else can do in your mind?

JANE: (3) *Actually, it explains to me a lot of points in the Bible that I don't get when I read.* Actually, our former minister did that a little more than Bob as far as really getting into reading more of the Bible, as far as taking one chapter and verses from one area. Bob goes back and forth, which isn't bad. Our former minister, he really just explained a lot of things I would read at home, and I'm like, *"What exactly does that mean?"* *I come here, and it seemed like it's always the next week just what I'd been reading, trying to understand.* After he explained it, "That was easy. Why didn't I get that?"

INTERVIEWER: It really instructs you about things that aren't clear to you in the Bible.

JANE: Yes. Or even there have been different sermons that after we've left, I've got to know more. I didn't get enough in that half-hour. I go home and read more. Some of them really energize you and get you ready to go.

INTERVIEWER: I know this is hard. Can you think of any specific sermon where you really have felt energized?

JANE: There was one. Now this wasn't here. Two years ago, we were visiting my aunt in Florida. We had never been to the church before. They did a reenactment. Although the congregation had kids, they did a reenactment of the death on the cross and the resurrection. I can't even think what the name of the song was, but there was a guy that sang this long song about it while they were doing it. (4) *I don't think there was a dry eye in the congregation when it was over. It was one of those that just really moved you. Really.* Bob has had a couple that really got to me. He had a backpack one time. This was actually when he was just visiting preaching. He had a backpack just totally loaded down. He was talking about burdens and worries. People carry them and we need to let them

3. Jane isn't simply interested in feeling a relationship with others and the minister; she wants to learn and understand. I wonder if Jane not only wants the security and safety of relationship, but wants some solid direction on how to live life. Both safe relationships and clarity of understanding reduce anxiety.

I wonder if the preacher knows that more careful attention to clarity of purpose in his sermon would enhance Jane's experience of logos.

4. Jane has identified some moving experiences she has had in church. Tears seem to be a sign of energy and power. Pathos signals that something important is happening. The way the very concrete presentations of drama, song, and illustration speak to Jane seems to point to the importance of being able to visualize. When Jane visualizes even painful and difficult circumstances (the crucifixion), she feels connected to something mysterious and maybe divine. Embodiment and pathos seem to contribute to making the message realistic and useful to Jane.

go. (5) *That one really got me. Then there was another one. He had us singing "How Great Thou Art." We went through it the first time and it didn't really get you. Then he explained each of the verses and had us re-sing it. By the end it was another one of those, where there was not a dry eye in the place. I'm more visual, I guess, or something. All three of those got me.*

INTERVIEWER: Say some more, because that seems important, but we usually don't sit down and think about all the reasons why. That's what I'm interested in hearing. Why would you say any one of those was particularly moving to you since you're more visual? Is there anything else that you can identify about why it touched you so much?

JANE: They were so positive, even with Jesus' death on the cross. Of course you were upset, thinking he went through that for us, but then as you come around...(6) *The negative thing that you turn around to the positive. He did that for us! It's just so positive.* Like the book bag. Yes, people do carry around heavy burdens, and we don't need to. I like the positive a lot, too. They talk about judgment and wrath and that kind of stuff, straight from the Bible, but they harp more on the positive, I guess. I've read different books where different people have talked about churches they've gone to growing up with preachers yelling and screaming and harping on the bad stuff. You're going to go to hell. (7) You're going to go to hell. *You hear that, but it's more positive. It makes you really want to get to know the Lord, because he loves you and not just because you're going to go to hell if you don't. It's more loving, I guess.*

INTERVIEWER: You said there wasn't a dry eye in the house, that it wasn't just your own response.

5. Notice how Jane is moved to tears by the music and the reenactment. Tears seem to be a sign that Jane has connected with somethng divine as well as with the human community. Pathos validates the words spoken and the message delivered.

6. Notice here that the logos of preaching persuades Jane when the preacher couches the hard things of judgment in the context of the more positive hope that is a part of the gospel. She feels the need to be challenged to live a faithful life but is not open to it unless there is some chance of a positive outcome.

7. This reminds us of the depth of emotional need in the listener. The experience of hell (isolation and separation) is powerful. The desire for love is also powerful. In Jane, these seem to commingle. Preachers can be reminded that listeners need words that take seriously judgment and grace.

JANE: (8) *Oh, no. Even my husband was crying, and that's...Even to get me to cry is a lot. But even my husband cried.* The one in Florida, the reenactment of the resurrection, even the singer... Of course, I'm sure... Halfway through he'd have to stop. This was a huge congregation. Here, we've got just a small one. This was a huge church, huge congregation. I bet there was probably two hundred people there, at least two hundred. It was moving. (9) *You could just feel the energy.*

INTERVIEWER: For you, what does make a sermon true?

JANE: As long as it comes out of the Bible. As long as it's not just taking one verse here and one verse there. I like to read the verses before and the verses after to make sure that what they're saying...There are even times I've gone home and I'll read it after, (10) *because Bob skips around a lot. I'll go home, and I'll look at a verse and read the verses before and the verse after to make sure. Not that I don't believe, but I want to read it myself and make sure that he's telling me the truth. I don't want to be blindly led.*

INTERVIEWER: You trust him, but you don't just take it blindly.

JANE: Yes.

INTERVIEWER: You're doing your part.

JANE: Yes.

INTERVIEWER: Do you think that all sermons should begin with scripture or be based on scripture?

JANE: No, not all of them. Well, yes, I guess so. Bob's sermons before always talked about family, raising your kids, what husbands should be, what wives should be. (11) *He goes above and beyond the Bible, but he'll find scriptures in there that pertain to what he's talking about. I really like those, too. Self-improvement, I guess.*

8. Notice again how tears seem to reveal that something important is happening. Pathos is very important to this listener.

9. Jane seems to equate energy with shared emotion. Large numbers of people with shared tears feels like energy to her. She might identify this as the work of the Holy Spirit.

10. Jane struggles to comprehend the meaning of the Bible. For her, logos is very important. She longs for more clarity and knowledge of the faith. She is especially interested in how the Bible helps her live in the daily business of family life. Because she is connected to Bob personally, she trusts that his interpretation of the Bible is correct. Logos is validated by being nested in the ethos of community and the personal relationship with the pastor.

11. Jane seeks logos to improve herself. She wants words that will help her order family life. The fact that her minister is married and has a family helps Jane identify with his teachings. Jane wants help in becoming a better person and her minister's similar life situation gives credibility to what he says.

INTERVIEWER: You gave me three examples of sermons or worship services that really moved you. Can you think of one in particular that left you flat?

JANE: There was one here…This has just been a few weeks ago. I don't know if he felt that the church was splitting or something. (12) *I don't know exactly. But his sermon was about being united. That one just didn't really set well, because I didn't feel like we're splitting or anything. He's got ideas he wants to do and what we're used to as the church. That kind of left me a little flat, I guess.*

INTERVIEWER: It was because you felt that it was off target?

JANE: A little bit, and maybe a little berating I guess. Yes. I don't know. Maybe it wasn't on target with some. I don't know. But for me and my family, including my in-laws, it just didn't pertain, I guess, is what I'm saying.

INTERVIEWER: Let me ask you a slightly different question. Are there sermons that bore you and why?

JANE: Yes. There are some. If someone is sitting back here just really…I guess I'm not used to it, him being new. I'm visual again. I like to be able to go home in my Bible and read. (13) *He's flipping back and forth so fast. By the time I get to the next one, he's already read and he's on to the next one. After a while, I'll sit back, okay. I don't like the flipping back and forth. A few, that's fine, but when you're reading ten, fifteen, twenty verses just back, forth, just flipping back and forth. You can look around and most everybody is trying to flip back and forth in their Bibles.*

INTERVIEWER: Too much of that jumping around in scripture loses your interest.

JANE: Yes.

INTERVIEWER: Sometimes people say, "That sermon really changed me or changed the

12. Jane seems to get anxious when she can't follow the line of thought or when the movement back and forth in scripture is too fast. There seem to be two things that bother Jane—one is the inability to follow the thinking and the other is when the topic doesn't relate to her directly. Jane was left "flat" by a sermon in which the preacher felt it was important to talk about "unity" and she didn't feel that the church was "splitting." Since it didn't affect Jane directly, she thought it was not a good sermon. Jane is touched when the preacher helps her connect her life to a divine presence with insights on how to live more meaningfully.

13. Jane is persuaded by logos. But words from the Bible must be clear and coherent. Logical ordering of ideas is important. Simply quoting from the Bible because it is the Bible is not helpful to people like Jane.

way I thought·about things or what I believe." Can you think of a particular sermon or set of sermons that have impacted you in that way? I'm not saying you should.

JANE: I feel like that a lot. At least once every month or two, we'll get one that just really will explain something. I'm like, "Wow." (14) *Like raising your kid, marriage with your husband, committing... Yes, that stuff really gets me thinking. It does change me, my husband also.* Well, this was a year ago, *he had a marriage series. It was about a month long, raising kids one weekend and then other things the next few weekends. We had big long discussions. We got the Bible out and read some verses.* (15) *Let's look at wives submitting. That was a biggie for me. We got it out, and I read it in context. Don't have to be doormats, okay.*

INTERVIEWER: There's a difference between submission and being a doormat.

JANE: There have been other ones like that. Let's see. I like Moses and the burning bush, not wanting to do...You feel that connection. There are different things that are hard to change, but in the end, you're better off. That kind of thing.

INTERVIEWER: Those are good examples. That's helpful. What about the church as a whole? Can you think of specific sermons or things that he preaches about that really impact who the church is or what the church does? That's hard because it's like, "Well, I don't know what's going on in everybody else's mind."

JANE: (16) *Like the singing "How Great Thou Art" and going over it. That one you could tell the whole church was moved. It was just a different energy in the air afterwards.* I can't really, honestly think of another one off the top of my head, other than that.

14. Again we have the desire for a word that will help the family be a better family. Logos is an important strategy for improving their lives.

15. Jane wants help in living to be grounded in biblical understanding. She needs to have the biblical word interpreted so that it is both consistent with the Bible and does not violate her sense of herself as a worthwhile individual. She wants to be submissive without becoming a doormat.

16. Pathos is a most important key to good preaching for people like Jane. When the whole church is moved, there is an energy that overcomes Jane.

INTERVIEWER: What do you think Bob thinks he's doing when he preaches? You've told me a lot about what you're perceiving and how you're taking it. What do you think they think they're doing?

JANE: *I'm going to say some of it is doing what God tells him to do, just because there is so often he gives sermons and it's like they're personally talking to me.* It's something I've read about that week or been praying about that week or something. (17) *It can't be coincidence as often as it happens. The Lord is definitely telling him what to preach on. For Bob, I might say he's better at the family unit, as far as raising children and husbands and wives, how you treat each other. He is. I think he is bettering the family unit.* (18) *That makes it very good to listen to. He'll leave you with a lot of examples about things they do and scripture also. He does definitely better family units and stuff.*

INTERVIEWER: Can you say anything more about those sorts of stories, personal stories, out of preachers' lives or their experience? How do those come across to you?

JANE: No. I like to know that they're living as they portray themselves, which if you didn't know them personally, you wouldn't know. *We've really gotten to know Bob and Jill in the last six months, maybe. Even our former minister and his wife, for that matter. You really know them. To an extent most of the people in the congregation. There are some that we don't know real well outside the congregation and stuff, but you still feel like you know them pretty well.*

INTERVIEWER: Do you see any potential problems with that?

JANE: (19) *No. I'm just thinking if it were me personally or my husband up there telling stories about something I've done. I don't know that I'd care to hear that up there in front of everybody. I don't think he really gets into quite that detail. He doesn't say, "My kids have this week been*

17. Jane believes that God is speaking through the preacher when it touches her personally. God's words are those that help her with her personal needs.

18. Again, Jane seems to be reinforcing the importance of ethos in her listening. She believes that the pastor intends to speak from the depth of his spiritual connection with God and that is verified in the way it connects to her own life (pathos). The preacher must be speaking for God because he speaks about things she wonders about. Through the connection with the context and the pastor and feeling moved, Jane seeks words which will help her live life faithfully. She seeks words to help in marriage and family life. Logos is very important in her feeling the meaning she seeks.

19. Although Jane wants the ethos of preaching to be strong, she has some understanding about the boundaries between pulpit and personal life. She believes that self-revelation helps her understand the preacher, but she is uncomfortable if the revelation is too personal or contemporary.

horrible," or something. He doesn't comment to that extent. It's a broad range. It's not, "My wife has done this and made me mad." Nothing that way. It's just all broad stuff.

INTERVIEWER: It seems appropriate to you.

JANE: Yes.

INTERVIEWER: Let me switch gears just a little bit and talk about what helps you to actually listen in terms of delivery. It's one of those things you take for granted until it's a problem usually. What makes a sermon easy to listen to in terms of the way they speak, mannerisms? And also what makes them hard to listen to?

JANE: The first thought that came to mind when you said that was, we had a revival here couple years ago. I don't know where the preacher was from. I couldn't even tell you his name. (20) *We came the first night and this guy just screamed the house down. It was every two minutes, he was wiping his mouth. He was screaming so that he was drooling. I know. I'm talking about my in-laws along with my family also, we still joke about that now. We didn't come back after the first day. It's our church, but we didn't like that. You felt like he was berating you. It was horrible. Now I've noticed even Bob raises his voice, yelled before. Just one or two words, just to get your attention. That's not bad. Even my daughter, she'll raise her head up and look around because it's just so unexpected. That's good when it's done in the moment.* There was another time. I can't even remember what the sermon was now, but he threw a book on the floor. Everybody just jumped. It's got its moments. Just like you're talking normal and just changing the tone of voice. Bob, and our former minister at church, both for that matter, it's more like he's talking one on one with you. Not talking at you, talking to you personally. That guy from the revival...Oh!

20. How the preacher embodies what is being said is very important to Jane. For Jane to hear what is being said, the preacher must be authentic. When her former minister got out of character after listening to the guest preacher, Jane had a spiritual crisis. She and her family had to pray about their ability to be present in the congregation. Fortunately for them, he got "back to normal" and used his own familiar pattern of speech and tone of voice. Ethos is so important to Jane that she has a hard time listening if there is incongruence between the person in the pulpit and the person she knows out of the pulpit.

INTERVIEWER: His intensity was over the top.

JANE: Yes. Honestly, even after that, our former minister, for about the next month he was really getting tense like that. I kept telling my husband, "I can't do this. I can't do this." We prayed. We really did. It was about a month, month-and-a-half maybe and he got back to normal. We thought "We're going to have find another church."

INTERVIEWER: What is normal? You said he got back to normal.

JANE: Just normal tone of voice, just like he was talking to you one-on-one. (21) *I don't mind you yelling once in a while if you're making a point, but the whole time where he's just pointing his finger and shaking it at you—that was way too much. Way too much.* We would have been at that revival every night, but no, not if it was going to be the same guy there the whole week. No.

INTERVIEWER: If you could tell one or two things to preachers that you think would make their sermons more engaging or more energizing, what would it be? Your chance from the pews to say to all those preachers out there, "Why don't you…?

JANE: (22) *Be visual. The visual with me again. Just the backpack. It was just so heavy. That really made an impact with me. The positive stuff, too.* You have to put in the judgment and wrath, and going to hell and that stuff. You have to put that in there, too, but don't harp on that. Harp on the positive, which that really doesn't belong here because they do. This church definitely emphasizes the positive.

INTERVIEWER: What do you think God is doing through the sermon?

JANE: Sometimes when I'm reading the Bible, and I don't understand and I say, "*Please help me understand this.*" Sometimes that's an answer to a prayer that way. When it's really just that week it's what I've been

21. Conventional styles of preaching which accuse and attack do not communicate well to persons like Jane.

22. Jane reminds us again that logos receives power when it is made visual for her. The ability of preaching to persuade is related to how visual the preacher can be.

reading about. (23) *Then I come to church and that's what the sermon is about. God is talking to me personally.* Sometimes that's not good. We had a sermon one time where... It must have been a few months ago. Bob was talking about, "Lord, put your hand over my mouth so that I don't open my mouth and insert foot," whatever. "Make my words sweet as honey." That one I felt like he was talking to me, too. *There's the good and the bad with it. I can't say every one I feel like he's personally talking to me, but there are a lot of them.*

INTERVIEWER: Anything else along those lines in terms of what God is doing in the sermon?

JANE: (24) *Making his presence known. Making sure we're saved.*

INTERVIEWER: Is there anything else that you feel like you want to make sure is heard here about preaching?

JANE: I really can't think of anything. In the last week I've been thinking, "What am I going to say?" I thought, "I don't know the questions," so I didn't really have anything thought of ahead of time. I think we've covered everything I thought of anyway.

23. Jane's understanding of preaching leans toward a rather individual theology of salvation. For her, effective preaching impacts the way one lives. The persuasive power of a sermon is related to the way it hooks her emotions and effects her relationships.

24. Where there is real concern on Jane's part for words that assure personal salvation, she has a communal understanding as well. Her sense of energy that comes when many people are touched is communal. Presence of the holy is related to "making sure *we're* saved." Family and community are important to Jane and her theology.

Listening for Preaching

Jane is a listener of sermons who seems to be looking for an authentic and nurturing pastoral and communal ethos (1). She desires empathic connection with her preacher and the environment. Jane's relationship to the environment and the preacher (ethos) is related to her feelings about the words she hears (pathos), but she is sometimes moved even when she does not have a relationship with the pastor or the environment is not familiar (3, 4). The power of the word (logos) to persuade is related to how the preacher is present (embodiment) when he speaks (18, 19, 20).

It is important to note how a healthy familiarity and a "normal" embodiment of the real personality of the preacher help a listener like Jane. This familiarity extends to the logos of preaching. She is able to hear the preacher better the more personal connection she has with him, others around her, and the topic of the sermon.

Jane's confidence in the preacher is connected to her knowledge of who the preacher is. It seems important to her to be connected to one she believes has power. When the preacher came to her house, she felt like "Jesus was coming"(1). At the same time, her knowledge of the life of the preacher contributes to her ability to trust his word. If he speaks contrary to what he lives, she finds that a barrier to trust (2, 17).

But she wants to know not only the preacher. She wants to know others in his world who relate to him. Knowing his wife and children is important to her ability to listen to him. When Jane feels that her preacher knows her because his life has similar characteristics to hers, this helps her trust level. It also provides the preacher with messages that connect with her life, especially those related to "bettering the family" (9, 10, 13, 14).

She is also offended if the preacher seems to be putting down the listener. The revivalist who seemed to shout and judge left her out in the cold. She was able to accept words of judgment and wrath from one who also shared the mercy and the joy (2, 5). The attitude of her ministers toward her and the congregation make it possible for her to hear their critique of the human situation.

Jane's motivation to "go and do" what the preacher says seems to be related to her confidence that he is living what he says. The communal shape of living is reinforced by this attitude. We are not simply islands who each determine our behavior on the basis of the way we process our perception of reality. We are influenced in our behavior by the actions of others we know and for whom we have respect. The actions of the preacher seem to help set a communal standard for behavior that is consistent with the words used to define and motivate that behavior.

This might suggest to the preacher that awareness of his doubts could contribute to the integrity of his speech. When the preacher shares the same human struggles as the listener, then when the preacher comes to some affirmations of faith, he models for the listener the relationship between doubt and affirmation (10). Robert Dykstra, in his book, *Discovering a Sermon: Personal Pastoral Preaching* claims that the internal journey of the preacher can shape and inform the preacher in such a way as to create connection that encourages and motivates the listener to a transforming life.[2]

A second factor is important in order for Jane to hear effectively. When she is moved to tears, she has a sense that something meaningful is happening. The power of the sermon is related to how it makes her feel (4, 18).

Jane listens to the sermon through pathos. For her, a good sermon is one in which the message speaks to her felt needs or moves her directly. She likes the sermons where the issues dealt with are ones that she has been struggling with. She believes that God is speaking through the preacher when the words "hit home" to her (16). When the preacher spoke of a possible split in the church, an issue about which Jane had no knowledge, it left her flat. Sermons about family and human relationships that were personally familiar to Jane were ones that had divine inspiration.

Jane has a strong desire to understand what God would have her do so that she can live her life faithfully. It is important that the logos is preached in a clear and compelling way. Jane finds her emotions engaged when she gets insights on how to live a better life with her family (12, 14).

The words of the preacher are made most powerful when the preacher helps Jane visualize what he is saying. Jane was moved by the dramatization of the crucifixion (3). The emotions of sadness and joy overcame her as she experienced the crowds and the solitary figure of Jesus. Listeners such as Jane seem to be concrete listeners. She connects with words that create some drama, or music that hooks her emotions. The pathos of preaching is reinforced by embodied drama and music as she frequently comments on how both her family and others in the community were moved or touched by the same thing. When others around her are impacted in a similar way, Jane feels that there is energy. One might call that the movement of the Spirit.

Ethos and pathos are not enough for Jane. She also is a logos listener. She wants to know how to live her life. She wants to know how the gospel helps her in her primary relationships. She listens for content. She reads the Bible and wants to understand in her mind what it says. She does not want simply to feel or be moved. She wants to know. She wants her cognitive skills to be stretched. She likes to know stories such as "Moses and the burning bush." She wanted to know what the Bible says about family and couple relationships. She seems to want to live well according to some set of values larger than herself. She wants to live according to values she perceives to be Christian.

This part of the story ought to challenge every preacher who wants people to develop skills of thinking to teach the critical skills of Bible study. Jane believed that she was being taught what the Bible said (14). She refers to teaching about submission of wife to husband. This kind of preaching that superimposes the culture's patriarchy on the patriarchy of the Bible sets up occasions for abuse. She seems to experience presence and grace, and those seem to motivate her to live a life of healing relationships. Careful biblical exegesis and interpretation would help the logos affirm and undergird the grace she experiences in the culture of the congregation.

Preachers should also note how important presence is to listeners like Jane (19). Jane was turned off by the overpowering physical presence of the revivalist. She didn't like his drooling and sweating. His shouting and mannerisms made it impossible to listen to him. In fact, when these mannerisms were adopted by her pastor, it so angered her she had serious doubt about going back to the church.

Jane was also sensitive to the way her own preacher was out of character when he adopted the mannerisms of the revivalist. The ethos she had come to trust was undermined when the minister tried to act like someone different from who she had come to know him to be. There is authority in embodied authenticity. When a person's life and embodied representation of truth are consistent with her/his words about truth, a sense of integrity is experienced by the listener. The integration of word and body creates power that is not there when there is a dissonance between tongue and body.

This interview with Jane reflects the complex relationship between logos, pathos, ethos, and embodiment as they interact in the relationship between a listener and a preacher. Attention to each of these factors will help improve the work of the preacher who seeks to persuade and influence through the work of the pulpit.

Listening for Theology

Theology has both personal and communal dimensions. Many people in congregations come to worship on Sunday morning seeking a personal relationship with God through the event of the Word. Effective preachers try to respond to that hunger with clarity by working to connect with the personal life experience of the listener. Preachers can often facilitate this connection through stories and witness that reflects something of the life of the listener. Jane responds very positively to such preaching.

From broader Christian perspective, of course, a preacher needs to help individuals realize that their personal relationships with God bring them into community with other Christians, and commission them for ministry in the world beyond the congregation. The preacher could encourage Jane to move in that broader direction by helping her consider how her love for her family can help her understand God's love (and the congregation's love) for others. For example, the preacher might invite her to respond to an abused child from a dysfunctional family in the way that Jane would like for someone to respond to her own children. Sermons could help her see that God's love for children who have lost their parents through war or AIDS is similar to her love for her own child. Christian theology affirms that God welcomes us where we are, but it also prompts us to welcome others with the same unconditional and compassionate welcome with which God welcomes us. Jane's remarks do not lead us to think that she is privatistic or self-centered. She may simply never have realized the wider claims of God's love on her life.

According to Jane, preaching can also be more effective and realistic when it reflects a theology of both transcendence and imminence. Some of life is very clear and manageable. There are things we do that can make a difference. Good advice on how to live with family and how to do our work is helpful. But, all life can't be reduced to manageable size. Events occur that remain mysterious. They are without clear answers. Multiple dimensions of life are experienced as mysterious and overwhelming. If preaching is only words that guide us in "how to live better," the listeners will find themselves wanting in faith when life is experienced as so overwhelming that they can't be managed with "how to." Preaching that points to the awe and mystery of the holy and does not assume to reduce faith to "how to" can serve the listeners when they are overwhelmed with the more unmanageable parts of life.

For Jane, effective preaching is related to embodiment of the preacher. The faith professes that God is made present in flesh. The way we are physically present in the pulpit and in the words we speak empower or disempower our preaching. At the same time, embodiment requires boundaries. When the preacher does not reflect boundaries that respect the space of the listener, some listeners are unable to hear.

Boundaries reveal respect. Pulpits function the same way. If we sense the power of the material with which we are working, we will seek to offer it to others as carefully as possible. If the gospel is power, it doesn't require that we push it onto people. The pulpit represents the distance that is necessary to access the holy terror. When we wander around and get in people's faces, we do not reflect respect either for the holy awe in the other or the holy presence in the words that we speak.

Jane is one of those listeners for whom the whole experience reinforces her capacity to hear and access the preacher's words. The safety and comfort she feels in the environment opens her to hearing the words that are spoken. She has more comfort when she is in the presence of a congregation and pastor whom she knows and trusts. Her experience of the word is reinforced (and affirmed as divine) when it is a shared experience of the word. She also identifies its divine qualities in its resonance with her own questions and her own experience. Guidance for living is received when integrity is present in the embodied experience.

Preachers can gain insight into preaching with integrity by listening to people like Jane. Her intuition about what she hears opens her to those who have both courage to speak what they believe and humility to recognize what they do not know. The personal life of the pastor matters to her capacity to hear, and some vulnerability on the part of the preacher enables Jane to understand what she hears.

When there are listeners like Jane in the congregation, the preacher must attend carefully to his relationship to the congregation (ethos), the way he helps the Bible speak to personal and familial needs (logos) and the emotions that are generated by stories and illustrations (pathos). Clarity and authenticity are critical for people like Jane. The preacher who works hard to be an effective pastor and who takes the teaching vocation seriously will communicate effectively with listeners like Jane.

Challenges for Preaching

1. How can our preaching reveal something about our life that will help listeners for whom ethos is important know and trust us?
2. How does our presence in the pulpit reflect appropriate boundaries?
3. What can we do to assure that our demeanor in the pulpit does not assume more authority than is appropriate to the people's knowledge of us?
4. How much time do we spend attending to clarity in our preaching?
5. Are we preaching messages that explain the meaning of Christian faith for daily life (families, marriages, etc.)?
6. What forms of visual stimuli can we use that will help people *see* what we mean?

CHAPTER 7

"The Sermon Is the Central Point. If That's Not There, the Whole Thing Goes Down the Drain."

A Small Group: Historic Downtown Congregation

RONALD J. ALLEN

This chapter considers an interview with a group of five parishioners in a historic congregation in a mid-Southern city with a metropolitan area population of about 250,000. Average worship attendance is about 160 and has been stable for many years. The church, made up primarily of middle-class professionals, self-consciously identifies with the liberal theological tradition and with liberal social causes. Indeed, some people in the wider community describe it as a "cause-driven congregation." About 12 percent of the members are African American, with about 88 percent Caucasian. This community officially welcomes persons with gay and lesbian orientations. The congregation is served by a female minister (Ariel) and a male minister (Rob) who is new to the congregation.

The interview took place about a month after the September 11, 2001, terrorist attacks. Several times the group refers directly to this event. All five members were at the service of worship on the Sunday afterward. The interviewer visited the congregation on the same day, and heard the sermon and reports that the group had deep feelings around that service. The following persons are included:

Jack is a fifty-one-year-old African American male who has been a part of the congregation for four years and leads a department in a government bureau. Jack, who had spent most of his life in a more theologically conservative congregation, joined this one after his partner brought him. Jack finds the congregation religiously liberating. He states that the "sermons are one of the reasons I came here."

Jerome, a thirty-eight-year-old Caucasian male who works in the financial world, has been in the church for ten years. He became of part of the congregation because he found it to be the more inclusive kind of church he was seeking.

Martha, an eighty-year-old Caucasian female, is retired. She was a member of another congregation of the same denomination in the same city for fifty years, but began attending this church when she knew a woman minister who preached here occasionally, but who had cancer and needed help with certain things. Martha starting attending this congregation to help the woman preacher, was attracted to the inclusiveness of the congregation, and transferred her membership.

Susan is a forty-eight-year-old Caucasian female connected with the legal world who has been in the congregation for seven years. She was formerly affiliated with a more conservative congregation but felt excluded. She said she always had "a critical inner dialogue" with the sermons in the previous church because "the minister would be talking about men [males], and everything was about hell and how horrible we were, and how we were going to pay unless we got saved…I was always answering everything and being really critical of his sermons." When she visited this congregation she felt immediate welcome and inclusion.

Derry is a sixty-two-year-old Caucasian male who has been in the church for forty years and works with technology. Although Derry has gone to other congregations, he returns to this one because "the beliefs expressed here are better than any place I have been."

The group represents the general age distribution in the congregation. However, the female population in the congregation at large is slightly larger than the male.

The group setting affects the interview. The people in the group prompt and respond to one another. An insight, feeling, or memory from one member of the group sometimes sparks related associations from others, or sets in motion other trains of thought. Communal life is a strong theme in this interview. These listeners have a strong sense of the sermon and its effects in congregational community.

Excerpts from the Transcript

As the interview begins, members of the small group tell how they became a part of the congregation. The woman minister on the staff preached in the service earlier in the day.

INTERVIEWER: Tell me about a pastor you have had who was also a good preacher.

MARTHA: You heard her today.

DERRY: Ariel's great (murmurs of agreement).

JACK: When I first started coming to [this congregation], we had another male reverend. I found him to be very powerful...I was a bit apprehensive of who was going to replace this person. When Ariel got here, I was mostly happy with her.

SUSAN: I think for me part of it is *emotion and passion.* I guess it's a combination of emotion and I don't know if the right word is "intelligence," but you know what I'm talking about. Both Rob and Ariel talk about both. They pull things out of books that are pertinent to the sermon, and it's very thought provoking, but (1) *it also strikes a chord inside.* So it's not just all...Like I tend to think of churches [in our denomination] being kind of cold and intellectual. It's intellectual, but it has a pull, because we talk about how to live your life as Christ would want you to. Doing that out there, not just like [another church] do all inside. It's very visible. I think the really good preaching that I've heard here has been intellectual, but it also has been, (2) *"And what are you going to do about it?"*

JEROME: It's very meaningful to me to have both Ariel and Rob. It was very, very refreshing to me to have a pastor who didn't

1. Susan reveals immediately that pathos is important to her: She feels most deeply spoken to when her emotions and passions are engaged. She appreciates logos material (e.g., things out of books that are pertinent to the sermon) but these things are most important because they "strike a chord inside." Logos sometimes generates pathos for Susan. The preacher who wants to connect deeply with Susan needs to include material in the sermon that touches the emotions, and that even excites passion.

2. For Susan, the pathos in a sermon is not an end in itself. The purpose of pathos should be to help her figure out how to live faithfully. A sermon is not complete for Susan until it offers her practical guidance. Her preacher needs to help her identify "what she is going to do about it."

have the answers, (3) *who struggled* with some of the tensions that you would have in your faith, grace, and good works or whatever. To be open enough to share that with the congregation. (4) *Plus especially Ariel, knowing her life and the way she lives it, and that she practices what she says from the pulpit. That did mean a lot to me.* Not that I came from churches where that didn't happen. I don't think I had terribly hypocritical [pastors] before, but that's just very meaningful to me.

DERRY: I remember what it was that struck a chord [in an earlier part of the interview in response to another group member's remark that sermons in this congregation help people in the congregation accept one another]. (5) *Politics in churches can really get vicious. My wife is a citizen organizer. She just gets involved in all these churches and their politics, just tears them up.* This church now…It did have some politics before, but now I'm outside the [church council] I don't know what's going on in the [church council]. (6) *It looks like politics here are just nonexistent. There's no factions or struggles or power struggles. You talk about emotions.* From the back [prior to the start of the interview] I answered this question about what touches my emotions. It [preaching that promotes positive relationships in the congregation] does.

INTERVIEWER: So your emotions are being approached through your intellect.

DERRY: That's right.

INTERVIEWER: Tell me about a sermon that you really found engaging.

MARTHA:: The one that I remember I heard years and years ago on a Youth Sunday. A person who was of course a young man then, probably high school age, was the

3. Jerome identifies with the preachers when they struggle with the same tensions that trouble Jerome. The content of these struggles is a logos matter, but preachers sharing their struggles in the pulpit creates a preacher ethos bond that encourages Jerome to take seriously logos content. Preachers can engage Jerome by sharing their own struggles.

4. Jerome is likely to take the message seriously because of the preacher's integrity. This is an ethos phenomenon. Hypocrisy turns Jerome off to the preacher and the sermon.

5. Derry thinks that sermons at this church promote positive relationships in the congregation. He perceives the sermons contributing to a lack of vicious politics in the congregation and to persons respecting one another's differences. This reinforces his confidence in sermons since fractious congregational ethos is negative to him.

6. For Derry, logos (content) sometimes creates pathos (feeling). Sermons that call for respecting one another in the community help create mutual respect. This insight is important: putting forth strong, clear *ideas* in the sermon is a way to excite the emotions of some listeners.

preacher. (7) *I remember the line that he used, and I've thought of it a thousand times. That is, "God has no grandchildren." The idea is that each one of us make our own relationship, and I don't get what my mother had, and I don't get what my grandfather had. It's my relationship.*

SUSAN: I think about the time when I first came to [this congregation] and [a well known woman preacher from another city] was [visiting] here [to speak at a service], and she was like…She reminded me of Lily Tomlin, a Southern comedian and such a presence. She had this vibrant stole on, and it was like seeing a performer…I just felt like I had come home. (8) *I can't even say I can pull up anything she said, but it's just I'll never forget that sermon. It's changed my life. It was her passion, and it was her presence. (9) It was visual, and it was feeling that Spirit of God.*

INTERVIEWER: Particular gestures?

SUSAN: Yes. She's *very animated, very animated,* and not to say you have to be a standup comedian to catch my attention. Maybe part of it was the first time I'd been in church for a long time, but it was just (10) *the whole package.* I'll never forget it.

7. Martha speaks of relationship with God and her relationship with her grandchildren—motifs with both individual and communal elements. A logos concern predominates: She remembers a line with a specific content that the young preacher used. She talks about the significance of this line as an idea.

8. Given Susan's prior negative history with a man's preaching (mentioned in the opening remarks of this chapter), the embodied presence of a woman in the pulpit is a key to establishing ethos between Susan and the preacher. This suggests that preachers need to recognize the simple fact that their gender (and perhaps other factors) sometimes affects the dispositions of the hearers toward them.

9. Susan was engaged by the passion and presence of the preacher, a pathos response. This listener speaks of *"feeling* that Spirit of God" in the sermon. The physical appearance of the preacher, an aspect of embodiment, is also important to Susan. Visual appearance is important: This listener remembers how the preacher looked. Even without being able to recall the content of what the preacher said (a logos perception), the encounter "changed my life."

10. Susan again calls attention to the importance of embodiment for her. Preachers might profitably reflect on "the whole package" that they are in the pulpit.

JEROME: I had a really (11) *meaningful* one here at this church seven or eight years ago. I personally was in a place where I was in uncharted territory for me. *I was just really floundering in life. The title of the sermon was* (12) *"Marching Off the Map."* It was the story about the Roman army that sent word back to Rome and said, "We don't know where we are right now. We've marched off the map." That was just really meaningful to me. I look back over the seven or eight years, and I still *think* of that sometimes how God is with you even in those times when the area you are in is so uncharted for you. You've never been there before. You have no experience to draw from to deal with that. When all you've got left is your faith, that will get you through sometimes.

JACK: I think for me it was…Actually this was a Catholic Mass in North Carolina. I was going through a very rough time in my life at that particular time. I wasn't suicidal or anything, but (13) *I was very despondent, and I was searching for my own personal goals, my own personal needs, my own personal self.* The sermon or the Mass was about how to relate to others, have them relate to you and when they don't relate to you, love them just as well, just as much. From that moment on I learned to love just for the sake of loving, and I think that's a very powerful

11. Jerome remembers a sermon from a time when his life "was just really floundering" because he was "in uncharted territory." The sermon performed a logos function by naming Jerome's feeling (pathos) as "marching off the map." That was "meaningful" (a logos notion) for it helped Jerome to live through the uncharted territory with a pathos response—feeling that Jerome can make it through uncharted territory. Preachers might keep an eye out for those in the congregation who are similarly feeling unsettled, threatened, even fearful, and for whom the sermon can perform an important pastoral functioning by naming their experience.

12. Note the importance of sermon titles. Years later Jerome remembers "Marching Off the Map," which is not only the title of the sermon but an image that names his experience. Such titles endure. This one originated with Halford Luccock more than fifty years ago and has been passed from generation to generation of preachers. See Halford E. Luccock, *Marching Off the Map and Other Sermons* (New York: Harper and Brothers, 1952), 11–16.

13. Like Jerome, Jack cites an example of an engaging sermon from a crisis point in his life. Jack felt despondent because he did not perceive a goal for his life. The sermon addressed his despondency by the logos means of offering an identity for him. From the sermon he *learned* to relate to others, particularly through loving others even when they do not love you. The logos of teaching triggers the pathos of loving for the sake of love.

thing. Be it a Catholic Mass or (14) *any preacher or reverend who's going to give a sermon should do it in a manner that the delivery is not only knowledgeable but is very understandable, and is something that we the flock can take home with us in our everyday lives.*

MARTHA: I have one that really turned me around. This was at the [national meeting of the denomination]. (15) *I'd gotten pretty negative about the whole concept of missionaries and missions and so on. I knew about a bunch of negative aspects of it...*I believe the [national leader's position] name was [recollects name]? All right. He preached the sermon on the Sunday there. When that man who was [the national leader] of the whole [denomination] stood up and said, "I'm a product of your missionaries. They brought me here. This is who I am." I thought, "Okay. Shift gears. *You've got something to learn.*"

SUSAN: Another sermon that was really memorable to me here was...again I hadn't been coming here long. Rob preached a sermon and had people from the congregation come up and talk about [some of their own experiences]. I guess there were people that had big changes in the last year of their life. You remember that? (general agreement)

SUSAN: That touched me so much because...When you listen to the gospel, sometimes you have to pay attention...You may be really down and somebody has made a gesture that's not significant to them, but has totally changed the person who is down in their life. I know that happened to me at [this congregation]. Somebody just said, "You want to go out to eat?" which was no big deal, but to me it meant everything.

14. Jack makes a general recommendation to preachers: Sermons should contain knowledgeable content, be understandable, and contain content the congregation can take home and apply to life.

15. Martha remembers another engaging sermon that combines ethos and logos elements. Before hearing the sermon she *knew about* negative aspects of missions and missionaries. The ethos with the preacher at the national meeting prompts her to change her prior opinion. "I thought...You've got something to *learn.'*" Here, the embodied presence of the preacher functions to teach Martha. The presence of a person prompted Martha to change her mind.

(16) *Even though it was a bunch of laypeople talking, and it wasn't really a sermon in the traditional sense, it made me realize you have to pay attention to the words. You have to listen to God's voice no matter what the situation is, because it makes all the difference. It has to me.*

INTERVIEWER: Let me ask about a sermon that did not interest you and left you cold. What was it about it that turned you off?

SUSAN: I can say any number of sermons that I've heard in [another] church.

JACK: Any number of sermons that are judgmental, derogatory. (17) *For me I didn't feel the presence of God and understand what all that had to do with anything.* Just a lot. This is not saying that all sermons in [that] church are all bad, because they're not.

(18) *But at the same time I think when you're searching for something to come from the pulpit, say a sermon or a lecture or whatever it might be, and you don't get that, then you're certainly disheartened by not hearing the Word of God.*

SUSAN: I did not realize how important inclusive language was to me until I started going here. When I learned the first day God's a mother, I was like, "This is wrong. God is a woman? God is a man?" Now, I hadn't always criticized preachers that I heard [in the other denomination]. But, everything was "Man, man, man." When I heard it, I just…Now I can't go back there [to the other church], because inclusive language, even though people say that "man" really means "woman," it doesn't.

16. Susan describes a memorable sermon in terms of congregational proclamation. When she was feeling *down*, some people from the congregation invited her out to eat. Susan sees that invitation and the conversation of the people at the meal have the effect of a sermon. Susan affirms that God speaks in multiple ways (not just through sermon in the service of worship) when she says, "You have to listen to God's voice no matter what the situation is." At this meal, the doctrine of the priesthood of all believers is in action as Susan's dinner companions perform one of the classic functions of preaching: interpreting God's presence for her and, indeed, embodying that presence.

17. Jack connects the preacher's presence with the doctrine of God: In churches where the sermons are judgmental and derogatory, Jack does not recognize the presence of God. This observation should give preachers pause: Does our demeanor in the pulpit adequately represent God?

18. Notice that for Jack, the way he thinks (logos) shapes what he feels (pathos). The wrong logos (judgment) creates the wrong pathos (disheartened feeling). God, for Jack, cannot be condemnatory. Based on his earlier remarks (no. 13), we surmise that the "Word of God" for Jack centers in the news of God's love for the world. Preachers need to be aware that the ideas we state often have emotional consequences in our listeners. Are these consequences theologically appropriate?

(19) *If you're a woman in the congregation and everything is "man," for me it just totally turns me off. I feel like I'm not being spoken to.*

JEROME: I always find it ironic sermons that don't particularly move you when you're talking about it after church. Someone says, "That's just what I needed to hear today," and I'm thinking, "Okay, I'm glad someone got something out of that message, because it left me just a little flat." I'm not sure that every sermon is really for everyone.

MARTHA: Mine was at [a nearby megachurch with a conservative theological orientation]. I didn't want to go, but I had this friend who kept saying, "Will you come?" I said, "I won't like it. I know I won't like it." So anyway finally she kept on until I said, "All right. I'll go this time, and we'll never mention it again." She said, "Oh, you'll like it." I knew I wouldn't like it, but (20) *I didn't realize I'd get so angry. I really felt like salt was coming out of my tears. The whole thing…Men took up the collection. Men served communion.* One woman was up front singing somewhere. But anyway, I can get bristly just thinking about it. We never talked about it anymore.

JEROME: Did you get her to come here?

MARTHA: No, because she's happy there. She's very happy with it. It's a megachurch. Actually in my judgment, the man lied. (21) *He was using weird definitions for terms.* Their old cultures don't define the way he did. When you got through listening to him, he had used this definition and made his point the way he wanted. But in my judgment he was just not telling the truth.

INTERVIEWER: Are there any particular gestures that turn you off during the sermon?

19. Susan calls attention to the importance of language in ethos. Susan felt alienated from her former preachers as well as from her former congregation because their male language excluded her. The language of "man, man, man" caused her to "feel like I'm not being spoken to" (negative ethos). To take a sermon seriously, Susan wants to feel positive relationship with the preacher and the congregation. Susan's response underlines the importance of the preacher using language that invites positive ethos by inviting people into the sermon and forming connective relationships with the preacher and the congregation.

20. When visiting another congregation, Martha is angered by the male dominance in leadership of worship. In the broad sense, this is a case of congregational culture that produces a pathos response (anger, bristling) in Martha. Martha's statement illustrates one culture coming into conflict with another: the gender-inclusive ethos of Martha's congregation with the less inclusive style of the congregation where she visited. Again, congregational culture is key for her.

21. Martha raises a logos concern. She thinks the content of the sermon is deeply flawed because the preacher distorted and manipulated the truth. Martha reminds the reader that the preacher does not speak to persons who are blank slates but to people who bring their perceptions and experience to the sermon. A preacher wants to get as fully as possible in touch with what the congregation brings to the moment of preaching.

JEROME: (22) *I can't stand pastors that walk back and forth across the chancel while they preach. [Such a preacher is] like a duck in a shooting gallery.* That is just a personal problem I have, I know, but I get really uncomfortable when pastors do that.

MARTHA: Where I used to be, we had one that not only paced, but he gave his sermon closer to joke telling. (23) *That kind of a person is not funny, because he has to do it.* I think he got onto it [in another church]. Somebody told me he did better then. He's a nice man, and I felt kindly toward him, but it makes you tired to listen to that. I'm surprised they let him get as far as he got. Calm him down a little bit.

INTERVIEWER: There was fair use of humor in the sermon this morning.

MARTHA: (24) *Yes, but it wasn't compulsive, and it didn't go on and on, and it didn't force you to laugh when you really didn't think it was funny.* She's good.

INTERVIEWER: This is kind of a theoretical question. When does a sermon have authority for you?

MARTHA: It's speaking to my condition. When I walk in, I want... (25) *When I go in hungry, and I feel like I've been fed.*

DERRY: When it's s*cripture-based.*

MARTHA: I'm assuming that. Maybe that's not a valid assumption.

DERRY: (26) *I think for it to have authority, just around half the sermon should be spent interpreting what the scripture lesson was.* The preachers do it here. They might not realize it, but people say maybe this is not a biblically based church, but if you listen to the sermons, about half of what they talk about is what happens in the scripture and explains the historical reference. The authority comes in that text, just basing it on the scripture. *Then the other half of the*

22. For Jerome, there is a connection between embodiment and pathos. The preacher's walking back and forth generates a feeling of discomfort. Preachers need to determine the kinds of movement in and around the pulpit that help the congregation feel comfortable enough to stay involved in the sermon.

23. The preacher's joke-telling style (reminiscent of a stand-up comic's routine) made it hard for her to pay attention to the logos of the sermon. The preacher's mannerisms overshadowed whatever logos there was in the sermon.

24. Preachers can learn from Martha's comment: She values humor that is not extraneous but is organic to the sermon and that respects the freedom of the parishioners to laugh or not.

25. Although Martha acknowledges, with Derry (following) that a sermon must be based on scripture to be authoritative (a logos appeal), she uses pathos language to say that it must feed her hunger. To be authoritative it must speak to *her life.*

26. For Derry, an authoritative sermon is not only one that is biblically based but, like Martha, must apply to the daily life of the community (a logos concern). Apparently, a sermon that only explains the Bible in its historical context would not be authoritative for Derry. In this respect, he shows an awareness that is typical of his denomination: The sermon should speak to the culture. Taking a cue from Derry, a preacher might ask of each sermon, "How does this message relate specifically to the life of the congregation?"

sermon would be applying it to our daily life. Half the sermon should be about that for me.

JEROME: We were raised Methodist. (27) *We were raised with the Wesleyan quadrilateral. It had all four things: science, the Bible, personal experience, and church history.* Those four things should speak with one voice for anything to be authoritative. Maybe I bring that baggage with me.

SUSAN: When a sermon has authority for me, (28) *it may not have ever. It's not necessarily something that I believe that I hear, but when I hear it I know it's true. It's a heart thing.* I believe it's true. It makes sense. It also has the power of God. It seems right.

JEROME: Just to elaborate on that. (29) *When it makes me feel good. When I believe it's true. Even if I question it, I want to go out and use that to better my neighbors or better my life and everybody that I'm associated with.* It allows me to reflect on biblical teachings that I had as a child and to put those teachings into practice.

DERRY: (30) *I would say in our church, our preachers have all attended seminary. They've got this good biblical foundation.* So you pretty well believe what they say and their interpretation of scripture. There are some churches, of course, that don't require seminary education to be a preacher. They can interpret it any way they might see fit. Our church is not like a lot of churches that way.

INTERVIEWER: What do you think God is doing during the preaching of the sermon?

27. Jerome uses a logos approach to determine the authority of a sermon. A message is authoritative when it satisfies what Jerome remembers as the four criteria of the Wesleyan quadrilateral. Even when Jerome highlights experience (pathos) later, it is in a logos frame. Jerome also recognizes that authority is contextual when he describes the quadrilateral as "baggage" that he brought with him from his prior denomination. Again, the preacher is reminded that listeners bring perspectives that shape what they expect in a sermon.

28. For Susan authority is shaped by appeals to pathos—her "heart." A sermon "makes sense," i.e., is authoritative, when it *feels* right. She may not be able to say, in advance, what she believes, but she feels it when she hears it. The authority of experience looms larger for many listeners than preachers typically expect.

29. Jerome acknowledges a pathos element in authority (when a sermon makes him feel good) but feeling is not enough. To be authoritative a sermon also needs to help Jerome improve his life and the life of the broader community, and to help him reflect on (logos phenomenon) the Bible and act this reflection.

30. For Derry, the education of the minister adds to the authority of the sermon. A preacher can increase the credibility of a sermon, for Derry, by referring in the sermon itself to study that has gone into the sermon. For him authority is increased by appeals to ethos: the education of the preacher.

JACK: (31) *Speaking to the minister.* That's what I think.

MARTHA: I think so, too.

INTERVIEWER: You're saying God is working through his flock?

MARTHA: Yes. Including the minister.

JEROME: Helping to interpret that.

MARTHA: That's an interesting question.

JACK: Powerful question.

INTERVIEWER: You were mentioning sermons that don't affect you might affect somebody else. That could be related to this question about what God is doing.

JEROME: (32) *Maybe it's not God's problem that the sermon didn't mean anything to me. Probably more rightly my problem. Maybe I wasn't quite tuned in.*

SUSAN: I like to think about God as…I read this in a book. It's certainly not original. God is not God, the Father, and God, the Son, but it makes more sense to think of God like a Spirit and breath. I guess what I like to vision, (33) *what I like to picture God in church is like Pentecost. It rushes in and touches your heart.* As far as being one person, it's working on you or doing something. *It's more just like a presence. You can feel it. You can't see it. You just have to feel it.*

INTERVIEWER: Picking up on some of the things you have just been talking about, can you recall a sermon during which the congregation was particularly moved?

JACK: I can. (34) *The one that Ariel gave that Sunday after September 11 [2001].*

DERRY: I would have to say that was probably the best one I've heard.

JEROME: I think the Spirit was moving that day.

INTERVIEWER: Say more about that.

31. All who speak agree that God speaks to the minister and even helps the minister interpret the divine message. However, this group does not name criteria by which to gauge when a statement is of God and when it is not. A preacher can help a congregation articulate such criteria. Otherwise, the community will have difficulty sorting through different, competing, and even contradictory claims as to what God wishes to say to the community.

32. Despite God's initiatives in preaching, Jerome acknowledges that communication with God must include human response. What can a preacher do to help the congregation "tune in"?

33. Susan again makes an intuitive pathos response. For her, God is active in preaching by "touching the heart," i.e., through feeling. The same question must be pressed here as in response 31 above. What criteria can distinguish a feeling that signals divine activity from other random or even contradictory feelings?

34. The sermon after September 11 spoke directly to the issue that was most deeply on their minds and hearts. Note how often in this book listeners report that a sermon was especially moving when they heard it at a point in life when they confronted a major personal or social issue. While every sermon does not take place in a crisis context similar to post-September 11, a preacher can still try to correlate the message with what is on the hearts and minds of the congregation.

DERRY: It wasn't a big service for us. What, 165 or something.

JEROME: Okay. Well, maybe more. I think there were at least a hundred more than we have on an average Sunday. Anyway, Ariel made a point in the sermon that some people could have been offended by. It could have been construed as being critical of the United States' policy in the Middle East. (35) *It's interesting the lack of tension that you could feel in the service, because of the graceful way she worded it.* I was ready to feel like everybody was upset about it, but I thought nobody is upset by this, because they heard it the way she wanted it to come across. It was just very...It was just an interesting spirit that you felt in the sanctuary that day.

INTERVIEWER: Can you say what it was about that sermon about September 11 that was so moving?

JACK: I think it was the (36) *comfort that everyone needed and felt from her sermon.* The congregation, as Jerome said, was like the Spirit of God or the spirit of people, all the sadness and all the sorrow just came in at one time, and *you left with this feeling in your heart.*

JEROME: What do you do in a church like this one that tends to be a pacifistic, peace-making church with the rage you felt that day, that you were ready to take your gun and go shoot somebody? How do you temper that with the attitude that we have in this church as being very much peacemakers. (37) *That was a good balance in the service of outrage, yet tempering it with mercy and justice and compassion.* And the fear that America would quickly react in retribution and revenge more than justice, which I think most of us were watching. I was very concerned about that Sunday that we would respond as a nation so quickly. We would be out for blood.

35. The sermon after September 11 contained a prophetic element criticizing U.S. policy. While this theme could have ignited a hostile reaction, Jerome believes that it did not "because of the graceful way she worded it." The preacher confessed that it was painful for her to speak critically of her nation at such a painful time, and she acknowledged that some in the community would disagree. Often a preacher can frame a prophetic point in such a pastoral and empathetic way that the congregation is more open than if the preacher simply confronts them with it.

36. For Jack, the appeal to pathos in the sermon was most important: "You left with this feeling in your heart." The sermon had a cathartic effect.

37. For Jerome, both pathos and logos elements were important in the service and sermon following September 11. He was glad for the opportunity to express feelings of sorrow and outrage. Yet, it was also important to consider the meaning and requirements of justice. It is key for Jerome that justice be defined in such a way as to include love and compassion, and to omit the possibility of simple revenge. For Jerome, the logos (gospel) helps modulate appeals to contradictory feelings (pathos). Jerome, like many listeners, yearns to know what the gospel had to say to his vengeful feelings.

MARTHA: I might be uncomfortable over that, but I get a whole lot more uncomfortable in a lot of other places.

JEROME: Revenge. Justice means revenge to them. *A lot of justice without love isn't justice.*

INTERVIEWER: Do you think there are issues that are just too explosive, too dangerous for the preacher to deal with in the pulpit?

MARTHA: (38) *I don't think there are any issues like that, but I think not everybody has the skill and the ability to do it well.* I think that would...I don't know anything that...I think God could handle it. As far as the minister there are some things I'd probably be afraid to do, because I'd be afraid I'd not do it quite...

38. Martha sounds a theme shared by all in this group: A preacher can and should deal with all issues, but dealing with explosive issues does call for pastoral sensitivity.

SUSAN: (39) *It seems like to me if you can't deal with explosive, divisive issues in church or especially in this church, where can you deal with them?* You've got to deal with someplace in a loving, forgiving community. I think that people assume the best of people here. For example, if something was said from the pulpit that maybe didn't ring true with the people, I don't think the congregation would be backbiting and trying to find fault. You would assume the best of the minister or a person in Sunday school. It seems like to me I can't think of any issue that's too divisive to bring up, because if you can't bring it up then maybe the church isn't doing what the church is supposed to do.

39. Congregational culture is important when the preacher considers a controversial topic. In a congregation with positive relationships, the community is likely to stay with the preacher even when members question the preacher's position. In a congregation with fractious culture, the reaction might be quite different. To help create an environment for preaching on explosive issues, ministers will be more effective as they help the congregation as a system develop a positive, loving, forgiving community.

JEROME: That's what we try to do is how you live out your faith when you're not here on Sunday morning. That's really important to us, to people in this church. I think that's meaningful. (40) *I can't think of a single issue that we haven't broached around here that could have been very explosive.* We have disagreement on lots of stuff like the death penalty for example. We've got people on either end of the spectrum in this church. Somehow we keep it together.

40. Jerome indicates that the congregation has a high degree of consciousness of itself: The congregation as congregation expects to be able to discuss explosive issues in an environment that maintains trust and communi-cation and that respects difference of opinion. In this congregation, respect for differences is critical to the community's self-understanding.

INTERVIEWER: How do you think the sermon or preaching shapes this congregation and helps you become who you are as a community?

DERRY: Sermons at this congregation are… (41) *That's it. If a sermon is no good, then everything falls apart, I think. We've had preachers here that could not do a sermon, and the church just went downhill.* The hour was all right. The worship service was okay, but *the sermon is the central point.* If that's not there, the whole thing just goes down the drain.

JACK: Sermons here in this congregation, they unify us. *They bring us together as one.* The sermon enables us to feel as though we are all one. We're all God's children— black, white, interracial, whatever, all nationalities, all faiths. (42) *No matter what your beliefs are, the sermons here at this congregation bring us together.*

MARTHA: (43) The whole hour is special. There isn't any part of it that I don't…But I would not want to give up the sermon. *I guess they teach me,* because offering is supposed to be the climax. Isn't that what they are supposed to do?

DERRY: Mm-hm (nodding).

MARTHA: Our response to everything else is what we do then. I've been thinking about this really all day before I got to here. I didn't spend much time before that, but I thought about it today. I was thinking about the whole service. Music is splendid and unusually good to me. The way it flows together, and the way people manage it, the way Derry polices the sound system, runs it.

41. Derry views the sermon as central not only to worship but to the whole life of the congregation. Ineffective preaching has contributed to the church going downhill in the past. While systems thinkers would likely say the causes of congregational decline are more complicated than simply vacuous preaching, Derry calls attention to the pivotal role of the sermon for this church.

42. Jack points out that sermons directly affect congregational culture. This culture is important as people identify with one another. Jack's last sentence suggests that for him, congregational culture (being together as one) is more important than logos (that is, sharing beliefs/ ideas). A part of the congregational style is that the members agree to disagree.

43. Martha and Derry see the sermon shaping the congregation through logos: by teaching. The denomination of which the congregation is part has historically understood teaching as the purpose of preaching.

SUSAN: I agree with Martha and I agree with Derry, because for me the service doesn't just focus on the sermon anymore, but (44) *if the sermon wasn't good, I think the time wouldn't be spent well in church and we wouldn't have that feeling of community and love.* Like I said, the Passing of the Peace is really special and when we do the Prayers of the People. That's something that's really special. So everything, the tone is set by the sermon. (45) *If the sermon is not relevant and if we don't respect the message, then the rest of the show doesn't matter.*

JEROME: That's true. It's kind (46) *of a major tenet of our tradition in the spoken word and the scripture is so central to your faith experience.*

MARTHA: One of my children in time became [a member of another denomination that has a more elaborate Sunday liturgy] because of marrying a member of that church. So one time I asked him, I said, "How do you like the liturgical aspect?" because there's part of me that I felt sometimes that I might like that. He's a medical doctor. He said he never did hold much with [a humorous caricature of one of the distinctive practices of the other church]. (47) *Actually, he said seriously, "I haven't heard a good sermon. The music. I miss the congregational singing."*

JEROME: Look at the focus of the Catholic or the Episcopalian churches. (48) *It's the communion. That's the culmination of the service for them.*

INTERVIEWER: Do you have one or two things you can tell preachers that would help them energize you when you are listening to a sermon? What would they be?

DERRY: I'm always energized when I hear [a certain minister] speak. (49) *He talks very slowly, and he emphasizes points very well and repeats them.* He'll say something, and he'll say it again slowly to make sure you get it.

44. For Susan, the service is a gestalt in which the parts work together. The sermon occurs fairly early in the service and plays an important role by setting the tone (a pathos dimension) for the whole. Susan speaks of her experience in worship in pathos terms: the "feeling of community and love."

45. Integrity between sermon and congregation is crucial for Susan: If the community does not live out the values voiced in the sermon, "the rest of the show doesn't matter." One of the preacher's callings is to help the congregation aim for integrity between what the sermon and the community say, and how the people live.

46. To Jerome, faith *experience* (a pathos term) derives in a logos way from preaching and the Bible.

47. Martha makes a comment that brings together pathos and congregational culture when she muses that she might like a church with a higher liturgy. However, solid preaching is important enough that she reports that her son misses it (and congregational singing—another aspect of congregational culture) in a church with a more elaborate liturgy.

48. Jerome recognizes that congregations centered in the weekly observance of the Lord's supper have a different culture than those centered in preaching. How might the weekly presence of loaf and cup affect your preaching?

49. Logos and embodiment are related for Derry. This listener likes a slow rate of speech and repetition to help get the point. All preachers might ask whether the speed at which they speak allows the congregation maximum opportunity to get their messages.

You don't know when to stop. I don't think I answered your question.

INTERVIEWER: Are you saying that he doesn't repeat too much?

DERRY: No. He'll repeat the last phrase and say it slowly. That's a technique for sermonizers instead of just going on to the next point.

INTERVIEWER: If you could talk directly to a preacher and tip them off about how they can really reach you, how would you?

JEROME: I had this one college teacher that talked about the concept of chasing a rabbit. (50) *When teaching a dog to hunt you have to train the dog not to chase the rabbit too much before he brings him back to you.* I think that's a good point for some pastors, not to chase that rabbit too long or too far, because eventually you'll forget where they were trying to take you with that.

DERRY: [A respected older member of the congregation] told me when he heard Ariel preach, (51) *the best thing about her sermon was when she quit.* She knows when she made her point, and she stops. She doesn't keep going for a half hour.

SUSAN: I'm thinking about Ariel right now, and I think the number one thing that she does that I really like, and it's not her...I mean I like her sermons but kind of the extraneous thing is her voice is very lyrical. It's very musical. It's up and down, and you listen to it. The other thing I really like especially are her (52) *hand gestures.* She does that very well. Again, it's *visual presence.* I guess it's all the senses. It's seeing, and it's hearing, *but it's also intellect* and her pulling out things that you might read or things that appeal to your intelligence and make them pertinent to your life.

JEROME: Three words from me: powerful, direct, and inclusive.

50. Logos and pathos concerns come to expression in the vivid image of the dog chasing a rabbit. The preacher needs to make the point expeditiously, that is, to bring the point home (logos) before the congregation gets too worn out to pay attention.

51. Derry, too, calls for concise sermons. This theme is persistent not only in this congregation but is found throughout other interviews from other churches. A preacher needs to ask, "Are my sermons an optimum length for the congregation to stay with me?"

52. As discussed in notes 9 and 10, embodiment is very important to Susan. She first describes her response to Ariel's preaching in pathos terms (Ariel's lyrical voice, expressive gestures, visual presence). For Susan, knowledge is a gestalt involving the whole self—senses working together with mind. Logos is important, too, as Susan comments that Ariel pulls out of her reading things that are pertinent to life.

INTERVIEWER: Do you want to elaborate at all?

JEROME: Powerful in that *to understand* what the sermon is about, what the preacher is saying. (53) *To make the congregation or to make me feel empowered to go out and do God's work or do God's will.* Direct, to the point, to overwork a dead horse. To leave me with something that I can use in my regular life to better myself as well as all humankind. We all heard the sermon this morning. Would you agree with me? I thought at one point when Ariel mentioned a former pastor of hers had said, "Why should we pray when we can worry?" (54) *I thought the congregation wanted to take a little more time to chuckle over that.*

INTERVIEWER: The movement in her sermons is really effective?

MARTHA: I've got a little phrase that I heard somewhere: (55) *depth, clarity, humor, creativity, and intellectually stimulating.* That's what I look for. I've learned a whole lot from Ariel. I think she knows pretty much everything. I don't even remember where she went to seminary, but she said you can tell somebody who went there...Anyway you can tell somebody who had been trained at that seminary. Talking about as a woman, their demeanor, their manner, the way they sit, the way they stand, the way they move. She said she does it. In other words, in addition to musical training and all that other stuff, she's had good preacher training.

DERRY: She practices every Sunday. She reads her whole sermon. (56) *She stands in the pulpit and reads it but it doesn't sound like she is reading.*

53. The fact that Jerome repeats earlier stresses on the importance of the sermon being clear, succinct, and providing practical suggestions for Christian living shows their importance to this listener.

54. At the end, Jerome calls attention to something many preachers could do better: give the congregation time to enjoy a moment of humor (or to feel a deep poignancy) before moving on.

55. Martha crisply enumerates five qualities of good preaching (depth, clarity, etc.). This laywoman's capacity to identify the marks of good preaching challenges preachers to do the same. What five qualities of preaching are most important to you? How do they compare with the qualities that your congregation most values?

56. Derry doesn't mind Ariel reading her sermons since they do not sound as though she is reading. It is important that the sermon have the quality of person-to-person address. Preachers might want to incorporate this quality in their embodiment. Derry's comment undercuts the clichés that preachers sometimes hear about the importance of preaching without (or with) a manuscript.

MARTHA: That is interesting to me because I never thought about that. (57) *But that was very distinctive manner and behavior. That if you didn't have any of this other stuff it would be sort of like a performance, but it's not like that at all.* At least that's the way I see it.

57. Per above, the fact that Ariel is a graduate of a seminary that Martha respects enhances the preacher ethos between Martha and Ariel. Ariel displays traits associated with that school. Preachers might discern whether their congregations associate particular styles of preaching with particular seminaries. If so, how do the congregation's associations with the preacher's seminary affect ethos?

Listening for Preaching

In this small group of listeners, we encounter a challenge that faces nearly every preacher in a larger way on Sunday morning: the diversity of qualities that people in a single congregation find engaging and not engaging. Martha, Jack, Jerome, and Derry say they are generally most engaged by logos, that is, content. They agree with the denomination's historic understanding of the purpose of the sermon as teaching (43). For Susan, however, the specific content of the sermon is less important than the feeling that the sermon arises from the preacher's passion (a pathos characteristic) and the sense of connection between herself and the preacher (ethos) and herself and the congregation (congregational culture) (1, 2, 8, 9). One of the most important functions of the sermon in the service to Susan is to "set the tone" (43). In the broad sense, of course, this is teaching.

However, a close reading of the transcript reveals that qualities of logos, pathos, and ethos are at work in all five listeners. Along this line, preachers often speak as if the self is divided into separate parts, as when someone says, "I try to preach to the head *and* the heart." The listeners help us see that ethos, logos, and pathos often relate for a single listener in complicated ways (18). Logos can enable pathos (1, 6). Aspects of preacher ethos and embodiment are necessary for some listeners to effect a hearing, and can even be more important than the specific theological content. In other churches, Martha and Susan found the congregational culture so troubling they were negatively predisposed towards the sermon (19, 20). For some listeners a sermon must generate pathos or they do not feel (!) that they have heard a sermon.

These observations suggest that the preachers should consciously consider how to incorporate elements into the sermon that appeal to logos, pathos, ethos, and embodiment. In the process, preachers will become aware of how all of these elements are related and intertwined. Preachers will also recognize that their lives, thoughts, and actions in ministry beyond preaching contribute to the willingness of the congregation to take the sermon seriously. On the one hand, the place of the minister in the congregational system affects how the congregation hears the sermon.[1]

On the other hand, the sermon affects the system (39, 40, 41, 42, 43, 45).[2] From this perspective sermons can contribute significantly to shaping and reshaping the congregation as community.

Three themes are found in almost all the remarks of the congregants in this interview. First, in varying ways and degrees, they found sermons especially meaningful when their lives were in transition, or in distress, or when they were vexed by a particular issue or question (11, 12, 13, 33, 34). The preacher who can correlate the gospel with such contexts may find that the context has created an unusual openness to preaching. Indeed, the preacher may find that people declare such sermons among the most important they have heard.

The preacher may also create such moments in the sermon itself, that is, moments that raise questions or evoke situations that call aspects of people's perceptions into question and, therefore, help them become more receptive to the sermon. For Susan, the experience of hearing a woman preach created such a moment that helped her name qualities in preaching that she now regards as essential (e.g., inclusive language) (8, 19).

Second, most of these parishioners explicitly say they want to know how the sermon relates in a practical way to everyday life (14, 25, 26, 27, 29, 53). Jerome, for instance, wants to know how the sermon will not only help improve his life, but how it will help him know how to work with God and with other people to improve the life of the community.

Third, these folk agree that a sermon should be concise and to the point (50, 51). A sermon in this church should not be long. The sermon should be organized so that people can follow it easily and so that it can do its essential work (make a point, create an experience, etc).

In this congregation, preaching is important to the overall health of the community. When, in an earlier time, the preacher "could not do a sermon," the church "just went downhill" (41). Good preaching is symbolic of the congregation in a state of good health.

Listening for Theology

This group manifests pluralism with respect to forms of theological awareness. As noted above, for Jerome, Jack, Martha, and Derry, theological knowledge consists of clear ideas that give them practical help with life. For Susan, however, theological insight has more to do with feeling and relationship (9, 28). Indeed, Susan speaks of a meal with friends as having an effect on her life similar to that of a sermon: The communal experience of the meal was the occasion of hearing God's affirming voice for her (16). The preacher who wants to try to communicate in depth with the whole congregation needs not only to articulate theologically precise ideas but to create moments in sermons that are imaginative and experiential.

Several of the listeners specifically think of the purpose of the sermon in terms that the denomination as a whole has understood it: teaching.

Although this subject is widely debated by New Testament scholars, in congregational life, sermons usually function as both *kerygma* (proclamation) and *didache* (teaching).[3] The preacher in this congregation might fruitfully ask of each sermon, "What do I hope the congregation will *learn* from this sermon?" Contemporary learning theory that emphasizes that people learn in different ways (e.g., through linear progression, by random association, through various media and modes, by means of feeling) suggests that the preacher might help the congregation embrace a wide range of approaches.[4]

We can never underestimate the redemptive role that preaching plays in human transformation. Martha takes evidence and the preacher's personal testimony into account when making a theological decision. Although she does not tell us *why* she had "gotten pretty negative about the whole concept of missionaries and missions," she changes her mind when confronted with a church leader who is a product of such efforts and whose ministry demonstrates missions can bear good fruit. One way to encourage redemptive transformation in preaching is to bring forth ample evidence that what the sermon asks the congregation to believe is true. For listeners such as Martha, the most impressive evidence is the appearance of the claim of the sermon in the life of a person. Indeed, according to theologian Bernard Loomer, the things that come to expression (or that do not come to expression) in our bodies are the strongest form of evidence.[5]

Almost all of these interviewees point to one of the ecclesiological functions of preaching: helping listeners name their individual experience from the perspective of the congregation's deepest beliefs about God and the world (11, 12, 13). When the preaching in this congregation named God as a mother and woman, those perspectives helped Susan realize why she had felt so out of place in her former congregation as well as why she felt so welcome at this one (8, 9, 19). Jerome remembers that when he was living "without a map," the preacher naming God's presence with him was a key to helping him make it through. Jack points out that naming the congregation as *community* helps the congregation *become* genuine community (42). Sermons can help teach the congregation how to be a faithful community (5, 43).

The listeners in this group *want* to be faithful. In the liberal spirit of this congregation, they recognize they can discern God's leading not only in the Bible but through other avenues, such as feeling and experience. However, the explicit *theological criteria* this group uses to identify phenomena as of God are vague (27, 28, 29, 31, 33). Preachers need to help congregations articulate clear criteria for evaluating qualities in life that are consistent with God's purposes. Clark M. Williamson, dean emeritus of Christian Theological Seminary, poses three criteria that might be helpful to this group (or to preachers more generally) to put to every idea, relationship, and situation (among human beings and including the natural world) as a way of trying to interpret the coherence of such things with the divine aims. (1) Is the idea, relationship, or situation appropriate to the gospel; that is, is it consistent with what we most deeply believe about God? (2) Is it intelligible? (That is, is it internally consistent with other things that Christians believe and do, and is it seriously imaginable from the perspective of the worldview of today?) (3) Is it morally plausible; that is, does it call for the moral treatment of all entities (including human beings as well as elements of nature)?[6]

Challenges to Preaching

1. What are the patterns of listening in your congregation along the lines of ethos, logos, pathos, and embodiment? Which elements are most valued by members of the congregation?

2. How do the elements of ethos, logos, pathos, and embodiment come to life in our preaching? How are these elements related in our preaching? Which ones do we favor? Which do we downplay?

3. Could we make some adjustments in our preaching to incorporate elements valued by the congregation, while maintaining our integrity, to give sermons a better chance to be positively received by the congregation?

4. What are our deepest beliefs concerning God and God's purposes for the world? Does the sermon represent these beliefs in ethos, logos, pathos, and embodiment?

CHAPTER 8

Insights, Discoveries, and Things to Watch

A pastor often makes discoveries about the congregation that may not be obvious to the surface observer, but that help the pastor interpret what happens in the community. For instance, a minister may notice that a certain matriarch is revered in the congregational memory and that connecting an attitude or idea with that matriarch (even long-deceased) invokes a certain authority in a meeting or a sermon. In a similar way, the writing team for this book has learned several things from reading the transcripts of the interviews in the case studies in this volume (as well as many others) that may not be obvious but that can help pastors when they listen to their congregants either through formal interviews or through informal pastoral attentiveness to what people say about preaching.

In this chapter we describe some key insights, surprises, and discoveries that have come to light as a result of reading the transcripts, and for which a pastor might watch, especially if conducting a similar study in one's own congregation. We divide our remarks into two groups. First, we highlight some things that will directly affect the pastor or congregation who seeks to interview hearers in their own communities. Second, we mention some ideas that pertain more generally to preaching and rhetoric.

Discoveries That Help Interviewing and Interpreting

Some things that surprised the project team may be of direct help to the process of interviewing in a local congregation and of interpreting the data. These include: the eagerness of many people to talk about preaching, the "messy" points of a listener's response as key moments for understanding how people listen, the degree to which images (and other forms of language) with which people talk about preaching provide important clues into how they interpret preaching, and how people's perceptions of the preacher outside the service of worship affect the attentiveness of many in the congregation to the sermon.

125

If You Ask, They Will Talk

We were surprised to find that many people are eager to talk about their perceptions of preaching. This interest shows up across the multiple spectra of the study group–among different racial and ethnic cohorts, in both genders, among all ages and locations, and in the different denominations and movements. Indeed, in a response to the question, "What would be missing in this congregation if there were no sermon?" several interviewees answered with the one word, "Me."

The commitment to preaching among the interviewees arises from a deep sense of the importance of the sermon. Many members of the community come to worship, week after week, to get help from the perspective of the Divine in making sense of life. They want to talk about preaching because it means so much to them and to their congregations.

One of the most dramatic demonstrations of this sense of importance came at the conclusion of a small-group interview in a predominantly African American congregation. The group members' responses to the questions had led to several interchanges among them in which they talked in detail about how particular sermons had helped them at crucial points in their personal lives and in the life of the congregation. The tape is electric with energy and feeling. The interview, which was supposed to last about an hour, ran over two hours, and concluded only because the interviewer took a strong hand in guiding it to a stop. As the group was about to end, one of the participants asked, almost urgently, "When can we meet again?"

A number of people in our study commented that no one had ever before asked them in a systematic or thorough way what they think about preaching.[1] To a person, the people making this statement said that they were very pleased to be asked. One person reflected on being evaluated at work during the week, "I learn a lot from those evaluations," and pondered whether preachers might "learn a lot" from hearing laity talk about preaching. To be sure, we stressed with laity and pastors that our study was not designed to "evaluate" the preaching of the local preacher but to gather congregants' general impressions about preaching. Nevertheless, the general insight has much to commend it: Ministers can learn about preaching from paying attention to what laity say about it.

In the movie *Field of Dreams,* one of the main characters says of the possibility of building a baseball park in a cornfield, "If we build it [a ball park], they [the fans] will come." In a similar way, we adapt this remark to the desire of laity to reflect on preaching, "If you [the preacher] ask them [in nonthreatening circumstances], they will talk [about preaching]."

"Messy" Moments in Listener Responses Are Often Key

Many interviewees respond to questions straightforwardly. When asked a question about a logos matter, they state clearly what they think about that logos concern. The analyst has a clear line of sight on how the interviewee understands a particular aspect of preaching. For instance, when asked what a pastor is doing when he or she preaches, a woman in her thirties says the preacher "explains to me a lot of points in the Bible that I don't get when I read." When heard in the context of the whole interview, this statement summarizes the main lines of how this woman listens to the sermon. She wants to know the meaning of the Bible so she can apply it to her life.

However, responses to questions are sometimes "messy," that is, some persons respond to questions that are intended to probe one category with answers not only from that category but from others. For instance, when asked a question about logos, interviewees might describe their reactions to the sermon in ethos or pathos language.

Initially, the project team was frustrated by such intermingling of categories. We had difficulty sorting through how such listeners process sermons. We wanted to be able to say, neatly and cleanly, how ethos, logos, pathos, and embodiment function for each listener. Eventually, however, it dawned on us that such complex occasions in the transcripts are at the heart of the way many people listen. The categories do not function in the self as carefully defined lines of rhetorical effect that operate on parallel tracks, but they impact one another in a gestalt that is unique for each person. To use the inexact analogy of the electrical parts of an automobile engine, it is as if ethos, logos, pathos, and embodiment are not only wired into the self to function like separate electrical components in the motor, but are cross-wired to affect one another in ways that are distinct to each motor (person).

Furthermore, we continue to find that the "messiest" responses in the transcripts are often the moments when the interviewees most deeply reveal what is important to them in preaching. These qualities point to an informal rule that the project team finds very valuable when analyzing transcripts: Pay careful attention to the "messy" moments in the listener's responses, as these are often the most instructive.

For example, in chapter 7, we find such a messy point. Susan, a forty-eight-year-old attorney is responding to the query, "Let me ask about a sermon that did not interest you and left you cold. What was it about it that turned you off?"

> I did not realize how important *inclusive language* was to me until I started going here. When I *learned* the first day God's a mother, I was like, "This is wrong. God is a woman? God is a man?" Now, I hadn't always criticized preachers [in the other denomination where she used to attend] that I heard. *But everything was "Man, man, man."* When I heard it, I just…Now I can't go back there [to the other church], because inclusive language, *even though people say it that*

"man" really means "woman," it doesn't. If you're a woman in the congregation and everything is "man," for me it just totally turns me off. *I feel like I'm not being spoken to.*

As this statement begins, the person analyzing the transcript suspects Susan will make a comment about the logos qualities of preaching that turn her off, as Susan first notes that the specific words that a preacher uses (inclusive language) are important to her. Then she cites a logos function of language: She *learned* that God is similar to a mother. Initially, the notion that God is similar to a mother was surprising, perhaps even objectionable, to Susan. But she soon has a dramatic "Aha!" experience, and embraces the new way of speaking.

Susan's response, however, becomes more complicated. The discovery that God is like a mother is not simply a datum to add to the information file in her mind. It is connected to her sense, as a woman, of being included or not included in the preacher's address and in the congregational community. In the other church, the leadership tried a logos strategy to help women feel included by saying that the *meaning* (a logos notion) of the term "man" includes women. However, in Susan's dictionary (so to speak) the word "man" refers to males.

This conflict of logos perceptions has, for Susan, important ethos and pathos implications. In her former congregation, Susan did not feel a positive sense of preacher ethos or of congregational culture. Both the preacher and the congregation said "Man, man, man," with the result that she was turned off and felt like she was not spoken to. The preacher was identifying himself with a chauvinist form of character (ethos) that, for her, was illegitimate. At the same time, for Susan, the logos *meaning* of "man" does not include "woman." All of these things added up to the desire to change congregations. She does not want to go back to the former church because the words that they use de-legitimize the message of the sermon (logos).

Susan's remarks are "messy" in that they bring ethos, logos, and pathos into a response to a question that was intended to prompt her to reflect on logos matters. However, Susan's response helps us realize the complexity of how she processes a certain use of language when it comes to sermons or to wider congregational life.

Congregational Culture Shapes Listener Expectations

As noted in chapter 1, each congregation is a culture with its particular combination of values, relational patterns, places and practices of significance, feelings, and organization. Congregational culture often plays an important role in shaping what listeners expect (and do not expect) from the sermon.

A number of responses to our question, "Tell me how you became a part of this congregation," reveal that people often join a congregation because they resonate with the culture of that community. For instance, some congregations stand for values that are important to certain people. Other congregations offer programs that appeal. The style of interpersonal relationships in some churches is important to some folk. Some people join congregations because of the content of the sermons or because they like the minister. Even when people cannot fully describe why they joined a particular parish or what makes them feel at home there, they often have an intuitive grasp of the character of the community.[2]

Most congregational cultures contain a sense of the place of the preacher and the sermon in that community (both in the service of worship and in the wider life of the parish). The congregation tends to be open to the sermon when the people perceive that the preacher and the message are in continuity with congregational culture. This matter involves the degree to which the congregation perceives the preacher as a part of the community and as a trusted authority. The congregation tends to authorize a preacher and a message when the preacher speaks or acts (in the service of worship or beyond) in ways that are consistent with the expectations of the congregational culture. Similarly, the listening community may be reluctant to take seriously a preacher or a sermon whose person, style, or purpose pushes beyond the boundaries of community culture. From this perspective, when the preacher adapts to congregational culture, we may say that the congregation often helps shape both the preacher and the sermon.

The interviewees in this study were quite interested in the degree to which sermons facilitate relationship among people in the congregation and with God. They believe that the preacher and the sermon do affect the ways in which people relate with one another. They also believe that the way the preacher relates to the congregation in settings beyond worship affect how they perceive the preacher and the sermon. While such concerns sometimes go beyond the boundaries of the rhetorical event of the sermon itself, it is clear that such matters affect how the listeners perceive the preacher in the moment of preaching. When the preacher is in relationships with listeners outside the service of worship that the congregational culture accepts as appropriate to the gospel and the purpose of the church, congregational members tend to listen more openly to the sermon than when the pastor's attitudes or behaviors run contrary to the expectation of congregational culture.

Of course, as we noted in chapter 1, the relationship between sermon and congregational culture is dialectical. Sermons sometimes affect how people understand the congregational culture, and can even bring about changes in how people relate with each other in the congregation.

Figures of Speech Reveal Depth Understandings of Preaching

Philosophers of language point out that a single figure of speech often evokes a whole way of thinking about some aspect of the world.[3] A figure of speech used by a person often reveals how the person understands (at least implicitly) the aspect of the world under consideration. For instance, the word "strategy" is from the world of military campaigns in which the object is to conquer other peoples. When speakers use the word "strategy" they imply that the context in which they speak is one in which they seek to conquer (or otherwise influence) others.

In a similar way, the project team notices we can learn much about how people perceive preaching by paying attention to the figures of speech (and other expressions) listeners use to describe the event of the sermon. For a figure of speech is often a window into a larger world of assumptions and expectations concerning how the listeners perceive the sermon and, in some cases, their lives, their needs, the world, and God.

This phenomenon is visible in the remarks of a male in his twenties. He is a homosexual man who has felt condemned by a number of preachers and congregations because of his sexuality. Ethos, the portal through which this listener begins to respond to the sermon, is visible in the following response to the question, "What do you think the minister is doing when he or she preaches?" The interviewee has just recollected a sermon focused on "judgmentalism":

> The preacher spoke of the *truth of light*, of when Christ came to earth, he gave us lights. In this church, the preacher said, *when we're baptized, you're handed a candle. It's not a flashlight, but members of this denomination seem to think that they're handed a flashlight to shine it in deep, dark, crevices of people's lives and expose hidden faults.* The preacher said that...if you're in the darkest of rooms, you're scared. You do not know if there's a bug going to get on you. You have no idea, so you start reaching for a match, and you light your candle. You hold it up, and when you hold that light up, *if there's something in front of you, you're going to see it as equally as it's going to see you, but if you have a flashlight, you're shining it on just that one object. They can't see you.*

Similarly, according to this listener, the preacher is not to shine a flashlight, but to hold up a candle in the midst of a shadowy and frightening world. The interviewee recalls, with distaste, that he has heard a preacher in another denomination who would take the Bible and use it in a congregation like a hunter uses a flashlight when going after a possum in a tree. The preacher would "put a spotlight on them [the congregation] and pick them off."[4] This young adult says, "That's wrong to do that." Leaving metaphors behind, the listener continues, "The main thing [a preacher is to do] is to teach people how to love and all the avenues that there is to love."

A sermon for this young adult is not simply a light, but a particular kind of light–a candle that illumines both the space and the person who is holding it. In a dark room even a source of light can be scary if the person who is holding the light uses it in the wrong way. For this listener, not only is the world often dim and scary, but preachers can be frightening when they treat you like a possum in a tree and shine a light on you in condemnation. Because of this listener's strong response to the appeal to ethos, preachers need to shine the kind of lights that do not condemn but, even more important, that reveal the preachers' identity so that this listener can feel a strong sense relationship with them. Without this positive preacher ethos, this listener will not give full credence to the sermon. Expanding the remark above about love, the interviewee later indicates that while he appreciates preachers whose messages are "politically correct," the key to good preaching is for the preacher to demonstrate acceptance and love for people.

Preachers do not have to conduct formal interviews to pick up the figures of speech with which listeners describe sermons. Members of the listening community often use figures of speech to talk about a sermon when they shake the pastor's hand at the door after the service, or when they drop by the church office, or in the midst of a board meeting or in ordinary conversation. By being alert to such remarks, a minister can often discover quite a lot about the ways in which hearers understand preaching.

The Bible Is Authoritative...but How?

The project team correctly anticipated that most of the lay persons interviewed for this study think the Bible is authoritative in the sermon. Indeed, when asked, "What role does or should the Bible have in preaching?" nearly 100 percent of the interviewees indicated that the Bible is important to preaching. Cassandra speaks for many when she says, "I know that you [the preacher] must be factual, which means you must have the Bible as your base of authority because there is no other base of authority when it comes to ministry." However, the statements of the laity in the transcripts underscore the fact that listeners have quite different understandings of *how* the Bible functions authoritatively. When a particular listener understands the Bible a certain way, that listener expects the preacher to deal with the Bible in the sermon in ways that are consistent with that perspective.

We can hear strains in this diversity simply by listening to attitudes toward the Bible in the interviews in this book. Jim, for instance, implies that the teachings of the Bible are valid in every time and place. After expressing appreciation for the fact that the preaching ministers in his congregation have the creativity to tell the biblical story in fresh ways, they do not change the story.

There is, I think, something that may be more important than everything put together: the fact that they [the preaching ministers] don't waver in what they teach. It's the Bible, nothing else. They don't take anything out of the Bible and say, "Well, that's not important." If it's in there, it's important. They never add anything to it that's not there. It's straight biblical teaching. I think some people may not want to hear that, but they appreciate it. I think that they learn to appreciate it and respect it.

Jim affirms that the heart of preaching in his congregation is fidelity to the Bible. The preachers "are not ashamed of it [the Bible]. If this is what the Bible says, then we're going to preach it...It doesn't matter if it's a topic that's controversial or not, [the preachers] are going to talk about it." The preacher really needs only to make clear what the Bible says. This respondent explains why.

> Most people would think, too, if your church is going to grow and be large, you've got to pander to the audience, so to speak. They've never done that. They don't water it down to try to get more people in here. I think because they've stuck so hard to their guns, that's why some people are attracted to it. There's probably a thousand different reasons why people would come, especially now, but from the very beginning, why would Fred be the one to grow [this church]? I think it's a God thing, and everybody here would say that...I do think one of the reasons for the growth has been because Fred, and now Tom, are both willing to stick to their guns on the issues and say it how the Bible says it, versus trying to water it down.

According to this understanding of authority, we can know God only through the Bible, and what the Bible teaches is in conflict with the prevailing mood in the culture. If aspects of the culture run against the grain of the Bible, then *prima facie,* the culture is wrong.

Jane also states a high degree of biblical authority, but her view is more subtle. When Jane is asked what makes a sermon true, she says,

> As long as it comes out of the Bible. As long as it's not just taking one verse here and one verse there. I like to read the verses before and the verses after to make sure that what they're saying...There are even times I've gone home and I'll read it after, because Bob skips around a lot. I'll go home, and I'll look at a verse and read the verses before and the verse after to make sure. Not that I don't believe, but I want to read it myself and make sure he's telling me the truth. I don't want to be blindly led.

Jane implies that the Bible is inherently truthful. However, while the Bible may be infallible, the preacher's interpretation of it may not be. Because the Bible is a reliable guide, Jane wants the preacher to explain its content, as she says.

Actually, it [preaching] explains to me a lot of points in the Bible that I don't get when I read. Actually, our former minister did a little more than Bob as far as really getting into reading more of the Bible, as far as taking one chapter and verses from one area. Bob goes back and forth, which isn't bad. Our former minister, he really just explained a lot of things I would read at home, and I'm like, "What exactly does that mean?" I come here, and it seemed like it's always the next week just what I'd been reading, trying to understand. After he explained it, "That was easy. Why didn't I get that?"

When the interviewer comments, "It [preaching] really instructs you about things that aren't clear in the Bible," Jane continues, "Yes. Or even there have been different sermons that after we've left, I've got to know more. I go home and read more. Some of them really energize you and get you ready to go."

Learning the content of the Bible is not an end in itself for Jane, however. She is asked, "Do you think that all sermons should begin with scripture or be based on scripture?"

No, not all of them. Well, yes, I guess so. Bob's sermons before always talked about family, raising your kids, what husbands should be, what wives should be. He goes above and beyond the Bible, but he'll find scriptures in there that pertain to what he's talking about. I really like those, too. Self-improvement, I guess.

Jane wants to know more than facts about the ancient world of the Bible. She wants the sermon to show how the Bible can help her life improve.

Furthermore, Jane operates with implicit norms regarding interpretations of the Bible that are acceptable. After being asked if she could remember a particular sermon that impacted her, she recalled:

At least once every month or two, we'll get one that just really will explain something. I'm like, "Wow." Like raising your kid, marriage with your husband, committing…Yes, that stuff really gets me thinking. It does change me, my husband also. Well, this was a year ago. He had a marriage series. It was about a month long, raising kids one weekend and then other things the next few weekends. We had big long discussions. We got the Bible out and read some verses. Let's look at wives submitting. That was a biggie for me. We got it out, and I read it in context. Don't have to be doormats, okay.

Jane seeks guidance from the Bible in family issues, but her sense of relief that she does not have to be a doormat is palpable. She has an intuitive norm: She wants the interpretation of the Bible to authorize respect for her personhood and a degree of freedom of self-determination.

Although Jane is committed to a high doctrine of biblical authority, her understanding of how the Bible functions is nuanced. The sermon that Jane will take most seriously interprets the contents of the Bible in a way that will help her improve her life and that authorizes certain qualities of life (such as not being a doormat). It is not clear how consciously aware Jane is regarding how the preacher interprets the significance of the Bible for today, but she has at least an intuitive grasp of this perspective.

Helen also regards the Bible as central to the sermon, but she is aware that all uses of the Bible contain interpretive elements. This view comes out when the interviewer asks, "What do you think preaching does in this congregation that no other thing does?"

> I'd say probably it's the main source of—this sounds hokey, but—spiritual enlightenment, if you will. What the Bible says. I think we really look to our pastor for that, because he's the one that does the Bible study and has time for that and knows. What does the Bible say? What should we be thinking about? Even if I don't always agree, which often I do with my pastor, what should I be thinking about in terms of what's going on in the world, in terms of what's going on in this city or this congregation? What should I be thinking about? Sometimes he gives opinions, and that's fine. There's probably sometimes where I don't always agree.
>
> I really think people get up, like I said, during sharing time and talk about the sermons from that point of view. "I needed to hear that right now," they'll say. Sometimes they're more specific and sometimes not. Our people are not...I've been in a lot of different congregations. Our people are very well-educated, sophisticated people, so it's not like it's a fundamentalist, very simple view of Christianity. So when people from here stand up and say those things, I think, "Oh, wow." I'm just real impressed.

Although Helen has reservations regarding "fundamentalist" approaches to the Bible, she does not articulate norms by which to gauge which interpretations of the Bible (and which perspectives on the things we should be thinking about today) are the most likely (or unlikely). However, she is clear that the meaning of such things is open to interpretation, and, moreover, that laity can come to interpretive perspectives that may differ from the pastor's but that can be even closer to the mark.

Derry regards a sermon as authoritative "when it's scripture-based." He initially seems to suggest a quantitative criterion for identifying an authoritative sermon.

> I think for it [the sermon] to have authority, just around half the sermon should be spent interpreting what the scripture lesson was.

The preachers do it here. They might not realize it, but people say maybe this is not a biblically based church, but if you listen to the sermons, about half of what they talk about is what happens in the scripture and explains the historical reference. The authority comes in that text, just basing it on the scripture. The other half of the sermon would be applying it to our daily life. Half of the sermon should be about that for me.

Later Derry clarifies that authority derives from more than the amount of time the preacher gives to explaining the Bible. Authority is also connected with the preacher's perspective on the Bible, as Derry continues.

I would say in our church, our preachers have all attended seminary. They've got this good biblical foundation. So you pretty well believe what they say and their interpretation of scripture. There are some churches, of course, that don't require a seminary education to be a preacher. They can interpret it any way they might see fit. Our church is not like a lot of churches that way.

For Derry, the interpretation of the Bible is authoritative (and, hence, the sermon is authoritative) when it is informed by the kinds of scholarship taught in seminaries. Derry's remarks do not allow us to know whether he is aware that there are significantly different interpretive perspectives not only among different seminaries but even within faculty members of the same seminary. Derry introduces a formal criterion (that an authoritative interpretation of the Bible is informed by a seminary-trained pastor) without clarifying the material or substance of that criterion (i.e., the marks of a seminary-trained pastor's interpretation) other than to say that such an interpretation respects the historical conditioning of the biblical writings.

Jerome, however, does articulate a set of material norms by which to evaluate the authority of a sermon's claims.

We were raised Methodist. We were raised with the Wesleyan quadrilateral. It had all four things had to be: science, the Bible, personal experience, and church history. These four things should speak with one voice for anything to be authoritative. Maybe I bring that baggage with me.

The components of the Wesleyan quadrilateral are usually identified as scripture, tradition, experience, and reason (rather than science). While Jerome does not explain how he understands the relationship among these four sources of the knowledge of God, Jerome's approach clearly opens the door to a conversational understanding of authority in which it is conceivable that claims of reason, experience, or tradition could challenge the claims of the Bible. The interpreting community then has to figure out how to resolve (or learn to live with) such a conflict.

To return to a theme that runs continuously through this book, a local preacher needs to go beyond general and soothing affirmations of biblical preaching to understand how the members of the particular listening community understand the Bible and its authority. As we hear in the texts and subtexts of the comments we have just examined, the issue of biblical authority is only part of the larger issue of authority in the church.

One of the most important things a preacher can do is to help a congregation name different understandings of authority at work in the congregation and in the broader church. The preacher can help the congregation understand the foundations and implications of each view. What is at stake with respect to the views of God presupposed in the different views? To what kind of community (both in the church and beyond) does the view lead?

If the Preacher Walks the Walk, the Congregation Listens to the Talk

A lot of congregations have an expression that is a good way to frame this discussion. They emphasize that a Christian must not only "talk the talk but walk the walk," that is, a person (and a community) must day-to-day live Christian values (walk the walk) in ways that are consistent with what they say Christians believe and do (talk the talk). In a similar way, the interviews reveal that many listeners are more attentive to the sermon when they perceive that the preacher's everyday behavior is consistent with what the preacher says from the pulpit. Put positively, if the preacher walks the walk, the congregation is likely to listen to the preacher talk the talk. Put negatively, if the preacher does not walk the walk, the congregation will not give full consideration to the talk.

This theme did not catch the project team completely by surprise.[5] We expected it to emerge from the interviews. We anticipated that it would be especially significant for persons who begin their listening with an ethos orientation (see below). However, this motif comes to expression in the interviews with much greater frequency and intensity than the project team expected. Fully 90 percent of the interviews mention it, and often with considerable energy.[6] Furthermore, integrity between the preacher's words and actions is important even to persons who initially respond to the rhetorical appeals to logos and pathos.[7] This pervasiveness does not mean that ethos is universally more important than logos or pathos but that many listeners place a very high value on it today.

This theme came out in the words of interviewees in several of the case studies previously discussed in this book. Jim, for instance says:

> I think you want to have a minister that is gifted at public speaking, but at the same time, *they have to carry whatever they preach over into their everyday lives.* One thing about [our ministers] is, I know them

well enough personally to know that these [two people] are *full of integrity.*

This motif stands out clearly in responses in the wider body of transcripts as well.

Consequently, this listener continues, "When [the ministers] say something from the pulpit, you can believe it."[8]

A Caucasian woman in her twenties speaks for many others in the study when she says that a preacher needs to be "honest and consistent." "You [the preacher] need to be consistent between your messages and your daily life. If you're going to preach against something, and then go out and do it, why am I going to listen to you the next day?"

A middle-aged African American woman comments that her pastor constantly talks about the importance of people in the congregation actively caring for one another. She was impressed by the fact that when this pastor began to serve the congregation, the pastor "visited every one of the members" in their homes.

> It didn't matter how far they [the members' homes] were from the church building. Every single one. I know this, and I went with him to quite a few. *This is a good thing: when you see someone not only talking about it, but actually putting it into practice. When he talked about it, it was like, "I know you're telling the truth. That's exactly what you do."* And we should all be doing it also. Sometimes people say things and you don't know whether they're just saying it, or whether they really truly believe it and live it. He lives it. He lives that. I know that for a fact.

The interviewee underscores the effect of integrity on her by telling about the pastor visiting a mother whose daughter had not been out of her apartment for several years. The pastor's call meant so much to the mother and to the daughter that the interviewee decided to begin making visits to people herself.

For most listeners, the preacher's life outside the pulpit contributes to the credibility (or discrediting) of the content of the message. Indeed, such matters as the pastor calling in the hospital, working in a soup kitchen, or treating another person with respect can help create a willingness on the part of the congregation to take seriously the content of the sermon.[9]

Discoveries of More General Interest

Some surprises are of interest not only to preachers but to others in the world of rhetoric. These ideas include the helpfulness of Aristotle's categories, and the discovery that many listeners begin to respond to the sermon through one rhetorical appeal (ethos or logos or pathos) and process other concerns through that appeal.

Aristotle Was Right (Mostly)

Aristotle has been one of the most influential figures in the study of rhetoric since he wrote *The "Art" of Rhetoric* in the fourth century B.C.E. In chapter 1 we summarized and adapted Aristotle's categories of logos, pathos, and ethos as used in this study. Although the primary purpose of our work was not to verify the validity of Aristotle's paradigm for understanding sermons, the fact that the three-fold notion of ethos, logos, and pathos has seldom been tested in empirical investigation of preaching gives us the chance to comment on the usefulness of that typology.

The main part of the title of this section of the chapter ("Aristotle was Right") indicates that we agree with the great philosopher that these three phenomena are central to understanding what happens in the hearts, minds, and wills of listeners when they hear sermons. The designation "Mostly" indicates that we believe Aristotle's understanding of these categories can be refined, at least with respect to preaching. First, we believe that because preaching takes place over time in a particular situation, the role of local congregational culture needs to be expanded in rhetorical analysis. Second, we find that the interaction of ethos, logos, and pathos is more complex for particular listeners than Aristotle describes. Indeed, the interrelationship of these three qualities in the listener is much more than simply adding up their effects. Each listener really forms a gestalt in which these dimensions influence one another in different patterns in each person and community. Third, whereas Aristotle reflected most fully on how these elements work together for individuals, we find that preaching affects a community as community. Preachers need to give increased attention to how preaching forms community in each congregation. Are a preacher's sermons offering optimum help to a community in taking shape in ways that embody the gospel? If not, what changes might a preacher make?

However, despite the obvious value of rhetoric for understanding what happens in preaching, rhetoric has not always been welcome in discussions of preaching (or theology) in the last eighty years. Thomas G. Long notices that the resistance of theologians and preachers to rhetoric can often be traced to the influence of Karl Barth. The great Swiss theologian "was scrupulous to speak of the Word of God as something completely outside of the human possibility, as an event of and from God and not at all dependent on anything from the human side."[10] The preacher would speak the Word of God in the form of the sermon and the Word would effect its own hearing. A number of authorities in preaching following in this vein spoke of rhetoric as human interference with the pure power of the Word. Disregard of rhetoric came to a height in approaches to preaching influenced by the Biblical Theology Movement. Long points out, however, that some voices in the preaching community have kept alive an interest in rhetoric and that this interest is growing. While confirming that they believe in the movement of the Spirit in preaching, these voices allow for creativity on the part of both the listener (responding to the sermon) and the preacher (shaping the sermon, in part, to account for the human fabric in the congregation).[11] Among the seminal voices in this track are Long himself, Fred Craddock, David Buttrick, Eugene Lowry, Christine M. Smith, Paul Scott Wilson, Lucy Lind Hogan, Robert S. Reid, Judith McDaniel, and Craig Loscalzo.[12] Our study lends further support to the idea that rhetoric can be a valuable conversation partner in thinking about preaching.

Many Listeners Begin Processing the Sermon in Response to One Rhetorical Appeal

Several of the members of the project team began this study with a presupposition that proved to be only partially true in how it placed the emphasis of the ethos, logos, and pathos. The presupposition was that ethos, logos, and pathos operate in each listener in about the same way and to about the same degree. That is, some of us thought each listener responded about equally to appeals to ethos, logos, and pathos. We had the sense that a listener might be more inclined toward one or two of the qualities than the other(s). We suspected, for instance, that some listeners would place more value on logos than on ethos or pathos, or that some hearers might value ethos more than logos or pathos. However, several of us assumed that each of the three categories functioned in parallel but not quite intersecting ways in the listener (rather like numbers in a column in a ledger) and that the effect of the sermon occurred as the listener was affected by each part (rather like adding up the numbers in the column and getting a total).

A more complex picture of the relationship of ethos, logos, and pathos in the typical listener emerged as we worked with the transcripts. Reading many transcripts, we began to sense that ethos, logos, and pathos relate differently in different listeners when we noticed that occasional listeners were asked questions dealing with one category, but responded with material from another category.

For example, a Caucasian woman in her sixties was asked, "If there were no sermon in this congregation, what would be missing?"

> I'm probably not the best person to ask because we're probably the newest members here. No, not the newest, but we've been going here for five years, and there are a few newer…I would have to say the relationships, because that's important to me. I've seen people let go of the church, and I don't understand it. It bothers me that they could walk away, having been here for years and years, some of them. They're elderly and move to the [home for senior citizens sponsored by the denomination]…and [that] is, I'll say, thirty-five miles away, maybe forty miles away. So it's a distance

thing, but still I feel like they're deserting us. To me, it's hard that they can do that just because of the relationship that they've had with the church over all the years. I don't know how they can do that. For me, it is a lot about relationships.

Her reply does not mention the sermon at all but initially deals more generally with the loss of relationship with people who leave the congregation, and concludes on a positive statement of relationship as the center of her Christian experience. "For me, it is a lot about relationships."

Although the listener does not reply directly to the question, her response suggests that congregational culture may be her point of entry into the sermon. This hypothesis is confirmed by a review of the whole transcript: Emphasis on relationships is not confined to this one remark, but she turns her comments in the direction of relationship in response to almost every question. She begins to listen to the sermon through the culture of her congregation and moves from there to consider the ethos of preaching, the way the preacher represents the best aspects of that culture. Hearing the sermon is an experience of relationship with the pastor in the context of the congregation. As she moves on to discuss the argument (logos) of the sermon, she makes it clear that that becomes meaningful to this listener as it reinforces relationships among members of the community.

The project team observed quite a few occurrences in the transcripts when the interviewer asks a question about one category but to which the interviewee gives an answer from another category. Usually the category through which the hearer replies to the question is the primary point of entry through which the listener begins to process the sermon. Even when a transcript does not contain such a direct interchange (and relatively few of the transcripts do), we can identify one appeal as the ground from which the listener takes in the sermon. The interviewee signals this starting point by talking repeatedly about it and by using vocabulary (especially figures of speech) that bespeak it.

Nearly every person in our study seemed to indicate that one appeal (ethos, logos, or pathos) is the point of entry through which they begin to process the sermon.[13] When we made this discovery, the project team used the terms "ethos listener," "logos listener," and "pathos listener" to speak of a person's initial mode of processing the sermon. However, we now assiduously avoid that language. Referring to a person as "an ethos listener" could be taken as reducing the person's patterns of processing the sermon to that one quality, as if for the "ethos listener" *only* ethos concerns matter. As we repeatedly see in this book, even when one element predominates, the others are operative, albeit in more intricate relationships than we previously imagined. We now borrow the term "setting" from the world of sound amplification and "mixing" to describe the primary mode through which a person listens to the sermon. The public address system of the congregation typically contains a console with dials that adjust the treble and bass qualities of the voice, as well as the volume. With the dials at different settings, the voice of the preacher sounds different. In a similar way, we may speak of listeners having ethos, logos, and pathos settings. Some listeners perceive ethos dimensions more keenly while other listeners respond more to logos or to pathos. Each person's mixture is unique to that person.[14] The other appeals come into play, but we can speak generally of nearly every person having a primary setting through which they begin to hear the sermon: The ethos focus is the initial receptor for some, logos for others, and pathos for still others. We did not discover anyone for whom embodiment was the primary orientation for hearing the sermon.

Logos Settings

The person *who responds first to the logos appeal* is not only interested in the content of the sermon, but is touched by other appeals. For such a listener, the appeals to ethos and pathos refract through logos.

We hear this plainly in an interview with a Caucasian male who left two other denominations because he did not like the content of their beliefs, and joined his current denomination because of "approach to theology." He states without ambiguity that preaching is "the cornerstone of worship" and emphasizes, "Give me the one thing that you demand out of sermons: it would be content." Expanding on what he means by "content," this interviewee says,

> I think we all like to hear our theological ideas confirmed. Theological beliefs, and this should not really be...I feel a little guilty in saying that, because I have listened to wonderful speakers who did not share my theology. I try to separate those. They do a wonderful job preaching. They do a wonderful job in delivery. Theologically, they are not where I am. No matter how hard I try to appreciate what they're doing, there's not a connection. I think it's automatically connected if they and I are theologically connected. I think this is what has meant a lot to me in the [name of denomination] Church is mostly the theological connection. I'm not saying I agree always with the theology, but it's much closer than any place else I have been.

At the same time, this cerebral listener is aware that people have feelings and that feelings can be very powerful. However, he sees a direct relationship between the ideas articulated in preaching and emotions. When asked if he had one or two things to tell preachers that could energize him as a listener to sermons, he replies,

> The one thing I would tell them is what they are doing in their role [explaining the theological beliefs of the community in the

sermon] is very, very important. They are probably looked upon, and I think traditionally the minister has been looked upon as a spiritual adviser, a spiritual leader of great importance *because our passions are formed from our spiritual ideas.* Spiritual ideas are formed from what we hear. I think preachers really need to take that seriously.

This listener recognizes that emotion can be very powerful. After mentioning a particular preacher who shares experiences from the preacher's own life that stir this listener emotionally, the listener explains further.

> There are a handful of preachers who do that for me [stir his emotions]. Another one that comes to mind uses a totally different approach, [preacher's name]. [Preacher's name] is a storyteller, but his stories are so beautifully woven…that *they move you.* I think that what [this preacher] does with stories, [the other preacher] does with content to make you want to be a better person. To summarize into one sentence: They make you want to be better. Now you've got to figure out, "How do I do that?" They haven't told you how to do that. They've left it open for you, but the content of what they have said, what they have illustrated for you, is a better life, a better way of living, a better way of doing things, *more passion.*

The goal of good theology in preaching, according to this listener, is to help the people live better. In the context of the whole interview, it is clear that for this hearer "to live better" is to live more faithfully. Such a life includes *more passion,* but the passion is important because it empowers the good life. This listener thinks that good theology evokes such passion. Indeed, the respondent notes that changes in human beings are typically cumulative, over time. "I don't think it's [changes in life] a dramatic thing necessarily. In fact, it would worry me if it were a dramatic thing. If I saw someone suddenly behave differently or perform an action, I think it would be much more on an emotional basis than a reasoning basis." Significant and lasting life change comes about rationally.

Ethos Settings

The person whose *initial response is geared to ethos* experiences the sermon through the lens of the character and role of preacher as preacher. For the ethos-based listener, the sense of identification with the preacher as a representative of the values of the congregation is the setting through which this listener experiences logos. Likewise, ethos perception fuels pathos.

We hear this phenomenon in a woman in her early thirties who is a university professor. From the opening words of the interview, she stresses that having a positive sense of relationship with others, especially in the congregation, is important to her. Indeed, when asked about the purpose of preaching, she says,

> I think they're instructors like I'm an instructor. They're trying to help people see *connections*. They're trying to help people feel *connected*, to have a *relationship* with God and to Jesus. I would assume they are working to create some *feeling of community* in the church.

One of the important qualities of preaching is that it "brings people together," that is, into close relationship with one another for mutual support. Elsewhere in the interview, she states that this togetherness is not only for its own sake but is to include empowering people for mission in the community beyond the congregation (such as working in shelters for the homeless).

As the interview unfolds, we discover that ethos plays a key role in helping this listener enter the world of the sermon and in bringing people together. While reflecting on her relationships with preachers over the course of her life (she has attended church all her life, including her college years), she repeatedly returns to the importance of feeling positive identification with them. When asked about a high point in her history of listening to sermons, she reflects,

> I can't think of a particular instance, no. But I think the things I do remember are when a minister or someone preaching will personalize the sermon a little bit. Disclose a little bit of something about him or herself that shows that person has grappled with the issues. That person is only human after all, as we all are. That person doesn't put himself or herself above the congregation in some way. I think those things, when they're connected to the main theme or lesson, for me are really poignant, and often times those are things that I remember long after a lot of the other material.

A sense of positive ethos with the preacher facilitates this listener paying attention to the logos of the sermon. This interviewee wants to know that the preacher is human in the same way that she is human, especially that the preacher struggles with life and its issues in ways that are similar to her own struggles.

This orientation becomes even more apparent when the interviewer asks, "Where does the authority lie for you when the person gets up to preach?" This listener responds, "I'm not sure what you mean." The interviewer continues, "If the [minister] is going to tell you something, what would give that something weight or authority for your faith life?" In response, the interviewee says,

I suppose the most...A lot of authority for me comes through a relationship with that person and feeling like I can trust that person and that person has really spent time grappling with issues and preparing and talking about issues related to worship and sermons. Some of it is through experience. Somebody can lose credibility if they haven't done those kinds of things. I think experience with a person over time and listening to a lot of sermons can make a difference for me. I don't think that I think about a minister as being an authority figure as much as a wise person who has leadership skills who can help me think about things differently. Maybe I'm bristling against the word "authority."

The interviewer presses a little. "If in the sermon the preacher is asking you to think about something in a new way, what would the sermon need to have in order to get you to think about it in a new way?" Again, the centrality of ethos comes into focus in the reply.

That's a good question. I think if it was consistent with the values that I already hold, it would have more credibility. If I could understand how it would certainly help people, either myself or others, and it was made clear, I think that would give it credibility. I think someone that I trusted in general, from experience, I would listen to more than someone new that I hadn't ever really known before. If I have a relationship with somebody either just from listening to them a lot or knowing them, that usually can give credibility if they are going to challenge me in certain ways.

This listener does not seek an outside authority who will give her answers. Indeed, earlier in the interview she stated flatly that she resists sermons in which the preacher seems to have too many answers. She will respond positively to preachers who, over time, demonstrate that they labor hard on her behalf, demonstrating a character of care, diligence, and integrity. In her own words, she is looking for a preacher who "really spent time grappling with issues and preparing." Indeed, this listener will typically enter into a sermon only when it is clear that she can have positive ethos with the preacher. In such a relationship, she is open to challenge.

Pathos Setting

The person for whom the appeal to pathos is the setting for listening to the sermon must be stirred at the level of feeling. Without a pathos experience, this listener does not feel that she or he has heard a complete sermon; the experience of pathos heightens the listener's willingness to pay attention to the logos of the sermon, and awareness of sharing a feeling with the preacher has an important ethos dimension.

We hear such a pathos motif in the words of a male in his late twenties who is asked, "When does the sermon have authority for you?" He states,

"When does a sermon have authority? A sermon has authority, in a very human way has authority when it has touched a point or hit on a point that I know deep down to be true even if, for whatever reason, I don't want to admit." The experience of the feeling of recognition–a pathos experience– is an important test of the validity of a statement. When that happens, this listener is open to reconsidering previously held beliefs.

Similar statements are a theme in this interview. When asked to recall a sermon that stirred him emotionally, he recalls two such messages.

> The sermon that was preached the day that I was ordained as [a leader in the congregation] was quite moving. Emotionally, I was pretty heightened that day. Basically, a sermon about hearing the call of God and that gift that all people of the church bring, I think, was a pretty powerful, impressive message for me...A year later when they installed and ordained the next class of [congregational leaders], our pastor preached that sermon as well. It was about hearing the call of God and heeding the call of God. I remember starting to cry in that sermon the same way I had the year before, because it was just a powerful message to say I don't always know why I feel compelled to do this or agree to do this, but I did feel called.

This listener's description of his reaction to these sermons shows that emotion functions as spiritual confirmation for this hearer. The feeling that came to him during the sermon affirms his sense of call to leadership in the congregation.

Several years ago, this listener had left the denomination with which the congregation is affiliated. Such an experience was key to this congregant's return. The story emerges when the interviewer asks, "Have you heard a sermon that caused you to think differently or to act differently?" This listener was visiting another congregation in the denomination located in another city.

> I'm trying to think exactly what the preacher's message was. The reason that I'm probably here today and what happened. I was worshiping at [name of congregation] and I found the preacher to be an incredibly effective preacher and an incredibly effective speaker and very emotional. The first time I saw him cry in the pulpit, I was incredibly, incredibly moved that he revealed his vulnerability to the hundreds of people that were sitting in that house of worship. Seeing his passion, and his sort of...He's a sort of hippies' crusader, if you will, for peace and justice and human rights. I had up to that point sort of emotionally resigned from the [name of denomination] church and said that the church is a mess. It's got to get itself together before I want to be a part of it again. Part of the word that was revealed to me that day was the fact that

you've gone around and visited different denominations and different places of worship and not become a member, just sort of stayed on the periphery waiting for the [name of denomination] church to smarten up. Once they get straightened out, then you'll go. I had this call about why not be a part of the solution. I was like, "Whoa." So now I can't wait for them to do it, then I can go join, but I have to take a role in helping to change or help it emerge, help it grow, help it evolve. While I can't tell you exactly what was being said in the pulpit at that moment, that definitely changed my course because I became a member of a church that really impacted me. That ended up bringing me to this [congregation when he moved back to the city in which it was located].

The experience of pathos–of feeling emotions stirred by the preacher–had a nearly revelatory effect on this listener. Here we see a dramatic aspect of pathos: When the preacher's pathos comes to expression in the pulpit (the struggle, the vulnerability, the weeping), it appeals to the emotions of this listener. The listener identifies with the preacher and is moved by the preacher's struggle. This kind of identification goes beyond legitimating the character of the preacher as a person of integrity who can be trusted. The hearer feels much of what the preacher feels and is profoundly affected by it.

Such experiences are not confined to private revelations. When recalling what happens after worship when the community has been moved emotionally, we are told,

People don't disperse very fast. They converse. There's a lot of people still milling around the sanctuary reflecting on something that impacted them during that service. That's the number one thing I can think. *There's a different level of energy. It heightens. It's almost palpable. You can almost feel it and see it jumping from person to person and emerging throughout that room. The hymns are also a little louder.* They sing louder. Yes, they do. They do. There's a little bit more movement. There's a little bit more movement when the people are singing. They're not just standing there still, holding their hymnals, but they might sway just a little bit. Even the most staunch of people, you see them sway just a tad. A little bit of nodding going on while they're singing.

This listener believes that pathos in the community intensifies the energy in the congregation.

In the full context of the interview, this listener expresses appreciation for logos and ethos. But when push comes to shove, the experience of pathos authenticates both logos and ethos. Without pathos, a sermon is incomplete. Healthy pathos not only touches this listener, but also, in his view, increases the energy field of the congregation as community.

Diagnostic Questions

To have a good chance to connect with as many parishioners as possible on a given Sunday, each sermon needs to appeal to ethos, logos, and pathos. A preacher might find it helpful to ask three diagnostic questions as a part of sermon preparation:

1. What qualities in the sermon (and from the preacher's wider relationships with the congregation) will help the person who listens to the sermon through ethos settings?
2. What qualities in the sermon will help the person who hears the sermon through logos settings?
3. What qualities in the sermon will help the person who tunes into the sermon through pathos settings?

While none of these surprises or discoveries turn a preacher's perceptions of what happens in preaching inside out, they are all worth watching for. We suspect they are manifest in different ways. Preachers who notice how such matters come to expression in particular congregations may pick up helpful insights into how the congregations process the sermon.

CHAPTER 9
_____

Approaches to Interviewing in the Congregation

The interviews discussed in this book reveal many illuminating perspectives on how listeners process sermons. Some, perhaps many, of the insights articulated by our interviewees apply to preaching and listening in almost any congregation. However, one of the most important discoveries in congregational studies in the last twenty years is that each congregation is a distinct community. Every congregation is a unique culture with particular values, practices, assumptions, and habits of thinking, feeling, and acting. Consequently, while the interviews previously discussed in this volume could be helpful to many preachers in many congregations, these materials do not reveal the listening patterns at work in the reader's specific congregation.

Because the congregational context in which listening takes place involves much more than simply the preacher and people in the service of worship, we begin this chapter with suggestions for moving toward an in-depth understanding of the congregation as a culture and listening community (with special attention to worship as the context of preaching). The chapter then outlines approaches by which ministers might deepen their knowledge of the patterns of listening at work in their particular situation through interviews with congregations conducted by the pastor or by others.

Getting in Touch with the Culture of the Congregation

Thomas Edward Frank, who teaches congregational leadership at Candler School of Theology, observes that faithful pastoral leadership (including effective communication) becomes possible in proportion to the degree to which the pastor has a deep sensitivity to congregational culture.[1] Congregational culture is the web of meaning, particular to each congregation, comprised of the interaction of the congregation's people, artifacts, values, practices, significance, worldviews, and ethos (or character).[2] A preacher comes to understand congregational culture by making a thick description of a congregation.[3]

Congregational culture includes things that are conscious and spoken, patterns that are assumed but unspoken, as well as dimensions that exist at the level of feeling and intuition and may not be fully speakable. Whether spoken or unspoken, conscious or unconscious, the force fields that make up congregational ethos are quite powerful. A minister needs to understand these force fields and how to work with the energy centers within them.

A pastor who is in touch with the culture of the congregation is likely to interpret interviews about preaching in ways that are deepened as the preacher hears resonance between the remarks of interviewees and the preachers' broader awareness of congregational culture. A preacher can often name significant aspects of congregational culture, but aspects of it are sometimes hard to describe; a preacher feels these dimensions, and in the deepest sense knows them, but cannot speak about them with precision.[4]

We draw on recent congregational studies to recommend several things that preachers can do to move toward understanding *congregational culture*: Determine who is present in the congregation, get a sense of how the congregation remembers its history, take account of the physical setting and its meanings, notice how people react with one another and their artifacts, note practices that seem to shape the community (and the values they embody), and describe the major service(s) of worship and what they reveal about preaching in the life of the community.[5] We call attention to how such studies can illumine our understanding of the place of preaching and varieties of listening in a local congregation.[6]

Before turning to the exercises themselves, we put some caveats on the table. While such exercises are usually helpful, they do not magically reveal the culture of the community. Congregational culture is a living organism or system in which the various parts constantly interrelate. A minister's vision of the community must sometimes transcend the bits and pieces of data that emerge from pastoral listening. At the same time, ministers sometimes let their interpretive imaginations take flight without sufficient grounding. Occasionally preachers become self-impressed or self-preoccupied with their own creative powers and become sycophants. An essential act of ministry is learning to interpret the community creatively in a way that is disciplined by awareness of the *actual* life of the congregation.

Who Is Present in the Congregation?

At the simplest level the preacher wants to know who is present (and in what percentages and spheres of influence) in the listening community according to:[7]

- Age (children, youth, millennial generation, generation 13, boomers, silent generation, World War II generation)

- Gender (men, women)
- Race and ethnicity (African American, Caucasian, Asian American, Hispanic, Native American, and appropriate subdivisions, e.g., Chinese, Korean)
- Sexual orientation (heterosexual, gay, lesbian, bisexual, transgendered, questioning, asexual)
- Social class (lower, middle, upper, and various gradations within, such as lower middle and upper middle)
- Make-up of households (singles, couples, single parents with children, foster homes, people living communally, etc.)
- Political orientation (conservative, liberal, Republican, Democrat, Libertarian, socialist)
- Educational levels (high school, technical school, some college, college, graduate)
- Displacement (From what geographical locations have people come to live in your city who are now in your congregation? From what other congregations and denominations/Christian movements have they come?)
- Religious beliefs (conservative, moderate, liberal? How do the actual beliefs of the congregation relate to the official beliefs of denomination/Christian movement of which the congregation is part?)
- What kinds of people are not present in the congregation
- Comparison of preceding factors with the preacher

The statistical representation of the congregation is less important in and of itself than for how it suggests questions, issues, attitudes, expectations, and values that are present in the listening community. Boomers, for instance, often manifest attitudes and behaviors that differ from Generation 13ers. Boomers tend to listen to the sermon with Boomer expectations.

A preacher may find it helpful to compare the demographics of the total membership of the congregation with those of the community who actually attend worship on a regular basis. If there are differences, what might they mean?

One of the preacher's tasks is to figure out not only which characteristics are present in the particular congregation but how they interact in the web of significance that is the congregation's ethos. How do they affect the ways in which the congregation listens to the sermon?

A danger of demographic statistics is that the preacher will read generalities that often characterize large segments of the population into specific groups and individuals in the congregation without taking account of the particularity of those persons or groups. Demographic statistics alert the preacher to the *possibility* of attitudes and actions associated with different cohorts, but ministers cannot *assume* that persons and groups in the congregation at Fourth and Elm will manifest these characteristics. Preachers must listen pastorally to the folk who are in their own congregations.

Get a Sense of How the Congregation Remembers Its History

A preacher needs to know how the congregation understands its history. This understanding is usually much more than the brute facts of when the congregation was established, who has led it, the buildings it has occupied, the rising and ebbing of attendance and influence. Robert Cueni, president of Lexington Theological Seminary, points out that a congregation usually has a story that tells how that congregation has seen itself in the past.[8] How a congregation remembers its history often contributes to how the community sees itself today.

Systems analysts point out that forces in the congregation often exist formally (officially acknowledged level), informally (recognized as influential but unofficial) and tacitly (unspoken but assumed).[9] Adopting a constitution and by-laws is an example of a formal action. Ideas about continuing (or not continuing) a pastor's service to the congregation among a group of influential members while watching football together on Sunday afternoons is an informal force. Everyone leaving Ms. Minnie's seat (on the outside aisle of the third pew from the left) empty is a tacit agreement. A preacher needs to be aware of all three levels of history and influence in the congregation. Ministers sometimes think that the formal statements and structures of a congregation are the actual means whereby a congregation determines values and decisions, when informal and even tacit relationships are the more powerful force fields.

A pastor can discover the main outlines of this story in two ways. One is by reading key documents from the church's past and present–church histories, official documents, newsletters, policy statements, and similar records. The artifacts that a congregation preserves and honors sometimes point to important memories.[10] When perusing such materials, a preacher can ask questions such as, "How does preaching appear in these materials? What do people seem to expect of the sermon? How do they regard the sermon function in the parish? How does preaching appear when these sources discuss the role of the minister?"[11]

An additional way to find out how the congregation interprets its history is to lead members of small groups in constructing a congregational memory time line. The leader draws a long line on a sheet of newsprint on the wall, and invites people to indicate what they remember about the congregation along the time line.[11] Thomas Edward Frank, who frequently leads congregations in this exercise, often asks participants to tell one story that encapsulates their experience in the congregation.[12] This exercise brings attention to aspects of the congregation's life that are very formative but that may not be evident from official statements and records. When participants remark about particular preachers or sermons, the leader can ask participants to amplify their perception.

Take Account of the Physical Setting and Artifacts

The physical setting (building, neighborhood, municipality) and the artifacts prized by the congregation often reveal much about a congregation. The location, condition of the building, the signage and condition of the exterior, as well as relationship (or lack thereof) of the building to its immediate surroundings, often signal how a congregation understands its relationship to its geographical context. The age and design of the building frequently signal how a congregation understands (or has understood) itself. The interior layout, signs, and upkeep provide clues as to what is more and less important to the community.[13]

Similarly, the physical objects that are important to the congregation can reveal much about what a congregation values.[14] What are the most important artifacts to the people? What is the network of associations that makes them important to this group? What do particular paintings, pieces of furniture, stained-glass windows, flags, or other artifacts mean to the congregation?

Along this line, Thomas Edward Frank finds it helpful to take small groups of members on "space walks." The group walks silently from space to space around and in the building, stopping at different places (parking lot, narthex, fellowship hall, Bible school classrooms, and kitchen) reflecting on what happens in that space and how it affects them. Members write down their associations and later share them with the leader.[15] In the process, the memories that come to the participants often bring to the surface much more than the importance of the different physical spaces in which the congregation lives.

To help focus on preaching, such a walk could include stops in the sanctuary, near the pulpit, as well as at the baptistery and table. The preacher would also want to think about how the shape and character of the worship space, the pews, and the pulpit (or other preaching space) orient the congregation to preaching. What do the size and placement of the pulpit, and its relationship to listeners, suggest about preaching in this community? Where does the pastor preach (from the pulpit? the floor?), and is that spot significant to the congregation?

The interviewers who conducted our study found it helpful to ask, from the time they approached the church building, what that setting suggested about the congregation. What did they see and feel as they approached the building? What did the kinds of cars (including bumper stickers and other things) in the parking area suggest about the make-up of the congregation and its values and world view? What did they see when they entered the building (condition, signs, indications of the kinds of activities)?

Pay Attention to the Congregation's Practices

In contemporary parlance, the term "practice" refers to things a community does repeatedly over time to constitute the identity and life of the community. Craig Dykstra identifies thirteen practices that are commonplace in most Christian communities: worshiping God, telling the Christian story, interpreting the Bible and the history of the church, praying, confessing sin to God and one another, tolerating one another, carrying out acts of service, suffering with and for one another, providing hospitality, listening attentively to understand one another, struggling to interpret the contexts of the congregation, resisting the principalities and powers, and working together to maintain social structures that support life as God intends.[16]

While such practices are found from congregation to congregation, their manifestation is always colored by how they are carried out in individual churches. Indeed, how a community embodies Christian practices from week to week and season to season shapes the character of culture of that community.[17] For example, the congregation does not simply "tell the Christian story" through preaching, teaching, mission, and other means, but *interprets* the Christian story.

Preaching is itself a practice that is part of the larger practice of worship.[18] Preaching also involves the practices of telling the Christian story, interpreting the Bible and the history of the church, struggling to interpret the congregation's contexts, listening attentively to one another, and helping the community envision how to confess sin, tolerate one another, carry out acts of service, provide hospitality, criticize the principalities and powers, and work together to support life. The preacher needs to employ the practice of listening attentively to the congregation to compare and contrast how these themes appear in the sermon and how they come to life in the congregation.

By putting together the pieces from such exercises, the preacher and others can sketch the values and world view of the congregation. The culture of the congregation comes into view.

Describe the Service of Worship and the Place of Preaching in It

As intimated already in connection with our suggestions about interpreting the significance of the worship space and about preaching as a Christian practice, the service of worship often symbolizes the place of preaching in the congregation. The preacher wants to locate the congregational ethos in the service of worship and how preaching relates to that communal culture. The preacher can pick up signs of this quality through the interviews themselves as well as through sensitive observation of the congregation. Here are some questions to move toward such reflection.[19]

1. What happens among people near and in the worship space prior to the service? What do these activities suggest about the relationship between the service and the community?

2. Returning to the space walk (above), describe the worship space. Note particularly the placement of the pulpit, the nature of the seating in that space and how the relationship between the pulpit and the seating orients the congregation to the preaching. Does the worship space contain symbols that are significant to the congregation?

3. How does it feel to be in the worship space? How does that feeling affect the relationship between preacher and congregation?

4. What do the pastor and worship leaders do prior to the service? How do these activities affect the service?

5. Where do people sit for the service? What does that indicate regarding their perception of their relationship to the service and the sermon?

6. Who participates in leading worship? What does that reveal about the congregation?

7. What do the worship leaders (especially the preacher) wear? What does this dress signify?

8. What is the order of service? What does this imply about the place of preaching in the service?

9. What actually takes place within the service? What do people actually do and say?

10. What is the feeling or tone of the service as a whole, and especially the parts surrounding the sermon?

11. What events in the service lead to the sermon? What do these suggest about the role of the service in the local community?

12. Describe the congregation during the sermon itself. How do they sit in the pews or chairs? What do they do during the preaching? What do you notice about their facial expressions? their body language? What relationship with the sermon do they embody?

13. Describe the preacher in the moments leading toward the sermon and during the sermon. What does the preacher telegraph to the congregation regarding the preacher's feeling about the sermon and her or his embodiment of it?

14. After the sermon, note how the congregation and the preacher seem to be affected.

15. In which moment(s) of the service does the congregation seem most involved? What role do these moments play in the service and in the wider life of the congregation?

16. When the service is over, observe what the people do (and listen for the content of their conversation) in the sanctuary, in the spaces nearby, and in the parlor or church hall (if the service is followed by a coffee hour). How do people relate with one another? Do they talk about the sermon?

Throughout, observers want to note how they (you) are affected by different parts of the service and the sermon. An observer's reactions are sometimes a window into (or a contrast to) the congregation's responses.

Through such observations, as well as through the questions that are pertinent to these issues in the interview questions in appendix B, the preacher can move toward assessing how the service of worship and the sermon feed into, and draw from, the wider life of the congregation.

Taking a cue from the Christian practice of listening attentively, however, the preacher needs to discern the degree to which the service of worship—and the role of preaching therein—reflects how the community truly perceives preaching. This discernment is necessary because some congregations adopt an order and style of worship at the suggestion of the pastor (who wants the service to be liturgically correct according to a historical and/or theological canon) but do not deeply embrace the change. Indeed, pockets of resistance may remain at conscious and unconscious levels. Over time, the practice of worship in the new mode may shape congregational culture, but even then some people may keep their emotional and intellectual distance if they resent the way the change came about.

Practical Matters of Interviewing

The pastor who decides to sponsor interviews of listeners regarding preaching faces several questions. [20] What is the purpose of the interviews? Who will be interviewed? Will the interviews be conducted one-on-one and/or in small groups? Who will do the interviewing? What questions will be asked? How will the data be recorded? Will the preacher analyze the data alone or with a community of interpreters? How will the preacher respond to the data? [21]

While we frequently use our own study as an example of one way to respond to these questions, we also refer to other possibilities. The dynamics that accompanied our presence in congregations differed in many ways from those that surround a residential pastor and congregational leaders. Readers in touch with *the culture of the congregation* in which they participate need to gauge the degree to which our recommendations and examples are useful or need to be adapted.

In the process of conducting the interviews on which this book is based, we tried to make it clear that the interviews are not a referendum on the current pastor's preaching. Nearly all of the interviewees seemed to catch the message that we wanted them to help us understand what works and does not work in their broad experience of hearing sermons and not to judge the preaching they hear from week to week.

At the beginning of each interview (as well as in materials sent to the subjects beforehand), our interviewers promised that we would use the material in the interviews anonymously. This promise seemed to free most listeners to be candid in the interviews.

What Is the Purpose of the Interviews?

The purpose of the interviews needs to be clear. What do the minister and others want to learn about preaching from the listeners? The purpose determines the character of the questions asked, and is sometimes connected to specific groups.

One basic decision is whether the interviewers will ask the interviewees to reflect on preaching generally or upon the specific preaching of their current pastor. This decision depends not only upon what the interviewers would like to learn but upon what the interviewees are likely to feel most comfortable speaking about. In many contexts, parishioners are more at ease responding to questions about preaching generally than about their current minister's sermons (especially if the interviewer is the preacher).

Since the teachers of preaching involved with this project work with students in seminaries that prepare women and men for preaching in the long-established denominations, especially in the Midwestern and mid-Southern parts of the United States, we focused our project on that constituency. Congregations that are largely African American or Caucasian make up most of the Christian communities in this area, so we focused upon them. Because most of our students become pastors of established congregations with relatively traditional worship orientations, we attended to listeners who regularly attend such services. The project interviewed a small sample of people from each congregation who approximately represent the congregation in categories of gender, race, ethnicity, and age. We designed the interviews in this project to help us learn more about qualities in preaching that listeners in the groups described above find engaging and disengaging. We hoped to identify characteristics of sermons that preachers could work into their sermons to improve communication between preacher and parishioners.[22]

A pastor or local planning committee similarly needs to identify the purpose of a set of interviews and (as pointed out below) identify a group within the congregation for interview. For instance, taking a cue from our study, the preacher might want to know what a cross section of regular attendees report as helping them listen to the sermon attentively. Interviews might also concentrate on a more specific purpose or on a specific cohort. The minister will likely need to recognize some principle(s) of limitation in regard to purpose and groups to be interviewed. What purpose (or purposes) seems most important at a given time in the preaching life of a local congregation?

We can further imagine interviews with people who seldom attend worship or who do not attend at all. Could interviews with such persons who are affiliated with the congregation help us understand how preaching may contribute to why they do not participate regularly in this key time in the community of faith? Could interviews with people who are not related to the church at all help preachers craft sermons that such persons might find of interest?

Ministers need to keep in mind that over time, interviews can be conducted for different purposes or with different groups. Preachers do not have to try to find out everything they would like to know in one set of interviews.

Who Will Be Interviewed?

We have already suggested that the purpose of the interviews often suggests persons to be interviewed. However, the groups identified for interview are usually too large for everyone to be consulted. A preacher and local organizing body can take one of three approaches to selecting persons for participation.

For one, the minister may follow a standard procedure in social science research and identify them by random selection. Within the target group, for instance, the preacher could simply tag every fifth name as they are found on the church roll. This approach has the advantage of generating a relatively representative group.

For another, the minister may have particular reasons for wanting to speak with particular people. In the study that underlies this book, our focus was on persons with a track record of commitment to the congregation and who attended worship regularly. We asked the pastor in conjunction with local lay leaders to identify persons for the study. We stressed that the interviews were not a judgment or referendum on the current minister's sermons, but were a reflection on preaching generally. We particularly urged the ministers and local leaders not to stack the interviewees with persons who were buddies (so to speak) of the current pastor and who would only say positive things about his or her preaching.

Although a minister can take yet another approach and issue a general invitation for people to volunteer, this method is seldom satisfactory. Persons who regularly volunteer for church activities and whose views are already at the center of parish life tend to sign up, while persons who are not in the inner circles of the congregation are less responsive. While persons in the power center may need to be heard, voices of persons who are outside the mainstream of leadership often alert the preacher to effects (or non-effects) of the sermon that the preacher may not notice because these effects occur in people with whom the preacher has little contact.

Will the Interviews Be One-on-One and/or in Small Groups?

Interviews are typically conducted either one-on-one or in small groups. The one-on-one session allows opportunity to explore the responses of the interviewee in breadth and depth. Many of our interviews generated such energy between interviewer and interviewee that the sessions ran far longer than the anticipated time.[23] A problem in the occasional one-on-one interview is an unfocused listener who has difficulty sticking to the subject.

A small group interview typically generates less depth from any one participant, but calls forth greater breadth of congregational perspective.[24] We used the small groups for two reasons. For one, they do provide information in their own right. For another, they provided a communal check and balance on the more detailed statements made by the individual interviewees.[25]

In the give-and-take of multiple interviewees interacting with one another, they can build on one another's insights regarding what makes a sermon interesting or uninteresting. Members of the group often offer different perspectives on the same aspect of preaching. Indeed, listeners sometimes disagree with one another. In the process, important aspects of commonality and diversity in congregational listening orientations come forth. Occasional problems in small group interviews include the presence of a single listener who (often unconsciously) dominates a group. Group interaction is sometimes so plentiful and intense that it is hard to move beyond a single topic or two, and sessions sometimes threaten to become unproductively long.

Who Will Do the Interviewing?

Naming the person(s) to do the interviews is an important decision, and one that can only be determined with sensitivity to congregational culture as to which approaches have greater and lesser chances of helping the interviews succeed.

Our project used interviewers who were neither members nor clergy of the congregations in which the interviews took place. Congregants generally felt quite free to talk candidly about preaching with these outside interviewers.

The pastor might be able to conduct the interview. This approach has the advantage of giving the pastor direct access to the full effects of the interviewee and the possibility of immediately following up on intriguing points. However, many parishioners are uneasy about speaking directly to the pastor about aspects of sermons that discourage them from being engaged. A pastor could feel devalued or attacked by a listener comment and respond in a way that interferes with the pastoral relationship and decreases the listener's willingness to attend to the sermon. Although the purpose of the interview may be to talk about preaching generally, interviewee and interviewer may have difficulty getting beyond the local preacher's own preaching.

Persons within the church might be able to conduct the interviews if they are trusted, sensitive, and known to maintain confidence. Some members will respond freely to questions from such a person. Other listeners may be slow to open up to an in-house interviewer, especially if the interviewer is known as a friend of the pastor, or as a power figure in the congregation who could limit aspects of the interviewer's   future participation in the community.

A local pastor or planning group could call a nonthreatening person from outside the congregation to do the interviews, collect the data, and help with the interpretation. While outside interviewers may not be optimally aware of congregational culture, they may be less likely than locals to be hooked by congregational issues that can distract the movement of the interview. For example, local ministers might engage in the equivalent of a pulpit exchange with respect to interviewing. That is, ministers might do the interviewing in one another's congregations. Ministers in a small group working on D.Min. degrees might interview in one another's churches. The congregation might hire a trained social worker with skills in interviewing or a speech teacher from the local college to conduct interviews.

What Questions Will Be Asked?

The questions asked should give an interviewee an opportunity to articulate ideas, feelings, associations, connections, images, and other things that help the interview move towards its purpose. Ministers and others planners often find it helpful to have a conceptual framework within which to develop questions. Such a framework identifies categories and subject matter that can provide both the focus needed for interviews to have a good chance to achieve their purpose and enough open-endedness to allow for the possible emergence of potentially valuable insights not specifically prompted by the questions.[26]

We found that the traditional rhetorical categories of ethos, logos, and pathos, supplemented by the category of embodiment, formed a fine conceptual structure within which to develop questions that would help the interviews achieve their purpose.[27] These categories allowed us to develop questions that took account of appeals by the preacher to the preacher's moral or spiritual character (ethos), appeals to arguments or ideas to persuade listeners (logos), appeals to emotions (pathos), and the use of appropriate delivery (embodiment).

Our questions are included in appendix B. The reader might like to try these questions to see if listener responses to them provide the kind of information that is helpful. Chalice Press, the publisher of this book, grants permission to ministers and other leaders to photocopy this page for use in interviewing in congregations.

How Will the Data Be Recorded?

Needless to say, the pastor and other planners should record the data from the interviews in a way that preserves it in a full enough fashion that the interpreter(s) can reflect on it. We tape recorded the interviews with small, unobtrusive recorders, and (for a modest fee) had the material on each tape transcribed. We now have fine paper transcripts with which to work.

The body language of the interviewee (including not only facial expression and tone of voice but posture and gestures) is sometimes important for understanding a listener's remarks. Videotaping can help with these matters, although even in this age of increasingly smaller and more convenient electronic equipment, the camera can be cumbersome and intrusive.

We have talked with interviewers in other projects who tried to keep handwritten notes made as the interview took place (and immediately afterward) as the primary record. This process proved unsatisfactory, as even the fastest note takers could not simultaneously maintain the kind of face-to-face contact with the interviewee that is often necessary for picking up subtleties of meaning, capturing listener expression, and keeping up with the flow of the interview.

Will the Preacher Analyze the Data Alone or with a Community of Interpreters?

Most preachers will want to spend some time by themselves with the transcripts from the interviews. Beyond that, we have found that having a small community of interpreters read the transcripts often allows us to hear more in the transcripts than we would have picked up by ourselves.

A pastor might read the transcripts with a small group within the congregation (e.g., the lay elders or the pastoral relations committee). Such persons may be able to provide illuminating (but not obvious) connections between the remarks of particular listeners and the ethos of the congregation. Taking such an approach, all involved would need to agree on (and honor) rules of confidentiality that are acceptable to all involved—preacher, interviewees, and local commentators.

The preacher might also consider the transcripts in dialogue with a clergy colleague group. Although the members of this group may not have intimate knowledge of the preacher's congregation, their distance from the community may allow them to raise questions or make observations that persons caught up in the local context miss.

Some preachers may find it too uncomfortable to look at the transcripts directly. They may be better served by asking another person from the congregation or another clergyperson to read the transcripts and interpret the data.

How Will the Preacher Respond to the Data?

Pastors can often learn much from the interviews that can help them reinforce and build upon characteristics of their preaching that listeners generally find engaging. Preachers can also work on modifying qualities that generally discourage congregants from entering fully into the world of the sermon. Toward these ends, a preacher might make a list of such qualities (both to reinforce and to modify) and conscientiously work on the items on that list in so far as the preacher is able while maintaining personal and theological integrity.

Our interviews, not surprisingly, turned up listeners in the same congregation who had very different reactions to the same qualities in sermons. A modified form of a cliché is true: A preacher cannot communicate with optimum effectiveness with all the people all the time. In such cases of radical diversity, the preacher needs to gauge the degree to which it is appropriate and possible to include different moments within the same sermon to speak to particular listeners or, perhaps, to shape whole sermons around a particular listener orientation.

Listening in Situations Other than Formal Interviews

Whether or not a minister and congregation decide to engage in formal interviewing, a preacher can learn a great deal about how local congregants process sermons by paying attention to what they say about preaching (and public communication, more broadly) in typical life settings. In meetings at the church, for instance, people will often make remarks (or use body language) that communicate what they value (or think they value) in preaching and what they do not. A parishioner in the hospital may recall a sermon that was meaningful. A gentle question or two may allow that person to explain more fully what made it meaningful. On the parking lot or in the midst of a home visit, the preacher may pick up clues that reveal qualities of preaching that are engaging or not engaging, or may signal a preacher as to how ethos, logos, and pathos relate for a particular listener.

People often disclose how ethos, logos, and pathos function for them when they are talking about subjects other than preaching, as well. A person who is particularly attuned to logos patterns of listening will often talk about ideas and issues. When commenting on the sermon after worship, for instance, this person might mention particular ideas that the preacher brought forward in the sermon. In a church council meeting, this person focuses on the intellectual principles that are connected with items of discussion and business. In a Bible study, this listener seeks an explicit articulation of philosophical or theological notions that interpret the Bible texts. Persons attuned to logos want to know the meaning of events. These people are motivated by ideas as ideas. The listener with a logos orientation seeks a logical rationale for why things are the way they are, or seeks to understand what a person or congregation should consider when making a change in thinking, policy, or behavior. This member is likely to volunteer to teach a Bible class. A preacher can often get quite a bit of insight into the logos concerns in the congregation by paying attention to the logos oriented remarks that people make in a formal or informal meeting, or the logos questions that people ask in the hospital or in crisis.

A congregant who is oriented foremost to ethos qualities in preaching frequently shows a concern for relationship with the preacher or for the preacher to be a person of integrity and education. When remarking on the sermon after worship, this listener often shows interest more in the person of the preacher than in the preacher's ideas. Such people are motivated positively when they have the chance to identify with the preacher and are also motivated by the desire to improve leadership relationships in the congregation. This member is likely to serve in a leadership role in order to monitor and foster enabling leadership in the congregation.

A person who is oriented toward pathos is especially sensitive to feelings not only in connection with the sermon but in broader dimensions of life. When commenting on the sermon after worship, this person is likely to do so in terms that evoke feeling. For example, this person may say, "That sermon brought me to tears." The preacher might ask, "What was it about the sermon that moved you?" When participating in a discussion on a policy or decision in the church council, this person makes a decision based on how people will be affected. These congregants are less concerned with principles than with emotional ramifications. Who will be hurt? Who will feel good? In a Bible study, people who listen from a pathos point of view often name the feelings with which they respond to the text. These people are often motivated by empathy. They may volunteer for a drama in worship that will express the joy of the resurrection. These members may be a part of a group sponsored by the church that gives people an opportunity to express their feelings about a major life issue such as divorce. A preacher can learn quite a lot about the pathos fields present in the congregation by not only noticing how people talk about feeling but by observing when feelings come to expression.

A preacher needs to handle carefully characterizations of listeners along the lines of ethos, logos, and pathos (such as the immediately preceding ones). We reiterate that all dimensions of listening are present (in varying degrees) in almost all listeners. A person whose basic frame of reference is ethos may initially respond to a particular sermon or event from a logos or pathos starting point. A person whose first response to the sermon is typically in logos or pathos terms could respond to a particular event or sermon along ethos lines. Furthermore, a preacher may need a sense of the context and fabric of the parishioner's wider life to interpret that parishioner's remark. When faced by a crisis, a person who begins from a logos starting point may ask, "Why is God allowing this tragedy to happen?" This person wants the preacher to offer a set of theological ideas to interpret the situation. A second person whose first filter for sermons is ethos may ask the same question in the same words but is not really looking for a theology of suffering. This second person wants to know that the preacher is with her, in solidarity during the season of tragedy. A third listener who is sensitive to the pathos dimensions of life may ask the same question, again in the same words, but not actually to raise the question as question. This listener asks the question as a means of expressing feelings of sorrow, pain, confusion, dismay, and/or fear. A preacher who hears someone ask the question, "Why is God allowing this tragedy?" needs to take into account the asker's frame of reference and to respond appropriately. When asking the question in a sermon, the preacher needs to address the question on all three levels—ethos, logos, and pathos.

Furthermore, the same behavior may arise from different places in different listeners. A person with a logos orientation may sing in the choir because of the great theological ideas in the anthems. A congregant with an ethos perspective may sing in the choir because she loves the sense of connection with other people during the act of singing. A listener initially motivated by pathos may sing in the choir because the music so deeply touches his emotions.

Despite the complexities of these things, over time a preacher can gain considerable insight into the listening profile of the congregation by noticing how people not only talk about the sermon but about how ideas, relationships, and feelings operate in persons and groups outside of the service of worship. We stress the phrase "over time." A preacher can seldom draw major conclusions about individual listeners or the congregation as a whole based on isolated remarks spoken in side conversations.

As indicated at the beginning of the book, while a minister wants to use approaches to communication that are as friendly as possible to the congregation, a preacher should not adopt listener recommendations simply because listeners report them. Listeners sometimes want qualities in the sermons that are contrary to the gospel. Clergy should adapt preaching only in ways that are consistent with their deepest convictions about God and God's purposes for the church and the world. Preachers who respond to listeners in the latter spirit will likely find the congregation growing in the gospel in response to enhanced communication from the pulpit.

Epilogue

We end with a confirmation, a caution, and a call. This study confirms that many people in congregations care very deeply about preaching. One of our respondents, a senior African American male, speaks for many interviewees in response to the question, "What would be missing if there were no sermon?"

> I always refer to the sermon as the main event. In other words, I think everything else leads up to that. If you don't have a sermon, it's kind of like going to dinner, and you don't get your main course. You may have some desserts, and you have some appetizers, which are always nice, but if you don't get the main course, you missed something.

We report this point of view not to downplay other elements of worship or other aspects of the congregation's life, but to underscore the value of the sermon to many listeners.[1] These interviews confirm that many people believe one of the central tenets of any good theology of preaching, namely that preaching is constituent of the identity of the church. The people care; the preacher is called to care.

The caution is to appropriately use the data from this study and other empirical investigations of preaching and other forms of communication. We run across preachers from time to time who think that by distilling "principles of preaching that really work" from studies such as this, they can control what happens in the event of preaching. However, explorations such as the ones described in this book do not give preachers tools to manipulate people. To the contrary, the interviews underscore the thick nature of communication among preacher and congregation. The most appropriate use a pastor can make of empirical examinations of preaching is to become more sensitive to the multiple layers of interaction that are taking place each time a woman or man stands up to preach.

The call is for humility on the part of the preacher. Because of the thickness of communication from pulpit to pew, a minister can never be sure what is going to happen when the gospel goes forth through preaching. One of the foundational beliefs of the Christian community is that God is present in every situation to help persons in that situation respond as fully as they can to the divine presence and purposes. Given the complexity of communication, the movement of the divine spirit, and the degree of a congregation's receptivity, a preacher is often surprised at the congregation's response to a sermon. When the congregation's response is positive, self-congratulation is less faithful and honest on the part of the preacher than thanksgiving. When the response is negative, the preacher cannot know, at that time, how the congregation's reaction might nonetheless help shape the congregation in the future.

An effervescent moment occurred when the writing team was together in the final stages of assembling this book. One member burst out, "This task [preaching] is really worth it! Everything that goes into it–the study, the struggle, the anxiety, the joy–all of it. It's worth it." Our prayer is that ministers who read this book will agree, and will recommit themselves to the call to witness to the gospel through preaching.

Transcripts for Analysis

This appendix contains unannotated transcripts from two interviews from our study. The first is an interview with an individual and the second with a small group. Readers have a chance here to practice the kind of analysis found in chapters 2–7. These transcripts have been abbreviated to save space.

An Interview with an Individual: Albert

Albert is a thirty-eight-year-old African American male, married and the father of three children, who attends worship three Sundays a month in a congregation that is affiliated with a long-established denomination with a formal approach to worship and liturgy and that averages seventy-five in worship. The church building is located in a neighborhood with an urban feel in a city of about 170,000 in the Midwest. The current congregation is composed of a merger of a former church (primarily African American), and a current church (primarily Caucasian). About two-thirds of the present membership is African American and about one-third is Caucasian.

INTERVIEWER: What do you think preaching does in this congregation?

ALBERT: With [this denomination] you have the [church council] which sometimes I feel can twist a pastor's arm and hold him at length. I think when it comes to his sermon, I think that's when the pastor can say those things that maybe the [church council] will allow him to do to a certain degree. It's a way of telling the masses, even if the [council] doesn't hear him. He can still go to his people and share his feelings through the sermons.

INTERVIEWER: The pulpit is very significant [in this denomination]?

ALBERT: I think it is. I think it is very important. Sometimes when I think about this church, the women play a large role in this church. Sometimes I feel if you don't conform to them, then they have problems with you. Pastor is one of those people who goes past that. He's not going to let you handcuff him because his reason for being here is to spread the word of Jesus. I know he respects the committees and the groups around him, but by the same token, his work is to do outreach and to tell people about God and Jesus Christ. Sometimes I believe he may bump heads with some of these people who don't like him to be strong about some of the things he says or his ideas.

INTERVIEWER: Tell me about your history as a person listening to sermons. Were there high points, low points? Was there any time when you almost walked out on a sermon?

ALBERT: No. I've never really wanted to walk out on any sermon. Maybe I'm a controversial person. I guess I like controversial sermons. I want sermons that make people scratch their heads and look around at other people in the congregation…I like sermons that move me. I don't come here for a reading. Then I go back home, and I feel something. I want to leave here a little more energized than what I was before I came. Some folks have a problem with that. Some people want to listen to the nice quiet sermon and then come to fellowship and then go home. Sometimes I don't get anything from sermons that are like that. I'm not saying that the pastor has to be ranting and raving in the pulpit, but I want you to wake me up.

INTERVIEWER: You go to church hoping something like that will happen.

ALBERT: Since I've become an adult and really understand Christ as I know him, each week when I leave church on Sunday and go back to my life and start work on Monday morning through Saturday, a lot of things come into play. A lot of just making it from one Sunday to the next. I feel like I come to church every Sunday with invisible suitcases that are filled with junk that's occurred all week and now Sunday is my way of coming to church, opening that suitcase. The pastor gives me a sermon. I feel like I empty everything that happened all last week. Take those empty suitcases back home. Then on Monday I start filling them up again. I at least get to start the week out with empty suitcases. By Thursday or Friday of that week, they start getting full again, but then Sunday is coming around. That's what helps me through. I wouldn't say I'm the most devout Christian. I don't leave church just Bible-beating my friends who don't go to church. It's for me. It helps me get from week to week. If you don't want to go to church, that's your own concern. I go because a lot of things are laid on my mind from week to week and situations that come up from week to week. That's what helps me. To me, my view of church is to empty those suitcases each Sunday. I want to be moved. I want to leave what's in those suitcases to go fight this next week.

INTERVIEWER: Can you tell me about a particular sermon that moved you?

ALBERT: I equate church to my father's death in 1997. Growing up in the [name of previous] church and coming here. Going from acolyte to usher to youth group president and youth choir and council and eventually one of the last vice presidents of the [name of previous] church before we came here. All those years of church in my mind built me up for my father's death. We all started in church. When we became adults, we could do the things we choose to do. I asked my brothers and sisters who strayed away from church. They're still believing God but just not getting up Sunday mornings and coming. I think with me coming to church all these years, I think it better prepared me for my father's death than it did the rest of my brothers and sisters. I knew death. I understood the purpose. They had a more difficult time dealing with it. I think spiritually that's the reason they were not able to come to grips. It was a sermon about death that had come prior that really made me sit back. I'm one of those people who sit back and think, "Mom and Dad are getting kind of old." That's when it was coming to me. "I'm about to lose these folks." It finally happened, and I was able to deal. Through a sermon that was a series, the regular preaching from week to week, got me ready. It's been almost four years now in November and I have brothers and sisters still having a difficult time.

INTERVIEWER: What do you most want to know about God when you hear a sermon?

ALBERT: As far as a sermon is concerned, you wonder why some folks are chosen over other folks in sermons. I'm still on death. As far as sermons are concerned...Sometimes I just want to know why God chooses some people. Why evildoers get to stay and then some innocent folks...Someone shoots a person. A man flies a plane into a building and kills innocent people. How do the people behind these things—the people who maybe not flew the plane but people who funded it to happen—those evildoers, how does God separate, or how does he punish folks who do things like that? If God is in control of everything, how can he allow that to happen?

INTERVIEWER: How do you see the role of the Bible in sermons?

ALBERT: It's a real powerful thing that's happened throughout the Bible, and the stories of Noah are some of my favorites, and Genesis about Sodom and Gomorrah. I didn't think those kind of things happened. When you read...man...maybe the first ten pages of Genesis, that's a heck of a movie right there. The way it starts out. Just like I think Revelations...to go back to death. Revelations is just as interesting to me as Genesis is. The beginning is just as good as the end. I guess they go hand in hand. Somehow I think you have to incorporate the Bible. I'm not a big fan of television preachers, but T. D. Jakes, he'll start out his stories straight from the Bible. They may be a little complicated, but then he takes it to the street. He'll tell you the same story in today's form. That's what makes his ministry so powerful. The youngest of people who watch him on television can understand to some degree what he's saying. I think in any sermon, it has to be both. The story has to come from the Bible, but you can incorporate it into today's times.

INTERVIEWER: Can you think of a particular sermon that didn't interest you at all?

ALBERT: I think there are some Sundays when the pastor or a pastor doesn't feel it. Maybe the pastor had a suitcase that was loaded that week, and he hadn't emptied his out on Sunday. Sometimes a sermon can go over your head. If he's feeling great, his sermon is going to be great. If he's not feeling his best, or if he's got things on his mind, it can't come off good, because even though he's speaking through God, the words come to him through the Lord, he's human, too. Sometimes something in his life may have knocked the wind out of himself on a particular Saturday or that weekend. Some Sundays you can come on outside and, "Whew! That was complicated," or, "That made a lot of sense," or, "What was he talking about?"

INTERVIEWER: What do you think is God's role in the sermon? What is God doing during the sermon itself while it's being preached?

ALBERT: I'm hoping that God's touching the speaker. Like I said, the words are supposed to be coming through. The pastor, he always says how he was sitting at home and how God brings the words to him. I'm assuming when he's standing in the pulpit, he's giving me exactly what he has gotten from God. I don't know how pastors do it, because I haven't had to teach it, but if he says it comes from God to him to us, then I have to accept that. Sometimes the pastor will let you have it. I wish he would let you have it every Sunday. For me, number one was emotion. I want to be touched by the sermon. I have to feel it. If I don't feel it, I wasted my time getting up that morning.

INTERVIEWER: Can you think of a sermon where the pastor let the congregation have it?

ALBERT: Yes. When he talks about finances. This church is slowly going downhill. The congregation is too small. The bills are above what is being brought in. Everybody's wallets are tight. You give what you can give. You give your time, and you give your money. It's still sometimes not enough to pay the bills. Then he wants you to dig deeper. Sometimes he lets you know that the only reason you live in your house, the only reason why you're driving that car, the only reason why you have any friends, the only reason why you woke up this morning is because of the Lord. So you need to think about taking care of his house. You're taking care of yours and the kids, but you won't take care of his house. Sometimes it takes a little waking up, a little slap.

INTERVIEWER: Are you saying that sermon moved you?

ALBERT: Yes. It makes you say, "Well, maybe I can come up with another ten dollars."

INTERVIEWER: Are there any other sermons like that you can remember that caused you to think or act differently?

ALBERT: Spouses, how they should be and how we sometimes take for granted. I guess if you've been around a person for a while, sometimes you can become kind of relaxed and don't do things that you used to do to make that person smile. Sometimes that can also help your suitcases get filled, too, at home is while you're at home, the problems that may be occurring. You could be making your life a little more fulfilled. You could be doing better things at home to make your life a little better, which could keep the suitcases kind of empty. It was a sermon on treating your spouses better or that significant other person, which would keep the cohesiveness of your house together. It just made so much sense to me. Sometimes I said when you're going through life just trying to figure out how to pay bills, sometimes you forget about those things that are really...You don't forget about them, because you live in a house with people and you don't forget about them in that sense. But sometimes you forget about the way you started, when you first met them. Keep that light going that keeps houses together.

INTERVIEWER: Do you think there are some issues that are just too explosive or too dangerous for the preacher to deal with in the pulpit?

ALBERT: No. I don't think there's any issue. If the sermons are based on the Bible, then there should be no sermon that's too biblical to preach. Maybe turn it another form, but there's no way. If it's in the Bible, then you can retell it. The Bible is the full authority. If it's written in the Bible, it can be retold, if it's the way it's supposed to be told. If we're telling it the way it was intended, then it's the one and only authority.

INTERVIEWER: What would be missing in the service of worship if there were no sermon?

ALBERT: It would be a major piece of the service. It's almost like when your pastor's out of town and they send in a substitute pastor who just doesn't hold your interest. You say, "I'm getting nothing out of this service." He may have been a very monotone person. He may be a great guy and a wonderful Christian, but something about the delivery just didn't catch on. You're here, but you spend more time looking at the kids or talking over here and you miss the whole sermon. Without it being there, you wouldn't have church.

INTERVIEWER: You spoke about monotone and delivery. What kind of animation do you like to see in a preacher when the preacher is preaching?

ALBERT: I like to see him moving around. The way our PA system is set up, the pastor has a lavaliere on his robe. He can leave the pulpit and walk around. He can walk down the aisles. He can move. I like the movement instead of just standing in the pulpit. I'm a teacher. One of the things when we were trying to get our certification for teaching, the one thing they stress is movement. Don't stand in one place when you're giving your lessons. Move around the room; touch people, so people can get a better feel. The kids will respond to you better if they see…If nothing else they wake up to the fact that you're coming near them. The movement keeps the people involved. Hand movements. Talk with movement and hand gestures. It's actually what keeps the eyes focused, along with your voice, but your movements keep people focused on you.

INTERVIEWER: Can you think of any stories in a sermon that were particularly effective?

ALBERT: You can tell a Bible story to where a person really, really feels it. That's when I'm being touched. That's touching you when the pastor is telling you almost as if he was there. That moves people. That's what keeps people coming to church. Most pastors in this church are nice quiet guys. They'll tell the stories with less emotion. I think that's just the [name of the denomination] way. Sometimes I think [with this church's way] and with these pastors, that's the reason a lot of churches are dying. People want to feel. People want to hear music that's up-tempo, upbeat. The hymns were beautiful, but people want more. It's almost being entertained as far as in the sermon, and with the music I guess that helps.

INTERVIEWER: What about different types of emotions? Feeling or anger or passion?

ALBERT: You can see the times and tell when someone has passion. You can tell the anger. Sometimes you can feel it. He gets to a point that maybe he feels that you're not listening. He needs to shake it up. He gets to the point where maybe someone is looking at him in a way which prompts him to say, "Maybe you're not understanding what I'm saying." He'll say, "I'm sorry if I hurt your feelings. I don't mean to." Sometimes he'll set it up before he throws the fire. He might say, "I don't mean to hurt anyone's feelings," or, "I'm not talking about anyone personally, but I want to say this." You can read him. You can tell if it's from the heart.

INTERVIEWER: If you had one or two things you could tell preachers that would help them energize you when you were listening to a sermon, what would they be?

ALBERT: I would say be firm. Be compassionate. But mainly touch people. People get up on Sunday mornings to be rejuvenated. You have to touch them. You have to make me feel I want to be here. That's how churches lose members…People don't get a good feel. They go to new places that I call more entertaining.

INTERVIEWER: What is it about being emotionally involved and participation?

ALBERT: Not participating. Not me but the preacher. The preacher has to make me…He can't just stand at the podium and flip papers and just read. I want to know personal stories. I want to know stories from the Bible. Tell me about what happened to your friend, Joe. Just normal folks. That's what I mean about being touched. You just can't read to me and then send me home. I want to feel it. Folks want to do that. I'm just speaking for myself, but I speak for the young folks of my age group, and they're saying the same thing. That's why their brothers and sisters don't come because they don't get nothing out of it. Everything is too monotone. You've got everybody sleeping.

An Interview with a Small Group

This small group is from a large and growing African American church (average Sunday morning attendance of 1,500) in an urban area with a population of about one million in the Midwest:

Geraldine, fifty-one, a professional woman;

Jerry, mid-thirties, office manager;

Maude, sixty-five, retiring from a profession;

Thomas, sixty, a professional;

Ann, seventeen, interested in going into the ministry;

Charles, forty, self-employed.

All these listeners are in worship every Sunday and are involved in study groups, mission projects, and congregational leadership.

INTERVIEWER: Tell me about a pastor that you've had that was a good preacher.

JERRY: Our pastor. I heard many, many pastors, and I think the thing that drew me to this church was listening to those pastors and maybe stacking them up in a manner of priority. [Our pastor] comes as close to anyone that I have heard in terms of getting inside of me…You can never reach the bar that he has for you, because you always have to keep reaching up, and when he sees that you have almost reached that bar, he seems to raise the bar just a little bit out of your reach to keep you reaching. I like that. I like that challenge. I like the discipline, the electricity. One of the things here I think is just prevalent of all who come and go is outreach. This is one of the few churches I know of, family congregation that seems to support any and all, whether you are or are not a member of this congregation. This church seems to support anyone, and I like that. I think he's an honest man. I think he's a Godly man. (general agreement)

ANN: I think that with our pastor, what you see is what you get. My grandfather was a pastor, and I was around a lot of pastors, so you can see the different personalities when they weren't at church. Sometimes that church personality didn't line up with what was outside of the church. Our minister, I've seen him on social occasions, and everything lines up. That always struck me growing up that I was going to a church where the pastor had to be this way, real pious, but then when he got out behind closed doors, he was like totally different, and he was acting the way that he was telling everybody not to act when he was in the church. And our pastor is not like that.

GERALDINE: I consider our minister my best friend although I don't have a social life with him. He is one that I can listen to, and I know he's going to bring me a word from God. I know that he's going to inspire me, and I know that he's going to lift me up. I know that when I am in distress, I know that I can go to him. I know that he's going to listen to me, and I know that he's going to set me on a Godly path.

CHARLES: He always teaches with the same principles in mind, biblical principles about faith, about obedience, about giving God first place in your life. No matter what the subject is, he always ends up that he asks you, "What is God saying to you? Not what am I saying, but what is God saying to you?" It's always scripture-based. What I really like about it is he always has a principle and a pattern in mind in his sermons and that gets you to want more. When I study the word of God, I don't just try to memorize the words. I want to know what principle God is trying to convey to us through His written Word. He's dealing with these people, but he's got a principle that he's trying to get them to model. How does that apply today? If you study the Bible, the key things that he makes you understand is who the writer is, what the writer's writing and what the subject matter is, who is he writing to, and what the subject matter is. So then you can take his sermon and apply it to your everyday life. My favorite sermon that I heard him preach was "Stay in the Boat." When the boat got shaky, and the disciples wanted to get out, Jesus said stay in the boat. So the thing you have to remember is no matter how it looks, how a situation looks, [how] your circumstances look, stay with Christ, because he's going to see you through. That's what the pastor preaches to me. When I hear him, he'll go all around and talk about different kinds of things, but when it comes up, it's Jesus and nothing else. It's so strange how his sermons that you can get on the roll with him. You know where he's going. He may surprise you how he gets there, but you know how he's going. To me, that's the greatest thing. So I always listen with tiptoe anticipation, because I know he's going to enlighten my soul on fire.

INTERVIEWER: When he gets up to preach, what are you hoping is going to happen to you?

CHARLES: I'm hoping I'm going to be fed, and I'm going to be excited about the word of God no matter what the subject is. No matter how much you anticipate how he's going to bring the Word and how you read it, he always gives it…I know he's going to create some excitement with that. He's a great user of words. Like I was writing something the other day, and he says, "Pursue your dreams," last Sunday, "with backbone, not wishbone." That will make you think. It's sort of the way Jesus taught the disciples. He used those parables. He met people where they were, and then he lifted them. Our pastor does the same thing. He meets us all where we are, and he lifts us through his words. I want to go from every Sunday with something that would last for six days and something that keeps drumming in my head that Tuesday ought to be nothing more than a forty-eight-hour extension of Sunday, and Wednesday a sixty-hour extension of Sunday and then next Sunday I'll say it again.

MAUDE: He challenges us to apply. It's not a matter of just sitting and listening to my sermon and getting emotionally charged, but then you take this message out. What are you doing out there in the world? The church gathered–great. We come to be filled, but the church scattered.

INTERVIEWER: Tell me about a sermon that really stirred you emotionally?

JERRY: I can think of one that's relatively recent where he was talking about that "I Am a Survivor." It charged me emotionally, I think, mainly because that point in time I was going through a major crisis as I thought. It just…What he was saying, the biblical truths, as we have said. Just makes the scripture come alive. Because of that, because of its practicality, it's reaching my emotions, my physical needs, all of that.

CHARLES: That entire sermon he had us to write down three things and put it in our billfold. In what we faced everyday, take that out. First one, "All things work together for good." The second one, "If God be for us, who can be against us." The last was, "Let nothing separate us from the love of Christ." It was so practical that everybody can take it home with them and get that out as something that somebody can take. That's an extension of his sermon. It was a great sermon.

ANN: I would have to say that my most emotional, if you will, sermon was not preached by our pastor. It was preached by [one of the assistant pastors], and it was just not too long ago, "Seeing What God Sees." It stuck with me because I'm a person who dreams, and I call them deja vus. I have them often, but it's my dream coming to life, if you will. I wasn't sure if it was God showing me these things. I thought, "Oh, I'm just dreaming, and it's coming true. Oh, wow. That's a good dream." But the more I listened to him and listened to what he had to say, it made it more real that I truly am seeing what God sees and seeing what God wants me to see and how he wants me to use what it is that I see. I think that was the most emotional because I had just had a deja vu that was so real it made me nervous. It wasn't anything bad or anything like that, but I'm able now to understand what it is that I dream about. When it actually happens, I'm able to understand to go back and say, "Okay, well, I know what to do in this situation, because I feel like I've been here before." Hearing what he said about his dreams, it just made it real to me, and it struck right then at the time that I was having these thoughts. I think that's what made it a great sermon for me, and it's also what made it emotional for me, too.

GERALDINE: When I came to this church, I would speak to people. Everybody spoke to me, and they would hug and kiss, and I would say to them, "How are you?" and they would all say, "Blessed." I didn't understand that. I didn't know what they were talking about. I thought, "why are these people saying 'blessed'"? What does "blessed" mean? "I feel blessed." You have to remember I was coming out of a very difficult time in my life. I was coming out of…I was looking for a family. I was looking for God's love. Then one Sunday morning, our pastor stood in the pulpit, and he preached a sermon on "Blessed to Be a Blessing," and at that moment, I just stood up and said, "Thank you, dear God. That's it. Wow." It was just like the clouds had opened, and I could just see clearly what the meaning of God's love was: that we are blessed because we have been given everything we need. It's already there. We have to be brave enough to pull it up and use it as Christ has taught us to do. From that moment on, I have fully realized that I am truly blessed, and I just have to…I say it all the time–I'm blessed–and really mean it, because it's just glorious, glorious, God-filled feeling.

INTERVIEWER: What do you think the pastor is doing when he or she gets up to preach?

MAUDE: I think that when they get up to preach that they know they have the task of sharing what the Lord has given them to the people of God. I think that they know that what it is they have to say has to pertain to everyone or at least they have to try to break it down so that most understand. I don't think they come up there to play or to joke around, but that they come in the seriousness in order to save lives and win souls to Jesus. I don't think they come just to talk for forty-five minutes, twenty-five minutes, however long they talk. I think they're up there to do a job, and that's what they do.

GERALDINE: I think the preaching comes just like a doctor comes to see his patients. He knows that they have a need, and he's there to fill that need, but he's also there to do some diagnosis also and to give out some prescriptions and also to give advice, such as to go out and evangelize. He's not preaching just to the saved, but he's preaching to the unsaved. The church is like a hospital. You're going to have all kinds there. You're going to have some that are a little sick, some that are real sick, and we all, because we all sin daily…We don't sin in that great abounds, but we all commit sins. The preacher is there to help us to know what salve to put on that sin in order to live right, do the things that are right and get well.

CHARLES: I think he comes to talk about, to focus us on Christ, because he continually talks about, "Don't get caught looking at your circumstances." Focus on God and the scripture that I am always reminded of: Matthew 6:33 says, "Seek ye first the kingdom of God, and his righteousness," and all the other things will line up. So if you start seeking something else, they ain't going to line up, because you're going to miss God. You've got to seek

Him, and he continually gets us to stop looking at that and look at God. He does it in all kinds of different ways, and he's really matured in how he delivers sermons and how he allows the Spirit to use him. He'll start off to make something, and the Spirit will move, or he'll go a different direction. He's just…Oh, my goodness…Because he's ministering at a different level to everybody in there, like you were talking about. Different people in the hospital—but the Master comes in through the pastor, and he allows him to let it flow through him to us and not kind of have his own agenda. He lets it flow.

INTERVIEWER: Tell me about a sermon that you found really engaging.

CHARLES: Well, there's so many with him. One, and I don't remember the name of the sermon; but it was about when David had decided to go get the ark of the covenant and bring it back to Jerusalem, and they made a fatal mistake. They put it on a cart, and when the cart rocked and it started to fall, Uzzah reached up to hit it, and it killed him. They became afraid. He started talking about that David was afraid of the Lord that day. They took it to Obed-edom's house, and while it was there it got blessed. Then they figured out what they'd done wrong. So what it was trying to tell us in our lives is that don't try to do it our way; you have to do it God's way. You thought it was terrible that Uzzah got struck down, because they were disobedient. Only the Levites carry the ark of the covenant. You don't build a cart for it. It really helped me in that sermon to see some things in my life that I was trying to do my way instead of the Lord's way, and I came out of there going…I didn't go in there expecting to receive that, but I came out of there with three or four answers of things that I was doing that really would have made me stumble and do some things I didn't want to do, but kind of gave me the word that Sunday.

INTERVIEWER: What do you think God is doing during the sermon?

CHARLES: If the minister, if the preacher is ordained…If the preacher is listening to God, God is ministering to people who need it, maybe one person in a way that they would never be able to receive it. When that happens…I know when it happened to me, I couldn't see anybody else. All I could see was the pastor. Words coming to me. I couldn't deflect that. Most people, you get it and deflect it. When you start being convicted about what the preacher is saying, you start thinking about somebody else's worse than you are. You start saying, "I only drink a little bit, but the guy over on the other bench, he's an alcoholic. So I know he's talking to him. He ain't talking to me." So until the Lord finally tells you, "Hey, I'm talking to you. It's me and you, not me and them. It's me and you." I think that's what's happening that he's delivering God's Word to those who are hurting as Geraldine had said earlier and it follows at different levels. That's the way the spirit of the Word is. It's not just for one person, but it can minister to people in different levels in different ways.

THOMAS: I think also…This is something our pastor talked about, I think, a couple of Sundays ago, teaching us to pray as God would have us to pray and to learn to listen. Just to be still and listen to God. Receive God's message, because we're being prepared for something much bigger than any of us might have any idea about. So I think God is working on us, to move us to that great place of eternity.

INTERVIEWER: Now tell me about a preacher whose physical presence in the pulpit is good.

GERALDINE: Here again, I'll talk about our pastor, because I've been under so many ministers, and I'm sure other people have, too, but I find our pastor to be just absolutely brilliant, knowledgeable, a scholar, a Godly man, and when he is in that pulpit, it's like everything else is just closed out, and we are here in one sanctuary. I just think that for me is truly my ideal.

JERRY: The church I grew up in, and that pastor is still there. I find his physical presence in the pulpit is very demanding, very commanding. I find him learned. I find him well grounded as our pastor in the Word and biblical scholarship. I like that.

ANN: Two ladies that have a wonderful presence are [a well-known preacher] and [another well-known preacher]. It's just when they walk down the aisle, go into the pulpit, you know that there's a Word there. It's just the way they stand. They have a commanding air about them without being arrogant. They have a humbleness about them also. Also you see them worship. One thing that [second woman preacher], I always notice her hands are going like this, and it's just like she's almost dancing with her hands. Their presence just stands out.

CHARLES: She's good. She's real animated. I remember that sermon she preached here not long ago about Jacob wrestling with the angel, leaping into destiny, and she leaped across there. She made you forget about how long she preached.

INTERVIEWER: What would you tell a preacher that would help energize you as you listen to the sermon? If there were one or two things, what would they be?

JERRY: To travel my mind. I want you to go after my mind (general agreement). I want you to go after something in my intellect and feed me something that I can hang onto.

CHARLES: I love metaphorical preaching. There are several men around the country that I've heard on radio who are…And [a well-known TV preacher] is one who is a metaphorical kind of preacher that he comes out of left field with stuff. Now our pastor is like that, but our pastor always seems to me, always hits my appetite for the Word better than [the TV preacher]. He gets my appetite for the Word. He's not the kind of preacher who says, or pastor who says, "I want you to study the word," and then he does a sloppy job preparing himself, and then you run on ahead of him, saying, "I thought he was going…" Our pastor doesn't ever leave you that way. He leaves me wanting more. "Man, I never looked at that scripture like that." The other way he exposits the scripture, and that's what I like about him, that he's an all around preacher. Some preachers are great teachers, and some are great whoopers, and I don't like people who whoop. I turn it off as [I would] a kid. Like you were saying about kids when they scream and holler, you don't remember what they preached about, but our pastor has that balance that I like. He preaches good. He sticks with his scripture. He's not making up stuff as he goes, and he just challenges my mind. So a lot of times I take a lot of notes. I was sitting next to a guy in church, and he asked me. He was a friend of mine. He watched me taking these notes during the sermon. He says, "Why are you taking those notes?" I said, "Because it spurs me to think about other things, and I write it down. I go read the scripture again and read what he's told me to read. That way it fills me." I never see anybody take that many notes, but that's what he has taught me how to do is to write some of the things down that he says and not just take the sermon and go. I'd look at it again.

ANN: Did you say it was a suggestion? What suggestions would we give? When you do the whooping, and I've heard some white ministers, but it seems that black ministers have that trait where they "uhhhh" breathe in. I can't stand that. It's like I'm choking when they do that. If I could ever in a book tell them not to do that. Please don't. I don't know what that does, because I'm not a minister and I don't know that they get so excited that they can't breathe or what it is, but it turns me off.

THOMAS: I just wanted to just say real fast, I would suggest that pastors learn a way to bring peace–among their congregation. I want to just give you an example. Yesterday we were watching the news of the world. I was very distraught, and then I came here last night, and we had a prayer vigil. Our pastor gave people a chance to pray, to stand up and pray, and he called out the topic that we were to pray on. Then he did a prayer that just brought us together, and that fear that I had come in here with turned into just love and peace. That is what I would suggest pastors to do.

MAUDE: I think one of the suggestions I would make is not to really try to be there for popularity contests and not to try to follow the greatest giver or elder or whatever or whomever, but just look to Jesus and whatever that Spirit tells you to say, preach that, because then that's what's going to reach your congregation.

JERRY: I like the idea that we are all the sheep and because we're sheep, we attract other sheep, and he is the shepherd that tends this flock. I like the analogy of being the sheep because sheep are dumb just like we are. We won't come in out of the rain.

CHARLES: I think our pastor is so great at uniting a diverse bunch of people, especially African American people coming from all kinds of backgrounds, attitudes. He's able to unite us together in the peace of Christ, uniting us. That's because God has given that ability to be able to read what people need. He doesn't talk to me the same way he talks to Thomas. He doesn't talk to me the same way he talks to Geraldine, because he knows us. It's amazing how he knows about his sheep, and he can sense when something's not going right with me. He can sense when it's not going right with Jerry. In his sermons he can know that there's unrest in the congregation, but when we come out of there, we're unified and peaceful no matter how you came in, you go out of there. So it keeps us bound together in that horizontal worship of Christ by treating one another right.

Sample Questions for Interviewing

This appendix contains the basic questions that our research team asked the interviewees. We say "basic" questions because sensitive interviewers often asked follow-through questions or rephrased these questions to account for local context. We pass along these questions as samples that you might take into account when preparing your own interviews.

Two qualities in these questions can usually serve as models for other questions. First, they are open-ended. They do not suggest that the listener answer the question in a certain way. They allow interviewees to tell the questioner what is on their hearts and minds. Second, they are simple and direct. A long and involved question is often hard to follow and hard to answer.

The questions are grouped according to the categories of ethos, logos, pathos, and embodiment. At times, the interviewers asked the questions in pretty much the order in which they appear here. At other times, a listener's response would suggest that the interviewer move to a question from another category.

All of the questions are on one sheet of paper so that the interviewer can see all of the questions to be asked. When skipping from category to category the sheet reminds the interviewer of questions still to be raised. By having the questions on one sheet, the interviewer also has a minimum of amount of paper to clutter the interview space.

Because small group interviews move much more slowly than individual interviews, we have marked questions to be asked in small groups with an asterisk.

Ethos

Tell me about how you became a part of this congregation.

What are the most important things that happen in this congregation?

* Describe a typical Sunday morning in this congregation.

Talk a little bit about your relationship with the pastors and preachers that you have had.

* Tell me about a pastor you have had who was also a good preacher.

Tell me what preaching does in this congregation that other things do not do.

What would be missing if there were no sermon?

Tell me about your history as a person listening to sermons. What are some of the high points? What are some of the low points?

Was there ever a time when you almost walked out?

Logos

* What do you think your pastor is doing when she or he preaches?
* Tell me about a sermon that you really found engaging.
* What was it about that sermon that engaged you?
* Tell me about a sermon that did not interest you or that put you off.

What was it about that sermon that left you cold or put you off?

* What does God do in preaching?

What role does/should the Bible have in preaching?

What causes you to take a sermon really seriously?

I'll bet you have heard a sermon that caused you to think or act differently, maybe about some big issue, maybe about some small issue. Would you tell me about that sermon?

What did the pastor say or do that prompted you to act differently?

Pathos

* When the pastor stands up to preach, what do you hope will happen to you as a result of listening to that sermon?
* I would like for you to describe a sermon that seemed to affect the congregation as a whole, as a community.
* What was it about that sermon that seemed to move the congregation?

Would you describe a time when the sermon stirred emotions that made you feel uncomfortable.

* Do you think there are some issues that are just too explosive, too dangerous, for the preacher to deal with in the pulpit? Would you name some of them for me and tell me why you think they are dangerous?

Embodiment

* Would you please describe for me a preacher whose physical presence in the pulpit was really good—whose delivery was really engaging?
* What are some things a preacher does physically (while delivering the sermon) that help you to want to pay attention?

How do the physical conditions of being able to hear and see the preacher affect the way you pay attention to a sermon?

**If you had one or two things you could tell preachers that would help them turn you on when you are listening to a sermon, what would they be?

Description of the Project

In this appendix we describe the project. Rather than undertake quantifiable study from a random sample and generating massive amounts of statistical data, we thought it would be of more help to preachers to do a qualitative study through extensive interviews. While wanting to be alert to patterns that listeners have in common, our primary purpose in this book is to ponder what the interviewees say from the perspectives of their local contexts. Indeed, one of the most dramatic revelations of this study is that each congregation, and each listener, is remarkably distinct.

As noted in chapter 1, the research team envisions this project as a first step in helping preachers develop ways of discovering how listeners respond to sermons.[1] Our sample of congregations is small and limited to selected denominations and Christian movements in parts of the Midwest and mid-South, We do not purport to be able to report on how people everywhere listen to sermons. We hope that other preachers and researchers will investigate other denominations, movements, and contexts.[2]

The project directors and advisory board used the following principles to select the congregations in a study that would be limited enough in scope to be manageable, and yet would provide enough diversity to allow for modest comparisons and contrasts.

Geographical distribution. We decided to work in congregations fairly close to Indianapolis because the advisory board is largely from that region, and members are familiar with that area and could easily invite congregations to be in the study. The congregations in the study are in central and southern Indiana, Chicago, central Illinois, eastern Missouri, northern Kentucky, and southwest Ohio, with one congregation from Tennessee.[3] Twenty-eight congregations participated in the study.[4]

Racial composition. We wanted significant percentages of both African American and Caucasian congregations since these are the two largest racial groups in the study area. In the study were nine predominantly African

American congregations, sixteen predominantly Caucasian congregations, and three congregations that are mixed.

Gender. We aimed to interview percentages of women and men in the study approximately similar to the percentages of women and men in the congregations.

Denominational make-up. We sought congregations from a variety of denominations that represent different liturgical styles and different understandings of the nature and purpose of the church.[5]

Protestant. The research was limited to Protestant congregations to keep the study in an arena in which project leaders felt competent.

Different localities. We recruited congregations from different localities. These included rural congregations, small-town churches, suburban congregations, and urban communities.

Different ages. Within each congregation, we tried to interview people from different age groups—older adults, middle-aged adults, and younger adults.

We selected congregations for the study by talking with judicatory leaders to determine healthy local churches that seemed to represent the various categories in the study. We do not, of course, have a full complement of congregations to represent each category in the study as outlined above.

Within each congregation, we interviewed five or six individuals for an hour to an hour and a half each.[6] We also interviewed a small group of five to seven persons in most congregations. We did not use the small groups as true "focus groups" in the manner of hard sociological research but as sounding boards for the perspectives from the individual interviews. We wanted to see whether what the individuals said about the congregation resonated with others in community and were not idiosyncratic. Slightly more than 260 laity were interviewed. [7]

The questions (discussed in chapter 1 and printed as a set in appendix B) invited people to reflect generally on aspects of preaching that they find appealing and distancing and to illustrate their answers (as possible) with recollections from specific sermons.[8]

The interviewers visited each congregation on two different weekends.[9] In addition to conducting the interviews, these interviewers visited the service of worship twice and not only described the service of worship but also the neighborhood in which the church building is located, the condition and décor of the building, and, most importantly, the character of the members' interactions with one another.[10] Such observations provide further context for interpreting the interviews.

Although the congregations interviewed in our study do not allow us to speak with the confidence that a large random sample would have, we believe the sample is sufficiently representative to allow us to put forth methods and conclusions that can be tested in wider arenas. We expect listening patterns in congregations in different geographical areas or social worlds, or with different racial and ethnic make-up, to manifest characteristics typical of those areas or constituencies.

Notes

Introduction

[1]Anthropologists use the term "thick description" to indicate a depth of understanding of community that includes not only obvious indicators of community life (such as public statements) but underlying feelings, mores, practices that shape community and communicate values, symbols, modes of social organization, and behavior. See Clifford Geertz, *The Interpretation of Cultures* (New York: Basic Books, 1973), 6–7, 9–10, 12–16, 25–28.

[2]The full membership of the advisory board is given in appendix C, note 1 (p. 196).

Chapter 1: Listening to the Heart, Mind, and Will of the Congregation

[1]For representative attempts to pay attention to the listener in preaching, see Ronald J. Allen, "The Turn toward the Listener: A Selective Review of a Recent Trend in Preaching," *Encounter* 64 (2003): 165–94.

[2]Bernard Meland, *Fallible Forms and Symbols: Discourses of Method in a Theology of Culture* (Philadelphia: Fortress Press, 1976), 28.

[3]We promised anonymity to all persons and congregations in the study. All persons and congregations agreed that we may use anonymous quotations and other citations in published works. We provide general information about the interviewees (e.g., gender, age, race, setting, theological or ecclesiological orientation of the congregation) when such perspective is important for understanding the material with which we are dealing.

[4]The focus of our project is on persons who listen regularly to sermons in a given congregation. We believe that preachers have much to learn about preaching from members who attend worship erratically and those who seldom attend. We further believe that preachers can learn much about preaching from persons who do not relate to church at all. However, such investigations would take us beyond the scope of this book.

[5]On thick description see above, note 1, Introduction. On congregational studies, see: James R. Neiman and Thomas G. Rodgers, *Preaching from Pew to Pew* (Minneapolis: Fortress Press, 2001); Thomas Edward Frank, *The Soul of the Congregation: An Invitation to Congregational Reflection* (Nashville: Abingdon Press, 2000); Stephen Farris, *Preaching that Matters: The Bible and Our Lives* (Louisville: Westminster John Knox Press, 1998); Nancy T. Ammerman, Jackson W. Carroll, Carl S. Dudley, and William McKinney, eds., *Studying Congregations: A New Handbook* (Nashville: Abingdon Press, 1998); Leonora Tubbs Tisdale, *Preaching as Local Theology and Folk Art,* Fortress Resources for Preaching (Minneapolis: Fortress Press, 1997); James F. Hopewell, *Congregation: Stories and Structures* (Philadelphia: Fortress Press, 1987).

[6]In the interview settings, the interviewers spent enough time in the congregations to recognize significant aspects of the congregational context and listener perceptions. Nevertheless, our interviewers were not able to pick up the full range of the richness and resonance that a preacher would recognize from being immersed (and critically reflective on) a congregational culture. In this book, we try to limit our interpretive remarks to the extent of the depth of our acquaintance with the persons and congregations who are subjects in the study. There are many things about these individuals and congregations that the interviewers and interpreting team simply do not know.

[7]On the adequacy of speaking of preaching as an event of persuasion, see the interchange between two prominent teachers of preaching: Lucy Lind Hogan, "Rethinking Persuasion: Developing an Incarnational Theology of Preaching," *Homiletic* 24/2 (1999): 1–12; and Richard Lischer, "Why I Am Not Persuasive," *Homiletic* 24/2 (1999): 13–16.

[8]Aristotle, *The "Art" of Rhetoric,* tr. John Henry Freese, Loeb Classical Library, vol. 23 (Cambridge, Mass.: Harvard Univ. Press, 1932), 17 (1.2.4–6). For lucid guides to the use of these categories in contemporary preaching and theology, see Lucy Lind Hogan and Robert Reid, *Connecting with the Congregation: Rhetoric and the Art of Preaching* (Nashville: Abingdon Press, 1999) and David S. Cunningham, *Faithful Persuasion: In Aid of Rhetoric of Christian Theology* (Notre Dame, Ind.: Univ. of Notre Dame Press, 1990).

⁹The questions are listed in appendix B, p. 182.

¹⁰Aristotle, *The "Art" of Rhetoric,* 17 (1.2.4).

¹¹Lind Hogan and Reid, *Connecting with the Congregation,* 50–65, make a distinction between internal and external ethos. The former is the perception of the congregation that arises because of factors that occur during the sermon itself, i.e., they are internal to the sermon. The latter refers to perceptions that are generated outside the preaching event itself but that the congregation brings to the sermon. While this taxonomy is heuristically useful, for the sake of simplifying the discussions that follow, we employ the term "ethos" broadly to include both phenomena. Furthermore, while we can imagine speaking of congregational culture (see below) as external ethos, such an approach does not seem to the authors of this book to do justice to the pervasive and thick relationship between congregational culture and preaching.

¹²Cunningham, *Faithful Persuasion,* 132–139.

¹³Lind Hogan and Reid, *Connecting with the Congregation,* 53–60.

¹⁴Cunningham, *Faithful Persuasion,* 127–31, 139–47.

¹⁵Lind Hogan and Reid, *Connecting with the Congregation,* 91.

¹⁶For a critique of "pure logic," see Cunningham, *Faithful Persuasion,* 157–64.

¹⁷The authors of this book are not quite sure where to place imagination in relationship to the categories of ethos, logos, and pathos since Aristotle does not include an extensive discussion of imagination as a mode of "argument" in *The "Art" of Rhetoric.* However, the great philosopher implicitly recognized the importance of this realm of human interaction by writing *The Poetics.* See Aristotle, *The Poetics,* tr. W. Hamilton Fyfe, The Loeb Classical Library, vol. 23 (Cambridge, Mass.: Harvard Univ. Press, 1932), 3–120. On the notion of sermon as imaginative experience, see especially Robert Reid, Jeffrey Bullock, and David Fleer, "Preaching as the Creation of an Experience: The Not-So-Rational Revolution of the New Homiletic," *The Journal of Communication and Religion* 18/1 (1995): 1–18.

¹⁸Aristotle, *The "Art" of Rhetoric,* 17 (1.2.5).

¹⁹Lind Hogan and Reid, *Connecting with the Congregation,* 83.

²⁰Ibid., 75.

²¹Kenneth Burke, *A Rhetoric of Motives* (Berkeley: Univ. of California Press, 1969, o.p., 1950), 69. For an approach to preaching that places identification at the center, see Craig A. Loscalzo, *Preaching Sermons that Connect: Effective Communication Through Identification* (Downers Grove, Ill.: InterVarsity Press, 1992). Similar themes appear in Loscalzo's later works, such as *Evangelistic Preaching That Connects: Guidance in Shaping Fresh and Appealing Sermons* (Downers Grove, Ill.: InterVarsity Press, 1995).

²²Karlyn Kohrs Campbell, *The Rhetorical Act,* 2d ed. (New York; Wadsworth, 1996), 132.

²³On the notion of negotiating a hearing, see further John S. McClure, *The Four Codes of Preaching: Rhetorical Strategies* (Minneapolis: Fortress Press, 1991), 12–13, 23–24, 28–29, 34–36, 40–42, 45–46, 67, 71–72, 79–80, 85, 110, 115–16, 120, 124, 131, 148–49, 157, 162, 165–66. McClure shows that negotiating a hearing occurs through identification. McClure extends this insight dialogically in his *The Roundtable Pulpit: Where Leadership and Preaching Meet* (Nashville: Abingdon Press, 1995) and accounts for difference (aspects of nonidentification) in *Other-wise Preaching: A Postmodern Ethic for Homiletics* (St. Louis: Chalice Press, 2001).

²⁴Indeed, according to Robin Meyers, preachers must persuade themselves of the worthiness of their messages. See his *With Ears to Hear: Preaching as Self-Persuasion* (Cleveland: The Pilgrim Press, 1993).

²⁵As noted earlier, participants in the study were guaranteed anonymity. The names we use are pseudonyms.

²⁶The average transcript is about twenty-five pages of double-spaced typing.

²⁷For a taxonomy relating historical and contemporary theological families, see Ronald J. Allen, *Preaching Is Believing: The Sermon as Theological Reflection* (Louisville: Westminster John Knox Press, 2002), 129–41; for a practical means of determining and reflecting on the actual theology that one preaches, see John S. McClure and Burton Z Cooper, *Claiming Theology in the Pulpit* (Louisville: Westminster John Knox Press, 2003).

Chapter 2: "Like I'm Dancing Right There without Dancing"

¹William B. McClain, *Black People in the Methodist Church: Whither Thou Goest?* (Cambridge, Mass.: Schenkman Publishing, 1984), 19–23.

²Readers may recognize a similarity between our rhetorical categories and the subject of learning styles. A couple of classics are Howard Gardner's *Multiple Intelligences: The Theory in Practice* (New York: Basic Books, 1993) and Kay Vandergrift, ed., *Ways of Knowing* (Lanham, Md.: Scarecrow Press, 1995).

³The work of Henry H. Mitchell is probably most representative of this perspective. See *The Recovery of Preaching* (San Francisco: Harper and Row, 1977); *Black Preaching: The Recovery of a Powerful Art* (Nashville: Abingdon Press, 1990); *Celebration and Experience in Preaching* (Nashville: Abingdon Press, 1990).

⁴For surveys of contemporary African American preaching theories and styles, see L. Susan Bond, *Contemporary African American Preaching: Diversity in Theory and Style* (St. Louis: Chalice Press, 2003); Cleophus J. LaRue, *The Heart of Black Preaching* (Louisville: Westminster John Knox Press, 2000).

⁵See Samuel D. Proctor, *Preaching About Crises in the Community* (Philadelphia: Westminster Press, 1988); and Samuel D. Proctor and Gardner C. Taylor, *We Have This Ministry: The Heart of the Pastor's Vocation* (Valley Forge, Pa.: Judson Press, 1996). See also Bond, *Contemporary African American Preaching*, 35–49.

⁶James A. Forbes, Jr., *The Holy Spirit and Preaching* (Nashville: Abingdon Press, 1989), 15.

⁷Henry H. Mitchell, *Celebration and Experience in Preaching*, 34.

⁸Please see John McClure's comments on Pelagianism, Calvinism, and the human possibilities for perfection in chapter 5.

⁹G. Lee Ramsey, Jr., *Care-full Preaching: From Sermon to Caring Community* (St. Louis: Chalice Press, 2000), 28. Ramsey's work has one of the most thorough discussions of theological anthropology in contemporary homiletical literature.

¹⁰Randy Maddox is a contemporary theologian who deals with the ongoing legacy of Wesleyan thought. See his *Responsible Grace: John Wesley's Practical Theology* (Nashville: Abingdon Press, 1994); see also the book edited by Maddox, *Rethinking Wesley's Theology for Contemporary Methodism* (Nashville: Abingdon Press, 1998). See a collection of other essays, edited by W. Stephen Gunter, *Wesley and the Quadrilateral: Renewing the Conversation* (Nashville: Abingdon Press, 1997).

¹¹See Melva Wilson Costen's excellent work on worship and preaching traditions within African American Protestantism, *African American Christian Worship* (Nashville: Abingdon Press, 1993).

Chapter 3: "All of a Sudden, I've Got to Concentrate on the Sermon"

¹I am grateful to Dawn Ottoni Wilhelm of Bethany Theological Seminary for her insights about preaching within the Anabaptist tradition, and for her constructive comments about interpretation of the gospel as a shared responsibility between the Anabaptist preacher and congregation. For further discussion, see David B. Greiser and Michael A. King, eds., *Anabaptist Preaching: A Conversation Between Pulpit, Pew, and Bible* (Telford, Pa.: Cascadia Publishing House, 2003).

²See T.H.L. Parker, *The Oracles of God: An Introduction to the Preaching of John Calvin* (London: Lutterworth Press, 1947).

³For a more complete discussion see G. Lee Ramsey, Jr., *Care-full Preaching: From Sermon to Caring Community* (St. Louis, Chalice Press, 2002), 19–23.

⁴For a comprehensive discussion of preaching as shared endeavor between congregation and preacher, see Lucy Atkinson Rose, *Sharing the Word: Preaching in the Roundtable Church* (Louisville: Westminster John Knox Press, 1997). Cf. John S. McClure, *The Roundtable Pulpit: Where Leadership and Preaching Meet* (Nashville: Abingdon Press, 1995).

⁵See Ramsey, *Care-full Preaching*, 59–77, for a discussion of how preaching shapes congregations over time. Also, Leonora Tubbs Tisdale discusses the theologically formative dimensions of preaching in *Preaching as Local Theology and Folk Art*, Fortress Resources for Preaching (Minneapolis: Fortress Press, 1997).

Chapter 4: "I Told You, It's about Relationship"

¹William H. Pipes, *Say Amen, Brother! Old-Time Negro Preaching: A Study in American Frustration* (Detroit: Wayne State Univ. Press, 1979; originally published in New York: William-Frederick Press, 1951), 90–91, 110–13, 120–21, 136, 148–55.

[2]Teresa L. Fry Brown, *God Don't Like Ugly: African American Women Handing on Spiritual Values* (Nashville: Abingdon Press, 2000), 27–29, 54, 58–59, 63–85.

[3]Theodore Runyon, *The New Creation: John Wesley's Theology Today* (Nashville: Abingdon Press, 1998), 150–55.

[4]Colin W. Williams, *John Wesley's Theology Today: A Study of the Wesleyan Tradition in Light of Current Theological Dialogue* (Nashville: Abingdon Press, 1960), 142–46, 150–55.

[5]Ibid., 41–44; Runyon, *New Creation,* 27–31.

[6]Thomas A. Langford, *Practical Divinity: Theology in the Wesleyan Tradition* (Nashville: Abingdon Press, 1983), 43–45.

[7]Williams, *John Wesley's Theology,* 132–35.

[8]Romans 8:22–25, NRSV.

[9]Williams, *John Wesley's Theology,* 66–68.

[10]Ibid., 182–87.

Chapter 5: "It's a God Thing"

[1]Aristotle, *The "Art" of Rhetoric,* tr. John Henry Freese, Loeb Classical Library, vol. 23 (Cambridge, Mass.: Harvard Univ. Press, 1932), 193–96 (2.4 1ff.), 225–27 (2.8 1 ff.).

[2]In Stephen Ray, *Do No Harm: Social Sin and Christian Responsibility* (Minneapolis: Fortress Press, 2003), 107.

[3]Ibid., 3–7. At the level of social relationships, this permits some people to be grouped together as humanly marginal or even "defiled" in their sinful "difference."

[4]See Karl Barth, *Church Dogmatics,* ed. Geoffrey Bromiley and Thomas F. Torrance (Edinburgh, T. & T. Clark, 1956–1977), especially vol. 1.2: "Revelation of God"; Hans Frei, *The Doctrine of Revelation in the Thought of Karl Barth, 1909 to 1922: The Nature of Barth's Break with Liberalism* (master's thesis, Yale University, 1956). See also Rodney Holder, "Karl Barth and the Legitimacy of Natural Theology," *Themelios* 26 no. 3 (Summer 2001): 22–37.

[5]See John Howard Yoder, *The Politics of Jesus; vicit Agnus noster* (Grand Rapids: Eerdmans, 1972); Stanley Hauerwas and William Willimon, *Resident Aliens: Life in the Christian Colony* (Nashville: Abingdon Press, 1989), a provocative Christian assessment of culture and ministry for people who know that something is wrong.

Chapter 6: "It Was like Jesus Himself Was Coming"

[1]Tex Sample, *Ministry in an Oral Culture: Living with Will Rogers, Uncle Remus, and Minnie Pearl* (Nashville: Abingdon Press, 1994).

[2]Robert Dykstra, *Discovering a Sermon: Personal Pastoral Preaching* (St. Louis: Chalice Press, 2002).

Chapter 7: "The Sermon Is the Central Point"

[1]On preaching and the congregational system, see Ronald J. Allen, *Preaching and Practical Ministry,* Preaching and Its Partners (St. Louis: Chalice Press, 2000).

[2]Indeed, according to Edwin Friedman, a rabbi and pioneer in thinking of congregations from the perspective of family systems theory, a leader's sense of self and mode of being in community is often the single most important dimension in shaping a congregational system. See Edwin H. Friedman, *A Failure of Nerve: Leadership in the Age of the Quick Fix* (Bethesda, Md.: The Edwin Friedman Estate, 1999). For more muted discussions of the place of the leader in the congregational system, see Friedman's earlier *Reinventing Leadership* (New York: Guilford Press, 1996) and *From Generation to Generation: Family Process in Church and Synagogue* (New York: Guilford Press, 1985).

[3]See C. H. Dodd, *The Apostolic Proclamation and Its Development* (New York: Harper and Row, 1964); and Robert Worley, *Preaching and Teaching in the Earliest Church* (Philadelphia: Westminster Press, 1967), whose views are now modified in scholarship, as reported by Allen, *Preaching and Practical Ministry,* 29–46.

[4]On different modes of teaching in the sermon, see Ronald J. Allen, *The Teaching Sermon* (Nashville: Abingdon Press, 1995); cf. Dan P. Moseley, "Teaching Leaders for Congregations," *Encounter* 63 (2002): 159–68.

[5]Indeed, according to theologian and philosopher Bernard Loomer, the most persuasive form of evidence is the embodiment of a truth or ideal in a person. See his "S-I-Z-E is the

Measure" in Harry James Cargas and Bernard Lee, eds., *Religious Experience and Process Theology: The Pastoral Implications of a Major Modern Movement* (New York: Paulist Press, 1976), 74–75.

[6]Clark M. Williamson and Ronald J. Allen, *A Credible and Timely Word: Process Theology and Preaching* (St. Louis: Chalice Press, 1991), 71–90; id., *The Teaching Minister* (Louisville: Westminster John Knox Press, 1991), 65–82. Ronald J. Allen, *Preaching Is Believing: The Sermon as Theological Reflection* (Louisville: Westminster John Knox Press, 2001), 51–58.

Chapter 8: Insights, Discoveries, and Things to Watch

[1]We did not ask follow-up questions that might have revealed *why* congregants thought they had not been previously asked about their perceptions of preaching, nor did we ask how they *felt* about not previously being invited to voice their impression of preaching.

[2]On congregational culture, see the literature cited in chapter 9, notes 1, 4, and 5.

[3]A classic study along this line is Mark Johnson and George Lakoff, *Metaphors We Live By* (Chicago: Univ. of Chicago Press, 1980). For a generation, preachers and theoreticians have given increasing attention to metaphorical (and other figurative) dimensions in the content of the sermon. We take this interest a slight step further to focus on how metaphors (and others figures of speech) parishioners use to refer to the act of preaching provide significant clues into the ways they perceive the nature and purpose of the sermon.

[4]When hunting possum, the hunter often goes at night to look for the animal in the tree. The hunter shines a light into the eyes of the possum in the tree so the animal freezes. The hunter can then fire at an unmoving target.

[5]Other commentators also call attention to this phenomenon, such as David Cunningham, *Faithful Persuasion: In Aid of a Rhetoric of Christian Theology* (Notre Dame, Ind.: Univ. of Notre Dame Press, 1990), 101–3; and Lucy Lind Hogan and Robert Reid, *Connecting with the Congregation: Rhetoric and the Art of Preaching* (Nashville: Abingdon Press, 1999), 50–53.

[6]The authors of this book suspect that this concern results from the many occurrences of failure in integrity among public leaders that have become increasingly publicized in the late twentieth century and early twenty-first century.

[7]However, about 5 percent of the persons interviewed said that the character of the preacher is of little significance to the way they deal with the content of the sermon. These persons (whose primary points of entry are mainly logos) say they listen for the degree to which the content qua content is trustworthy. Lack of congruence between what the preacher says and the preacher's life may trouble them, but they still listen for the content of the preacher's message. Indeed, as one woman says, "I can hear the truth from a person even if I don't like the person or even if I don't care for the person…If you are seeking the truth, the message will come through and you'll pick it up even if you have distractions in doing so."

[8]In the wider context of the interview, as John McClure points out, this listener wants the ministers to be morally and spiritually ideal while also being very human and "real" (a pathos value, p. 82).

[9]With respect to theology, such observations do not necessarily cancel out the claims of the traditional doctrine *ex opere operatum*. The efficacy of preaching, as with the sacraments, is not finally dependent on the character of the preacher. Rather, the observations of our listeners suggest that many do weigh clergy integrity as relevant for the authority of the sermon.

[10]Thomas G. Long, "And How Shall They Hear? The Listener in Contemporary Preaching," in *Listening to the Word: Studies in Honor of Fred B. Craddock*, ed. Gail R. O'Day and Thomas G. Long (Nashville: Abingdon Press, 1993), 174. In lyrical fashion, Long notes that the use of rhetoric to help understand preaching, beginning in the first part of the twentieth century, suffered a "Barth attack." Barth's work, along with some others, gave impetus to the Biblical Theology Movement that shaped much preaching in North America in the mid- to late twentieth century. For a description and assessment of that effect, see David G. Buttrick, *A Captive Voice: The Liberation of Preaching* (Louisville: Westminster John Knox Press, 1994), 5–32.

[11]Long, "And How Shall They Hear," 181–88.

[12]For bibliography, see Ronald J. Allen, "The Turn to the Listener: A Selected Review of Literature," *Encounter* 64 (2003): 165–94.

[13]Although the interviews probed listener perceptions of embodiment, as well as of ethos, logos, and pathos, we did not find a single listener for whom embodiment appears to

function as the primary setting through which the listener receives the sermon. The research team wondered whether there would be correlations between different styles of embodiment and hearing the sermon through the ethos, logos, and pathos settings. Would persons who listen to the sermon through ethos settings respond favorably to distinctive qualities of embodiment? Persons who hear through logos settings? Pathos settings? The only correlation we found along this line was a preference, among some folk who listen to the sermon on pathos settings, that the embodiment mediates and encourages feeling. Such listeners are drawn to sermons in which preachers display emotions that are appropriate to the congregational culture.

[14]We struggle to find language that adequately portrays the relationship between the appeal that is the point of entry into the world of the sermon and its dynamic relationship with the ways in which the listener responds to other appeals. For a fuller discussion, see Ronald J. Allen, *Hearing the Sermon: Relationship, Content, Feeling* (St. Louis: Chalice Press, forthcoming).

Chapter 9: Approaches to Interviewing in the Congregation

[1]See Thomas Edward Frank, *The Soul of the Congregation: An Invitation to Congregational Reflection* (Nashville: Abingdon Press, 2000), 61–66, 78–83. Frank uses the phrase "soul of the congregation" to include what we are here calling "congregational culture."

[2]Ibid., 78–79.

[3]On thick description from an anthropological point of view, see note 1, Introduction, p. 189.

[4]The interviewers who conducted the interviews for the study on which this book is based made participant observations of the congregations in which they interviewed. Their observations (on which we draw in the introductory remarks to the case studies above) provide a sense of context for the interviewees' remarks in the transcripts. Per Scott L. Thumma, "Methods of Congregational Study," in *Studying Congregations: A New Handbook,* ed. Nancy T. Ammerman, Jackson W. Carroll, Carl S. Dudley, and William McKinney (Nashville: Abingdon Press, 1998), 200–201, the interviewers described the demographic make-up of the worshiping congregation, the physical setting, the service of worship, interactional patterns in the congregation, the verbal and written content of the service, and the meaning of these things (as best the interviewers could make it out). The methods we propose in this book are much more detailed and presume that the observer (the pastor, members of the congregation, or consultants) have access to much deeper awareness of the congregation.

[5]To use the language of contemporary congregational studies, we think of the pastor as a participant-observer, that is, as someone who is participating in the fullness of life in the congregation, but who engages in disciplined observation of the community. See Thumma, "Methods for Congregational Study," 197–203, and Nancy T. Ammerman, "Culture and Identity in the Congregation," in *Studying Congregations,* 82–84.

[6]The simple exercises in this chapter are derived primarily from *Studying Congregations* and from Frank, *The Soul of the Congregation;* as well as from Leonora Tubbs Tisdale, *Preaching as Local Theology and Folk Art,* Fortress Resources for Preaching (Minneapolis: Fortress Press, 1997); James R. Nieman and Thomas G. Rogers, *Preaching to Every Pew: Cross Cultural Strategies* (Minneapolis: Fortress Press, 2001); and Joseph R. Jeter, Jr., and Ronald J. Allen, *One Gospel, Many Ears: Preaching for Different Listeners in the Congregation* (St. Louis: Chalice Press, 2002). Such ruminations can become a part of, and be enhanced by, regular pastoral listening to the congregation while calling in homes, hospitals, workplaces, schools, and leisure sites. For further guidance see Robert F. Schreiter, *Constructing Local Theologies* (Maryknoll, N.Y.: Orbis Books, 1985); James F. Hopewell, *Congregations: Stories and Structures* (Philadelphia: Fortress Press, 1987); Stephen Warner, *New Wine in Old Wineskins: Evangelicals and Liberals in a Small-Town Church* (Berkeley: Univ. of California Press, 1988); Allison Stokes and David Roozen, "The Unfolding Story of Congregational Studies" in *Carriers of Faith,* ed. Carl S. Dudley, Jackson W. Carroll, and James P. Wind (Louisville: Westminster/John Knox Press, 1991), 183–92; Don S. Browning, *Fundamental Practical Theology: Description and Strategic Proposals* (Minneapolis: Fortress Press, 1991); Samuel G. Freedman, *Upon This Rock: The Miracles of a Black Church* (San Francisco: HarperCollins Publishers, 1993); James P. Wind and James W. Lewis, eds., *American Congregations* (Chicago: Univ. of Chicago Press, 1994), 2 vols. For a study of how ethnography can have subversive outcomes, see Alex García-Rivera, *St. Martide Porres: The "Little Stories" and the Semiotics of Culture* (Maryknoll: Orbis Books, 1995).

[7]Tubbs Tisdale, *Preaching as Local Theology and Folk Art,* 70–71; Thumma, "Methods for Congregational Study," 200, 203–6. Nancy Eiesland and Stephen Warner indicate values in being aware of the demographics of the congregation's neighborhood in their "Ecology: Seeing the Congregation in Context," in *Studying Congregations,* 55–63.

[8]Robert Cueni, *Dinosaur Heart Transplants: Renewing Mainline Congregations* (Nashville: Abingdon Press, 2000).

[9]George Parsons and Speed B. Leas, *Understanding Your Congregation as a System* (Washington, D.C.: The Alban Institute, 1993), 9; cf. Carl S. Dudley, "Process: Dynamics of Congregational Life," in *Studying Congregations,* 107–8.

[10]Tubbs Tisdale, *Preaching as Local Theology and Folk Art,* 69–70.

[11]Thumma, "Methods for Congregational Study," 209–12; cf. Nancy L. Eiesland and Stephen Warner, "Ecology: Seeing the Congregation in Context," 43–47.

[12]Frank, *The Soul of the Congregation,* 163–64.

[13]For an approach to space, see William McKinney with Anthony T. Ruger, Diane Cohen, and Robert Jeager, "Resources," in *Studying Congregations,* 156–64.

[14]Cf. Nancy T. Ammerman, "Culture and Identity in the Congregation," 91–92.

[15]Frank, *The Soul of the Congregation,* 165–66. Eiesland and Warner, "Ecology: Seeing the Congregation in Context," 47–50, propose that the pastor and other persons take a space walk that includes the exterior of the building and grounds and the neighborhood in which the congregation is located.

[16]Craig Dykstra, *Growing in the Life of Faith: A Way of Life for a Searching People* (San Francisco: Jossey-Bass, 1997), 27–28.

[17]Frank, *The Soul of the Congregation,* 43–56.

[18]On preaching as a Christian practice and its place in the congregational system see Ronald J. Allen, *Preaching and Practical Ministry,* Preaching and Its Partners (St. Louis: Chalice Press, 2000).

[19]Many of these questions are inspired by Thumma, "Methods for Congregational Study," 200. Cf. Nancy Ammerman, "Culture and Identity in the Congregation," 91–92. The pastor can ask and respond to many of these questions. However, some are difficult for the pastor, as a worship leader, to pursue. A minister may find it helpful to ask other people in the congregation, or someone from outside the congregation, to help with such observations. A preacher could also ask many of these questions directly to individuals and groups in the congregation.

[20]We discuss only interviewing that makes use of open-ended questions, that is, questions that invite interviewees into relatively detailed responses to the questions. Listeners can thus express nuances of thought and feeling and can link responses and provide data in ways that are often bypassed on statistical instruments. Occasionally pastors seek feedback on their preaching by the use of paper survey instruments that invite parishioners to rate aspects of the sermon on scales similar to "most helpful to least helpful" or "1 as most effective to 5 as least effective." Such instruments have the advantage of being easily and frequently administered to large numbers of people and of guaranteeing anonymity to the congregant. Some instruments provide some open-ended questions in response to which parishioners can write a sentence or two. However, statistically based and short-answer questionnaires do not provide the same depth and nuances of response as sustained interviews based on open-ended questions. For examples of paper survey instruments of this type that invite congregational feedback on specific sermons, see William H. Roen, *The Inward Ear: A Sermon Evaluation Method for Preachers and Hearers of the Word* (Washington, D.C.: Alban Institute, 1989), 70; William H. Willimon, "Lay Response to Preaching," in *Concise Encyclopedia of Preaching,* ed. William H. Willimon and Richard H. Lischer (Louisville: Westminster John Knox Press, 1995), 302–4; I. Ross Bartlett, "Getting Honest Sermon Feedback," *The Christian Ministry* 26/4 (1995): 25–27. For statistically based surveys that reflect on preaching generally, see Eric Reed, "The Preaching Report Card: Today's Listeners Grade Pastors on What They Hear from the Pulpit," *Leadership* 20 (summer) (1999): 82, and Lori Carrell, *The Great American Sermon Survey* (Mainstay Church Resources, 2000). On the use of survey instruments and questionnaires, see Thumma, "Methods for Congregational Study," 217–29; cf. 240–53.

[21]On interviewing, see Thumma, "Methods for Congregational Study" in *Studying Congregations,* 203–8; and Tubbs Tisdale, *Preaching as Local Theology and Folk Art,* 65–69.

[22]We wish we could have included congregations of Roman Catholics, newer Christian denominations and movements, Jewish people, and perhaps Muslims. We would like to have

broadened racial and ethnic representation of Hispanic, Asian, and Native American communities. We could see the value of interviewing persons who listen to preaching in contemporary or alternative services of worship. However, finitude came into play. We selected a study group within the range of our funding, person power, and spheres of familiarity. We hope that broader studies will soon be undertaken. We also thought that the study of the groups we selected would be most immediately applicable to our primary vocations as teachers in seminaries serving the churches we described in the text.

[23]We aimed for a one-on-one interview to last about an hour.

[24]We found the following book to provide excellent guidance in small group interviewing: Richard A. Krueger and Mary Anne Casey, *Focus Groups: A Practical Guide for Applied Research,* 3d ed. (Thousand Oaks, Calif.: Sage Publications, 2000).

[25]While we valued the particularity of the perspectives of the individual interviewees, they sometimes spoke as if on behalf of the congregation. The small group interviewers provide some sense of the degree to which the comments of individual interviews represent the congregation (or currents within) and are particular or even idiosyncratic.

[26]On formulating questions, see Krueger and Casey, *Focus Groups,* 56–67, who suggest that questions should be open-ended, ask interviewees to think back, avoid using the word "why?", be simple, arranged so that the general questions come before specific ones and so that positive questions and uncued ones come before negative and cued questions. Cf. Thumma "Methods for Congregational Study," 220–26.

[27]For these categories, see pp. 7–16.

Epilogue

[1]Statements such as the one just quoted–representing many similar sentiments in the interviews–underline the urgency for congregational leaders to help the community understand the role, function, and importance of worship in the church, and the systemic interconnection of multiple aspects of congregational life. We do not argue that preaching *is* inherently more valuable than other things that happen in the congregation, but we are obliged by the study to report that many people regard the sermon as being remarkably significant. It would be interesting to know how people would respond to questions such as, "What would be missing if there were…no congregational singing? no breaking of the loaf? no Bible school?"

Appendix C: Description of the Project

[1]This project, funded by the Religion Division of the Lilly Endowment, was carried out through Christian Theological Seminary in Indianapolis. The project was directed by Ronald Allen, who teaches preaching and Second Testament at that seminary, and by Mary Alice Mulligan, who is director of chapel and visiting professor of preaching. An advisory board made up of teachers of preaching guides much of the work: Dale Andrews (Louisville Presbyterian Theological Seminary), Jon L. Berquist (Westminster John Knox Press), L. Susan Bond (Vanderbilt Divinity School), John S. McClure (Vanderbilt Divinity School), Dan P. Moseley (Christian Theological Seminary), Dawn Ottoni-Wilhelm (Bethany Theological Seminary), G. Lee Ramsey, Jr. (Memphis Theological Seminary), Diane Turner-Sharazz (Methodist Theological School of Ohio). In addition, Nancy Eiesland, professor of sociology of religion at Candler School of Theology, served as project adviser. Planning took place in the year 2000 with interviews in 2001 and early 2002.

[2]We fully expect other investigators to refine our conclusions, adopt different methods of research, and even to call some of our work into question.

[3]Keeping the research base close to Indianapolis also minimized costs and did not place too great a travel burden on the interviewers.

[4]Taking account of race and ethnicity, size, and location, the congregations in the study are distributed as follows: African American mega-urban (1 congregation), African American large urban (2), African American medium urban (3 congregations: 1 free church, 1 liturgical), African American medium county seat (2), African American small rural (1), Caucasian mega-suburban (2), Caucasian large urban (1), Caucasian large suburban (2), Caucasian medium urban (3 congregations: 1 free church, 2 liturgical), Caucasian medium county seat (2), Caucasian medium rural (1), Caucasian small urban (1), Caucasian small county seat (2), Caucasian small rural (2), Mixed small urban (3).

[5]The congregations in the study belong to the following denominations or Christian movements: African Methodist Episcopal Church (1 congregation), African Methodist Episcopal Zion Church (3), American Baptist Church (1), Christian Church (Disciples of Christ) (4), Christian Churches and Churches of Christ (2), community churches (1), Church of the Brethren (2), Episcopal Church (3), Lutheran (ELCA) (2), Mennonite Church (1), National Baptist (1), Presbyterian Church U.S.A. (3), United Methodist Church (4).

[6]The pastor (or designated representative), in consultation with lay leaders and project staff, selected the persons from each congregation for the interviews. Criteria for consideration included regular participation in worship for an extended period of time (attendance at least twice a month for a year) and capacity for critical reflection and for clear articulation of ideas. Pastors were assured that the interviews would not be a referendum on the pastor's preaching and were urged not to nominate only persons who were known to be personal supporters of the pastor.

[7]Each interview was tape recorded. The recordings were then transcribed. The transcriptions, edited to provide anonymity for each person and congregation, are stored at Christian Theological Seminary.

[8]We did not ask interviewees to listen to a specific sermon and then to respond to questions about that message.

[9]The interviewers were Dale P. Andrews, Bobbye Brown, Lori Krause-Cayton, Owen Cayton, Lisa Coffman, John McClure, Mary Alice Mulligan, G. Lee Ramsey, Jr., Edgar A. Towne, and Diane Turner-Sharazz.

[10]These participant observations followed the pattern suggested by Scott L. Thumma, "Methods for Congregational Study," in *Studying Congregations: A New Handbook,* ed. Nancy T. Ammerman, Jackson W. Carroll, Carl S. Dudley, and William McKinney (Nashville: Abingdon Press, 1998), 200–201, and took account of demographics; physical setting; the service of worship; patterns of interaction the interviewer could observe prior to, during, and after the service; as well as the verbal and written content in the service and in the times preceding and following worship; and the meaning of these things to congregations (insofar as interviewers were able to determine it).